IN LOVE WITH THESE TIMES

IN LOVE WITH WITH THESE TIMES

MY LIFE WITH FLYING NUN RECORDS

Roger Shepherd

HarperCollins*Publishers*

HarperCollins*Publishers*
First published in 2016
by HarperCollins*Publishers* (New Zealand) Limited
Unit D1, 63 Apollo Drive, Rosedale, Auckland 0632, New Zealand
harpercollins.co.nz

HarperCollins*Publishers*
Unit D1, 63 Apollo Drive, Rosedale, Auckland 0632, New Zealand
Level 13, 201 Elizabeth Street, Sydney NSW 2000
A 53, Sector 57, Noida, UP, India
1 London Bridge Street, London, SE1 9GF, United Kingdom
2 Bloor Street East, 20th floor, Toronto, Ontario M4W 1A8, Canada
195 Broadway, New York NY 10007, USA

National Library of New Zealand Cataloguing-in-Publication Data

Shepherd, Roger, 1960-
  In love with these times : my life with Flying Nun Records / Roger
  Shepherd.
  ISBN 978-1-77554-089-2 (paperback)
  ISBN 978-1-77549-126-2 (e-book)
  1. Flying Nun Records. 2. Rock music—New Zealand—History
  and criticism. 3. Rock groups—New Zealand —History.
  4. Sound recording industry—New Zealand—History. I. Title.
781.660904—dc 23

Front cover image: Roger Shepherd © Alistair Guthrie
Back cover image: Roger Shepherd in the Flying Nun office, Hereford Street, Christchurch, 1982 © Alec Bathgate
All photographs are from the author's collection unless otherwise credited.
All reasonable attempts have been made to contact the rights holders of photographs. If you have not been correctly attributed, please contact the publisher so that appropriate changes can be made to any reprint.
Cover design by areadesign.co.nz
Index by Michael Wyatt
Typeset in Baskerville MT Regular by Kirby Jones
Printed and bound in Australia by Griffin Press
The papers used by HarperCollins in the manufacture of this book are a natural, recyclable product made from wood grown in sustainable plantation forests. The fibre source and manufacturing processes meet recognised international environmental standards, and carry certification.

For Catherine, Missy and Lulu: I could not be luckier

*And for all of the bands I have worked with and
without whom there would be no story to tell*

CONTENTS

INTRODUCTiON

There was no one direct cause for what happened in music in New Zealand in the 1980s. But it cannot be denied that an extraordinary amount of wonderful music was created in that decade. Most of it was from the South Island, Dunedin in particular, or had some connection with these places. And much of it was connected to Flying Nun Records.

A small but creatively rich scene had developed in Dunedin from the late 1970s onwards. Through their relationship with the Flying Nun label, the bands were able to sell sufficient quantities of their records to create the cash and the confidence for us to work with other musicians from all over New Zealand. The label was then able to help create an overseas market for many of those bands, which allowed some of them to have a go at building full-time careers in music.

The Clean, The Chills, Sneaky Feelings, The Verlaines, Chris Knox and Tall Dwarfs, The Bats, Straitjacket Fits, Bailter Space, The Jean-Paul Sartre Experience, the Headless Chickens and Garageland all built international profiles when the world was a bigger and less connected place. It was original and exciting.

Just as the New Zealand bands on the label influenced each other, they began to exert an influence on independently minded artists everywhere. It was a subtle thing; nothing was wholly appropriated or adopted, but ideas and sounds filtered through and permeated particular bands and musical genres. Sonic Youth would namecheck the Gordons, Pavement toured New Zealand very early in their career to find out what was happening. The Magnetic Fields, Superchunk, Mudhoney, Yo La Tengo and REM were all open about how New Zealand artists were an influence. Cat Power and the Wooden Shjips have covered songs by This Kind of Punishment and Snapper.

It's no big deal, but I know the music is taken seriously by the international music community. It's a small yet uniquely important ingredient in the independent music world stew.

Money was always tight, but the imperative was to record and release as much as possible of the music being made during this extremely creative time. I was inspired to start Flying Nun because I was a fan of the music, not because I was looking for a business opportunity. However, it quickly became a business, with a growing artist roster and increasing sales in New Zealand and then overseas.

Communication was always stretched. The label was based in Christchurch and most of the bands were working from homes in Wellington and Auckland, as well as Dunedin. This was well before email and Skype. But collaboration was key, despite the rickety nature of keeping in touch by letter or the occasional phone call with the bands and other key participants, such as Doug Hood, Chris Knox, Ian Dalziel and Roy Colbert.

It was the best of times, yes, but there were some worst of times too. Mostly there was the stress of finding out how to do things from scratch, making costly mistakes, all the while being excited by and trying to fund new projects. There was the inevitable pressure of being fundamentally underfunded and growing too quickly.

There are plenty of books written about successful bands. A common theme is the up-and-down nature of the journey: things don't go as planned, people fall out, get sick — or worse, die along the way. There is no money for most of the story and a fair bit of luck involved. The planets need to line up and only a few complete the fairy-tale journey. Grief and disappointment are never far away.

Not as many books get written about record companies, but the same things happen. Naive, wild-eyed optimists get ground down by the realities and demands of the music business.

I'm not sure I had the necessary ego or strength of character to ever make my fortune in music. It's a cut-throat industry and one's success is invariably somebody else's loss. In the music business that can include the people you are working with, the artists who make the music your business is built on. I'm a music fan first and foremost, and I have always measured my success in terms of the actual music released and distributed by Flying Nun.

I was certainly very lucky to be in the right place at the right time, to be able to work with the bands I did. I started the label because I felt this music had to be recorded and no one else seemed interested in taking it on. No doubt some of the bands would have eventually released records through other labels, perhaps ones based in Auckland or one of the New Zealand multinationals. But the small Dunedin music scene would have developed very differently and I doubt a fraction of the music that was recorded would have been. The legacy would not be as strong without Flying Nun's artist-centric approach and general disregard for common business sense.

While not at all hard-headed in business, my strength was in managing to stay a fan. I had a fan's enthusiasm and a fan's persistence to keep the whole ridiculous show on the road so we could make more records and help the careers of more bands. Underpinning it all was the belief that the music was good enough to eventually break through and see a return that would make life easier.

Life never got easier, but some great records were made as well as a great number of enduring friendships. Fun was had, sometimes far too much fun. Occasionally, the fun became madness. Perhaps it was the madness that made it all happen in the first place.

The sheer busyness of the label and the number of bands whose careers developed simultaneously mean the structure of this book is not *strictly* chronological or sequential. These are overlapping stories, and a huge amount of material had to be left out — there was just too much and some of it was too scary. I am afraid that many bands I worked with do not get a mention. There were simply far too many stories to include. Generally, however, I've tried to follow the rollercoaster as I actually rode it.

The book's title is borrowed from the song 'I'm in Love with These Times', written by Hamish and David Kilgour and Peter Gutteridge during The Clean's early days, and recorded by Hamish, Alister Parker, Ross Humphries and Glenda Bills as Nelsh Bailter Space in 1987. I chose it because it says it all. It motors along optimistically, enjoying the moment, while more mundane and perhaps even sinister concerns lurk beneath the surface. It's hard to decipher many of the lyrics, which is also apt — a degree of chaos and confusion fits this story. The music veers off on tangents, but is always driven — stuttering but driven.

In love with these times, you bet. It's the story of my life with Flying Nun.

CHAPTER 1

1981

I must have been drunk. I had told someone I was going to start a record label. All around the world people had grouped together to form bands and often these bands and their fans coalesced into scenes. And around these scenes certain individuals were inspired to start their own record labels. That was me. I wanted to be more than just an observer. I wanted to be a part of what was going on. Earlier in 1981, around March or April, I had told someone and the word was out, and now I had to actually do this thing. Start a record label.

There was a vague sense that this new post-punk music was not so much a genre as an approach or sensibility. It was about the making and the selling of the music, too. This set it apart from the music industry as it had previously operated.

So a group could either get exceedingly 'lucky' and sign an old-fashioned record deal with a major record company, or simply get together with a local independent that had sprung up in the aftermath of punk. The independent may or may not be more ethical or artist-friendly than a major company, but for many groups back then the way forward was to sign with an independent, find a studio that fitted the budget, and get on with it.

There were alternative ways to record and release records, and it also felt like there was more international interaction. There was a great deal of connection between post-punk artists in the UK and USA. A process of decentralisation or regionalism was also happening: Orange Juice and Josef K with the Postcard label in Glasgow; Devo in Akron, Ohio; Cabaret Voltaire in Sheffield; Pere Ubu in Cleveland; and Joy Division (with Factory), Buzzcocks and The Fall in Manchester. They were all seen as being just as important as what was happening in London or New York. A scene could develop in Brisbane in Australia, Christchurch or even in Dunedin in New Zealand, and be just as valid as anything happening anywhere.

Major record companies dealt only with their own branch offices around the world, and it tended to be one-way traffic when it came to which artists were to be signed and which records were to be released. Independent labels tended to network with different companies in different countries for different artists. The networking increased between management, record companies, agents and promoters. Business was more flexible, more business was getting done and more music was being released.

The British music press — led by the *NME*, *Melody Maker* and *Sounds* — helped foster this by throwing the net wider, covering the New York scene and reviewing records from everywhere. New Zealand band Toy Love's 'Rebel' single was reviewed in the *NME* even without a UK release. Feature stories were written about US bands touring Britain. In turn, we picked up on those reviews and stories when the weekly music papers eventually turned up in New Zealand.

So in starting a record label in Christchurch, New Zealand, I felt like I was already part of something much bigger. This feeling of connection was vague and slightly contradicted what I knew to be true. That we lived in a small isolated place where the idea that the repressive mainstream was very backward seemed irrefutable. At the same time, the local and international and interconnected nature of what I was about to do also felt very true.

In New Zealand, 1981 was a bleak year. Robert Muldoon was still prime minister and more out of control than ever, as evidenced by his allowing the Springbok rugby tour to take place. There were barricades, but it was the police and not the protesters building them. I had always liked rugby but it was all too much to take.

Against the backdrop of the ensuing mayhem there were some subtle shifts taking place within the local music scene. Old Hello Sailor Dave McArtney had cleaned up at the New Zealand Music Awards, but the kids on the street were already firmly focused on a handful of Auckland acts signed to a new indie, Propeller Records.

The Newmatics, Blam Blam Blam and the Screaming Meemees represented a scene that had built up in Auckland as the original punk one died out. The Meemees had a number-one single on the national chart and a just-perceptible shift in attitudes towards local music was starting to influence music buying — new, original New Zealand music was okay, good enough to go and see, and good enough to buy on record.

Part of my personal motivation for starting a label was having seen a number of very good Christchurch groups (such as the Vacuum Blue Ladder and The Victor Dimisich Band) develop then break up without ever recording or releasing a record. The lack of an accessible way to record and release may well have contributed to their early demise. I thought I could offer a solution by taking on quality local projects that would sell enough records to a mainly local audience to break even. The record itself would be reward enough.

It was an admirable worst-case scenario, but I really did want to sell decent amounts of the records I released. Having managed a small group of Record Factory shops I knew it was all about selling records and I thought I was reasonably good at it. I'd noticed a number of post-punk artists were selling well and even charting without the usual necessity of radio play, making it on talent and touring. Joy Division and The Fall both made the charts that year, and with the success of the Propeller acts I could see the market was changing.

I had no intention of running around looking for conventionally commercial bands. This was my record label and I was going to sign the acts I liked. Like any record company owner, I was arrogant enough to think everything would flow from there.

* * *

So, I was going to do this thing. I was going to start a record company, with no business or record company experience. There was no one to help or give advice because no one in New Zealand really knew how to run an independent record company — with the exception of Simon Grigg at Propeller. And, really, he was just a little further along the road of finding out how it all worked.

It would take time and money, but the advantage was that I didn't have to do things the same old way. I could make it up as I went along. If I'd sat down and thought it all through, it could have seemed too daunting and nothing would have happened. An instinctive hunch is what carried it forward.

Simon Grigg was actually experiencing considerable success with Propeller. He had released a compilation album of mostly Auckland bands, *Class of 81*. Auckland bands always seemed to be more open to the rest of the world and more adept at absorbing overseas trends and sounds. The Newmatics were a white ska band with a strong political bent who were actively engaged in anti-Springbok tour protests. The Screaming Meemees were a mod-flecked New Wave pop group who had achieved the seemingly impossible by getting their song 'See Me Go' all the way to number one on the national chart. Blam Blam Blam were an unabashedly cerebral art-school band that grew out of the original punk scene. They wrote quirky, subversive pop songs that overflowed with wit and humour and occasionally featured the euphonium as a lead instrument. While the Meemees made hits, the Blams made genuinely classic songs such as 'Don't Fight It, Marsha, It's Bigger than Both of Us' and 'There is No Depression in New Zealand'.

Propeller was a serious and ambitious venture. A statement of intent was its national Screaming Blam-matic Roadshow, featuring all three bands. Drawing fans, the curious, and a bit of bother, all the dates sold out. While the costs of a tour this size would have seen little if any profit, it showed that life — and sales — existed outside Auckland.

Propeller's other statement of ambitious intent was the near-simultaneous recording of two albums by the Screaming Meemees and Blam Blam Blam at Auckland's Harlequin Studios. I have always thought of Doug Rogers's Harlequin Studios as being big and expensive, but the truth is that he had then only recently upgraded his facilities. Still, he was dedicated to recording music rather than ads, and he produced the goods if you could afford his services. Recording an album's worth of songs at a studio with a high hourly rate, with inevitable time and budget overruns draining already poor cash reserves, has been disastrous enough for many an independent record company. But to double that exposure by recording two at once was almost foolhardy. Propeller believed it had a special deal; that misunderstanding effectively closed it down as an active record label.

The pain might have been worthwhile had the results been better. When the two records were released in 1982, the Screaming Meemees' album proved a bit thin on ideas beyond the already released singles; it effectively signalled the end of the band. The Blams' album went to number four on release, but sounded lacklustre and incomplete apart from the central masterpieces. I got the feeling both albums were rushed into without enough material or with incompletely developed songs. And perhaps the big studio experience was too much for young bands at an early stage in their careers.

* * *

Watching and learning from the local music scene was one thing, but I had a more pressing concern — what to call this record label I had decided to start. Naming things can be hard. Around and around it went. Christchurch Sounds? Square Records? Garden City Music? Round Records? Rock Art Music? Flat City Spinners maybe? It needed to be of the place, Christchurch and the South Island, as well as universal, sophisticated, witty and modern. Everyday yet memorable. It needed to be about the music but more than just that.

Flying Nun Records.

I immediately regretted it. I'd settled on it under the duress of some imminent releases. I named it after a dire 1960s American television series featuring a young Sally Field. Sometimes people would get confused and call it 'Blue Nun'. It seemed rather apt to have your life's work confused with a cheap brand of mass-produced sweet German wine (except I'd picked the wrong German wine to sound like — 'Black Tower' might have done the job better). But, oh dear, 'Flying Nun Records'. It was silly and throwaway and didn't at all reflect how seriously I was taking the venture. What would everyone say?

Actually, no one would ever say anything. They were all too busy wanting to get their records released, or too busy wanting to buy them, to give two hoots. Fortunately, it was all about the music.

I thought it prudent to form a limited liability company. I felt it might give me some peace of mind. When your application was approved, all the bits and pieces you needed to run a limited liability company turned up a couple of weeks later in a little box. It all seemed a bit Masonic, with the company stamp and a heavy laminated nameplate for the door: 'The Registered Offices of Flying Nun Records Ltd'.

I had seen a new local band called The Pin Group a number of times at the Gladstone Hotel, on Durham Street opposite the old intercity bus terminal, and they approached me about releasing a single they had recorded. Like me, the band's singer and guitarist, Roy Montgomery, had a day job managing a record shop, in his case the EMI shop on Colombo Street, across Cathedral Square from mine. Roy had been born in London and spent some time living in Germany before migrating to Christchurch in the mid-1960s. He was tall, thin, blond and quietly baritone. In 1980, as a music fan, Roy went back to London to see what was happening and came back to Christchurch inspired enough to form a band.

The Pin Group were Roy on guitar and vocals, with Ross Humphries on bass and Peter 'Buck' Stapleton on drums. Peter had already been in bands such as the Vacuum, and would later be part of many others, including Dadamah (again with Roy), Scorched Earth Policy and The Terminals. He was a great hold-down-the-beat kind of drummer. Ross was a natural musician, a valued member of later Christchurch bands such as The Great Unwashed, Nelsh Bailter Space and The Terminals. He even moonlighted as a crooner when not running an antiquarian bookshop. An eccentric friend, Desmond Brice, wrote the lyrics.

In some ways it was possible to view Roy as the band's greatest weakness as well as its major asset. His guitar sound could be described as weak and weedy, and his singing voice was a low, tuneless monotone. The cruel called them 'Roy Division'. But these points of difference were a big part of their allure.

The Pin Group were a bit dark and mysterious, otherworldly, hinted at unrealised potential and possibility, and were very much in the new Christchurch tradition. Understatement was a big part of that. They had played a few gigs and I liked them a lot. Roy tended to wear a jeans 'suit' consisting of an impossible-to-find imported black Levi jean jacket and straight-legged jeans. (It was a look I was sporting when I almost froze to death in a snowstorm on Mt Tongariro ten years later.)

They had recorded a couple of songs, 'Ambivalence' and 'Columbia', at Arnie van Bussel's Nightshift Studio, and I'm not even sure I'd heard the recordings before agreeing to release them. I was more than happy to press them up as Flying Nun's first release.

Having a master tape ready to go meant I needed a pressing plant to make the records. There were two in New Zealand — EMI owned one in Lower Hutt and PolyGram had one in Miramar in Wellington (in a building now called the 'Record Press', which today houses part of Weta Digital). Like the British establishment institution that it was, EMI was very formal, with documentation and credit applications to be made. I really couldn't be bothered, especially when Ziggy, my new contact at PolyGram, was happy to just get on with it. We sent the tape off and while PolyGram cut and pressed the record we turned to the cover. All twelve-inch record covers were printed in advance so the records could be sleeved as soon as they were cooled after pressing. But the major record companies didn't print seven-inch covers for each individual release, instead using cheap generic sleeves pre-printed and ready to use.

While The Pin Group were musically a bit dark, their artwork was generally eye-catchingly colourful. Their gig posters were designed and printed by a local art student, Ronnie van Hout. They were beautiful, bright, screen-printed things bearing images of *The Man from U.N.C.L.E.* or Captain Cook, overlaid with slabs of bright colour, and they really brightened up the miserable Christchurch winter of 1981. Ronnie had the cover design ready to go for The Pin Group's single and said he would print the covers himself. Perversely, the cover of the first single was not at all colourful. It was a beautiful black-on-black image, and it was only years later I realised it was of helicopters — helicopters in Vietnam, black helicopters on black ops, I guess.

We released a second Pin Group single later that year. 'Coat', backed with 'Jim', wasn't dissimilar to the first release, despite Roy having a better handle on the equipment at Nightshift Studio. Ronnie designed the cover again — kiwifruit cut into sections, with each cover featuring a different colour combination.

Roy didn't really get on top of the recording issues until the band went into the EMI studio in Wellington the following year. The five songs, including a re-recording of 'Ambivalence', on *The Pin Group Go to Town* twelve-inch EP finally gave the listener a clear idea of the band. They really did sound great, very much a part of the Christchurch independent music tradition that stretches from the late 1970s to the present.

To a certain extent Roy was trying to conform to a traditional rock template with The Pin Group and while I liked what they were doing, their appeal was not universal. They were a bit out of time in a way. Still, the Pin Group releases sold and charted well in Christchurch, where the band was known. Things began to work better for Roy when he recorded as Dadamah and under his own name, allowing his voice and drone-guitar to be expressed as parts of soundscapes, rather than boxed into conventional songs. This later material is what Roy's international reputation is based on.

Meanwhile, I could see what was selling at the Record Factory and it was clear the novelty of DIY New Zealand releases had waned. Buyers were becoming more discerning. They wanted better quality and the profile of the band was more important. The record had to be good, but there also had to be a motivating reason for buying it — a tour or a good review, along with a groundswell of grassroots support.

I wanted to find a really good band that I totally believed in. One I could promote nationally, a special band that was comfortable in the studio and on the road. A band that people instantly, positively responded to. The sort of band that comes along once in a lifetime. I was to become very lucky.

CHAPTER 2

ARANUI

In 1959 my parents bought a section in a new housing development in Aranui on the edge of Christchurch's eastern suburbs. The speedway track was over the back fence and the city dump and sewage ponds beyond that. The quarter-acre section was on top of a large, flattened sand hill with no soil. They built a small three-bedroom house clad with light-grey Summerhill Stone and with a dark-grey concrete-tiled roof, built a fence all of the way round, shipped in some soil and planted a garden.

I was born in 1960, just after they moved in. My younger brother Frank was born three years later. Our other siblings were considerably older. I shared a room with John. My sister Lea and Frank shared another room. My eldest brother Terry slept in the living room. Frank and I found out about an older half-sister a few years later. Ngaire lived on the outskirts of Waimate with a hard-drinking, truck-driving husband and seven children.

Our part of Aranui overlapped with Wainoni and was almost completely made up of state housing — individual houses, semi-detached units and what I think we would now recognise as mini-tenements. It was the sheer size and concentration that

LEFT: Me aged four. I doubt we had a telephone connected at home at this time.
RIGHT: My brother Frank (right) and I still believed in Father Christmas in 1967. Meanwhile,
The Beatles were recording 'Strawberry Fields Forever'.

would create the problems and contribute to the area's infamous reputation.

We lived on Hampshire Street, which was the main route through the new suburb. The shopping strip was just down the road. These were pre-supermarket days so everything was there: a Four Square, an IGA, a couple or three dairies, a haberdashery run by a one-armed gentleman, a chemist and an incredibly busy fish and chip shop. It was at one time the largest piece of strip shopping in New Zealand.

My mother had not been keen on my mixing with other kids and picking up bad habits, so I led a closeted existence until the day I went to school. My mother escorted me down to Aranui Primary on my first day. I walked home when the bell rang. There was no one home. My mother returned to find me sobbing and took me straight back. The bell had been for morning playtime. It didn't get any better. I wet myself constantly. The toilets were scary. I found the boys to be loud and aggressive yobs and the girls not much better. I guess it was all like real life.

I had a succession of ineffectual teachers because the good ones didn't stick around. I had six different teachers in my Standard Two and Three years (the equivalent of today's years four and five). I suspect my school would now be identified as failing. A number of the teachers were older men who'd been fast-tracked into teaching after the war. Nice men mainly, but often sadly ineffectual or plain eccentric. One headmaster liked to play his violin at school assembly in a Nero-while-Rome-burns sort of way.

I was withdrawn and wasn't learning anything in an environment where no one was learning much anyway. I was shy but had friends — the usual inappropriate types — and was able to stand up for myself. There may have been occasional violence, but I was never bullied.

There were visits to the Ministry of Education child psychologists in town for tests. I had appalling reading and writing skills. I was ten years old and they weren't telling me anything I didn't already know. It was decided I was smart enough to grow through and out of it. I muddled through. I was curious enough to start reading the newspaper and books independently, and this connected me to the world beyond my suburban existence and fed my imagination. I did become a better dreamer.

My last two years of primary education were at Chisnallwood Intermediate. The teachers were better, but there were still some mad ones in the system. I knew strange stuff about the Russian space programme, wouldn't shut up about polar exploration, and could point out the capital of Nepal on a map. I mixed with some of the other nerdy boys. The girls were getting taller. Some of the boys were getting hairy.

I had a paper round. A big canvas bag was attached to the front of my bike and off I went. Hampshire Street had been recently described as the worst street in New Zealand in a national newspaper. This was not true. Carisbrook Street, which was on one of my two daily rounds, was much worse.

People were not really the problem, since they tended not to come out of their houses. Dogs were the biggest danger. I still have a phobic fear of them. No dogs were restrained in yards or on leads. One had to be constantly alert. Packs of dogs were an ever-present threat. It was a daily routine of fight or flight. I don't know how I stuck at it. It got worse. When I became the 'senior' paperboy, one of my jobs was to collect the outstanding money from accounts in arrears. This took me right up to the back doors and often inside houses of people who lived very differently from my family and who often seemed considerably poorer, if not totally desperate. But they still wanted to have the newspaper delivered.

The papers were at their fattest on Wednesday and Saturday, the days people preferred to place classified ads. Near Christmas these papers became huge and virtually impossible to roll, let alone fit in the ready-made metal tubes customers were encouraged to fit onto their letterboxes. I had preferred the old system where you secured the rolled papers with a rubber band and hurled them onto each property, but there was no protective plastic bag and sometimes it rains during a Christchurch winter. The new system was worse, though, because the barely rollable giant editions would get shredded if jammed into the tubes when wet.

Dad learned to drive when he was in his mid-fifties, towards the end of the 1960s. To start with, he could only afford worn-out prewar American cars, before he graduated to the English tradition of small, underpowered cars such as the Ford Anglia and Vauxhall Velox. We all felt liberated by the car. We could escape the claustrophobic little house in the dead-end suburb and get out into the countryside, and it made a huge impression on me. Not so much the farms and farmers — Dad had an intense hatred of all farmers after his experiences working on Southland farms during the Depression — but the landscapes, the shapes and contours, the textures and colours, the sweep and velocity of the clouds.

Towards the end of the Christmas holidays, late in January, Mum, Dad, Frank and I would head out of Christchurch. It was fairly random to begin with, with us just driving over to the West Coast, down to Central Otago or up to Golden Bay, just driving in these old breakdown-prone cars to see how far we could get and then look for a motel for the night.

Pretty soon my mother decided she couldn't cope with the uncertainty of it all and started booking motels in advance. We got to see most of the South Island over successive years and it all seemed so incredible. The mountains, lakes, the remote beaches, the beech forests and these strange little towns inhabited by old-timer eccentrics all seemed utterly fascinating. We were enthralled in a way that contrasts sharply with the experiences of my own children, who seem so uninterested in drives through the countryside. I think we were so awestruck because our previous carless lives had been so constricted and narrow.

There were times, though, when I was happy to be left behind in Aranui. Just the idea of accompanying Mum and Dad to the supermarket in nearby New Brighton was an agony. I'd stay at home and explore my new inner world. Books were part of our lives and there were an awful lot of them scattered around the house. I guess the psychologist was right; it was inevitable I would get bored and eventually pick up a book and start reading.

I powered through the books I found at home: my father's George Orwell, Aldous Huxley and Graham Greene. My brother Terry's science fiction collection was accessible and I became especially fond of John Wyndham. Reading became central to my life and I read all sorts of books.

We also went to the New Brighton library every Saturday. This was good for big art books. Dad read about and liked art but for him everything had turned to custard with Modernism. He had conventional tastes, so our visits were an opportunity to see what else was out there. The library had a huge Thames & Hudson volume on Dada and Surrealist art. This was how you connected to the bigger world in the late 1960s.

Despite my father working in electronics, television came late to our house. When it did we were not allowed to touch any of the knobs. There being only one channel meant we weren't even allowed to turn it on or off. We weren't allowed to touch the radio either, and I knew there were truly horrific options available there. For the time being I was satisfied turning the pages of my books. Nineteen eighty-four may have been a long way off, but I was dead keen to see how it all ended up.

Something else I was not allowed to touch was the stereo. Dad liked to read and listen to music. Where there weren't bookcases there were cabinets full of classical records. Classical music was made by men in wigs or with big hair and deafness. We weren't allowed to touch the records either. I wasn't so interested in them anyway, although I was reasonably up on what was what. Again, Dad didn't like anything too modern. His interest ground to a halt just before Wagner. In his mind, Schoenberg was just as bad as the Rolling Stones.

I was more interested in a couple of records my older brother owned. *The Freewheelin' Bob Dylan* didn't look like a bundle of fun. On the cover it seems that a southerly is blowing through New York City and Bob isn't dressed appropriately. I was disconnected before I even heard the first bar. And like Bob on that record cover, it still leaves me feeling a little cold.

But I really did connect with the other record. On the cover there are all these people, some of whom I recognised, and the band up front wearing these astonishingly colourful satin uniforms. It was a modern-looking bit of artwork that connected to all these different personalities and ideas. The title sounded a bit pompous: *Sgt. Pepper's Lonely Hearts Club Band*. I had heard my sister talking about The Beatles a year or so earlier, before she decided they'd lost the plot and she moved on to the Bee Gees.

Nothing had prepared me for what I heard that day. Playing both sides of the album, a whole new world of possibility opened up before me. Out there were people making music like this? I couldn't believe the creative energy, the variety in the material, the sounds, the melodies and harmonies at work and the outrageous experimentation. And presumably there were other people out there listening to it and being as excited by it as much as I was. Staggeringly, no one at school had any idea what I was talking about when I mentioned the album. It remained a private pleasure and a secret. I'd listen to it when my parents were out, ever alert for their imminent return.

A few years later I was conscious of what other kids at intermediate school were listening to, even if I wasn't all that interested. I needed to know so I had something to talk about. Music is an important way of socialising at that age. T Rex's 'Children of the Revolution' I liked. The Sweet, Slade and Alvin Stardust seemed, well, ridiculous. David Cassidy, The Osmonds and the Bay City Rollers were obviously lightweight. The overall impression was one of soft aural woolliness. Nothing too loud, sudden or alarming. Nothing that seemed to compare to the Beatles album I had independently discovered. I really didn't feel I was even working with the edge pieces of the musical jigsaw yet. I knew The Beatles were key. I knew Dylan was important, but I really couldn't see how. Perhaps he had good management.

* * *

The 1970s saw the New Zealand economy stumble after the international oil shock. From the bright but socially conservative 1950s, built on the back of high wool prices during the Korean War, a slow, declining drift had settled in. The Labour government of the early '70s had realigned our small country towards the modern world, but the rest of the decade saw the country run by the increasingly maniacal and egotistical Robert Muldoon.

Petrol was in short supply and 'carless days' were introduced. The cars were old and it was a good time to be a mechanic. People had stopped painting their houses. It was a time of dowdy neglect and rust. Television might have gone colour in 1974, but any feeling of brightness was becoming increasingly washed out.

I was mostly immune to the malaise because I was still at school. Shirley Boys High was a five-mile bike ride each way from home. Into the wind both ways it sometimes seemed, with a freezing southerly from the side for variety. The route followed a path along the Avon River — a path that was virtually all red-zoned land after the 2010 and 2011 earthquakes.

It took me a while to settle at my new school. Most of my friends from intermediate had gone to other schools closer to home. Aranui High was at the end of our street but mum had insisted, with little resistance from me, that I go to Shirley, where my brother Terry had been in the 1960s.

I knew virtually no one and the system and the demands were quite different. I floundered and managed not to attend for three weeks at one stage. Gradually, I got my act together and ended up doing well enough academically. Boys' schools like sport, as it supposedly curbs the natural tendency to masturbate. But I had seen enough of the changing rooms to know that team sports were not, and never would be, for me. Running seemed like a good solitary option. Running away, I guess.

I was a middling athlete but was captain of the cross-country and athletics teams. The truth is there was no one else. My most glorious moment would be the interschool 3000-metre steeplechase at the QEII stadium. The start line was at the start of the back straight. I had a good run-up to the water jump but landed awkwardly deep in the water and onto the concrete at

Me at the beginning of my last year in high school, 1977, just before punk changed my hair forever

the bottom, resulting in a hairline fracture in my heel. I limped down the home straight tailing the field to retire in front of a full grandstand. I never ran again.

My few friends with an interest in music had their tastes shaped by their older brothers or by their sisters' boyfriends' record collections — Black Sabbath and Led Zeppelin, along with King Crimson and Emerson, Lake and Palmer. Most of it was clunky and sedated blues-based rock, recorded simply. Anything that sounded different immediately stood out.

Frank Zappa and the Mothers of Invention were impressive musically but the satirical and pastiche elements were lost on us. Some enjoyed the toilet humour. For me it was the link to Captain Beefheart via their jointly credited 1975 album *Bongo Fury* that was significant. I remember being less convinced by albums by the likes of Mountain, Atomic Rooster and Iron Butterfly, blundering past with little to connect to. No doubt they were cast-offs, temporarily intercepted by us on their way to the nearby Bexley tip. I can't say that any of this music seemed to fit naturally into our lives at the time. Our lives or the place we lived in.

Glam rock wasn't something I was directly exposed to but we were all aware of David Bowie, T Rex, Slade and The Sweet. I had seen enough posters on bedroom walls to know this was a different kind of long-hair thing from the blue denim, beards and moustaches. One day a boy in my class turned up with a Bowie haircut that got everyone talking. That you could get a haircut like that in Christchurch seemed unimaginable.

We didn't listen to the radio. Commercial radio was simply not tolerated in our house and what I heard of it elsewhere held no interest for me. Ads and lightweight pop had absolutely no allure. Inoffensive, catchy, hummable pop music doesn't really appeal to pretentious teenage boys.

The little music to be seen on television was different but no better. The single NZBC channel (there would be two after 1974) seemed designed for a middle-aged, middle-of-the-road audience.

There were no longer shows like *C'mon* or *Happen Inn* from the late '60s and early '70s, which I remembered as being pretty zippy and exciting. But two acts snuck through on the *New Faces* talent competition and stuck out like sore thumbs, creating consternation and outrage.

Alastair Riddell and Space Waltz mimed to their own song, 'Out on the Street'. A song about street prostitution was risqué enough, but Riddell appeared in an androgynous glam outfit and camped it up for the cameras and everyone that cared to watch. It became a number-one hit. I liked it because there was so little else to relate to. It was really quite straightforward glam rock, but strangely alluring because it was local. Somehow this made it more meaningful, significant and relevant.

A band called Split Enz had been on *New Faces* the year before and also made an impression. They were quirky but not really glam, and their songs seemed a lot more complex. There was a novelty component that harked back to the 1960s and music hall before that. Early on, they seemed unique. I liked them enough when I saw them live over the next couple of years, but what really captured my imagination was their 1975 debut album *Mental Notes*. There was a lot to be wary of, with its progressive rock leanings, multiple tempos and key changes. It was art rock rather than pop and set somewhere between here and Gormenghast. I was reading Mervyn Peake at the time, so I felt a connection. The cover painting by Phil Judd depicted the obviously demented band set against a barren but recognisable New Zealand wasteland. It's a strange, surreal album that transports me to another, stranger world every time I hear it. Strange — but it was *our* strange, and one of the great New Zealand albums. Suddenly, anything seemed possible, even in New Zealand.

I had been a passive and apathetic teenager — the word 'lackadaisical' appeared on one of my school reports — but I'd got my act together enough to sit and get good marks in the School Certificate in my fifth form year in 1975, and was set to coast through my University Entrance year. I had the measure of school and what I had to do to get by. With this relative newfound confidence came a feeling that I knew what I was about.

By then I had saved up enough money to buy a car. Morris 1100s were notoriously unreliable and I had to have one. It was cheap to buy (because it was unreliable) and expensive to run due to breakdowns and repairs — the dilemma all young car buyers must face. You will still see older Morris Minors and Volkswagen Beetles on the road today, but not Morris 1100s.

I was supremely fit and owned a racing bike, which at the time were relatively rare. But having a car was crucial. You could get to places more quickly; when you arrived you would be drier and warmer. You could drive friends, and it was easier to meet and entertain girls. I had become bigger and hairier.

CHAPTER 3

THE RECORD FACTORY

Christmas holidays, late 1976, and my mother thought I needed a job. For the unconnected this involved looking through the situations vacant ads in the newspaper. I spotted one offering part-time work in a record shop. Perfect. I had to ring quite a few times, as the line seemed to be hopelessly engaged. It turned out others were also keen and there was some sort of interview process.

The owner, Del Richards, was a big, friendly, effusive man and possibly the first businessman I'd ever met. He was a natural entrepreneur. Had I seen the current ads for the new Genesis and Status Quo albums? (TV advertisements for records were a new thing.) I was indifferent to the first and hostile to the second, but managed to sound sufficiently interested, informed and keen to get the job. I was going to be working the school holidays and Friday nights in a record shop.

I have occasionally felt a little guilty for getting the job under false pretences. I think I was hired for my enthusiasm. Perhaps I didn't know all that much about music, but I knew a little, and I was keen to know more. I had an enthusiasm looking for something to be enthusiastic about.

My sister had worked in the EMI shop on Colombo Street by the Square through the 1960s. Her manager was singer Ray Columbus's own very glamorous sister. My sister's taste tended towards the mainstream — early Bee Gees and The Hollies. Her Beatles buying may have ended with *Rubber Soul*. She gave me the first Electric Prunes album because she didn't like it. They were a sort of manufactured US garage rock band, but there are two brilliant songs on the album: 'Get Me to the World on Time' and 'I Had Too Much to Dream Last Night'. I still have this record and I still play it.

I was very excited on my first day of work. It was a dream job for a teenage boy. How much better could it be? The Record Factory at 637 Colombo Street was a couple of blocks south of the Square, between Lichfield and Tuam streets. Like most of the buildings in central Christchurch it was later demolished, or destroyed by the earthquakes.

First, I was shown how the till worked — obviously a crucial part of a job in retail, and some people never lasted because they could never master it. Then I was on to vacuuming. I was going to be working my way from the floor up.

The shop itself was dominated by record bins down the middle and along one side wall. The other wall displayed cassettes. The counter was at the back near some wide stairs. The actual records were filed away behind the counter, and the cassettes were kept in drawers underneath the counter. Filing and retrieval demanded bureaucratic levels of process. There was meant to be a logic to it, but there were often disagreements as well as missing records. One developed an ability to understand the crazy catalogue numbering systems. Some numbers stay with you for life.

My first day of work was on the Friday, when shops in the central city were open until nine o'clock at night. Nothing was open on the weekend so the evening had a festive feel. I discovered it was a brutal twelve hours of being on your feet. I was fit, but not fit for this.

Still, the evening was special. There'd be school kids buying singles, parents shopping for gifts for their children and wanting advice, rural types in town to buy country and western, girls just hanging around because it was one of the places to be and I was obviously so very attractive.

As the evening wore on, the parents and younger kids would disappear and youths and young adults would congregate. Working-class couples and art-school graduates mixed while the music on the turntable became more and more frenetic. If you played the right things, they'd buy more. You could sell ten copies of Iggy Pop's *The Idiot* off the back of one play at the end of the night.

It was a very social time and I became friends with many of the customers. We talked about music and they would buy music off my suggestions, but it was genuine nonetheless. I hate having to remember this, but sometimes the manager, Neil, would play Led Zeppelin's 'Stairway to Heaven' as the grand finale on a Friday night. It seems clichéd now but seemed perfectly normal at the time.

There are a couple of Led Zeppelin songs I like, but I don't think I ever owned a single album, CD or download of their music until very recently. Males tended to be obsessed with the band, which was probably the biggest in the world at the time. Males continued to be obsessed with them long after the band was no more. When I started my holiday job, one of the two shop windows contained a display for the new film soundtrack for the ironically titled live movie soundtrack album, *The Song Remains the Same*. I was very excited because we were all given free tickets for the opening night.

I wasn't familiar with the rock movie genre but I soon knew enough to know this was a dud. The live footage was incredibly dull and the dramatic split-screen effect only doubled the dullness. But the short scenes of fantasy that revolved around each band member and their manager Peter Grant took the cake. 'Amateur and pretentious' would be a charitable description. Clearly they had no regard for their audience. Music movies were generally poor in the 1970s — cheaply made exploitations that a starved audience would pay to see. That the biggest band in the world would do it too seemed inconceivable.

* * *

I met Paul Smith through the shop's manager, Neil. Paul was a little older and about to drop out of university. He liked to read, so had washed up at the University of Canterbury bookshop. He wanted to write and be artistic, and most importantly he liked music. He was well tuned to what was new and what was coming.

Paul was the first person I knew in Christchurch to be enthusiastic about the Ramones, and the first person to know about Television. I realise now he was probably picking up a bit of information from the record department at the bookshop. I regret the university's move out of central Christchurch in the 1960s. Imagine what could have been if they'd simply extended it a block or so into Hagley Park. The inner city would have retained the dynamic student and academic atmosphere it later sorely missed. And Paul wouldn't have had to bring us his musical news all the way in from Ilam.

Neil was a bit of a smartarse with an outsized ego and he could be pompous. His pursuit of women was relentless and the chat-up lines cringe-inducing. Yet somehow we got on well enough. He was a fan of what we would call progressive rock — Gentle Giant, The Far Eastern Band, Jon Anderson's solo albums, Jade Warrior and Patrick Moraz. But his general musical knowledge and appreciation was broad.

While record and cassette sales were very healthy in the late 1970s, the range available in New Zealand wasn't particularly wide. Government-imposed import licensing meant that if a title wasn't pressed at one of the two local plants, you might struggle to find an imported copy. If you did, it would be expensive. Some titles may have had a limited release years before and then been deleted. The Velvet Underground, Can and The Stooges were all hard to find. So you started to hang out with those guys (they were always male) who had really good record collections.

One of my co-workers invited me back to his house after work one night. He had the ideal setup, with a massive sleep-out behind his parents' house. But what, no girls? That didn't seem like this guy. I began to feel uncomfortable. I got stoned for the first time. Not bad. I was feeling very relaxed and just a little spaced-out. What was going on here? Two blokes sitting in the dark together?

He wanted to play me some of his records. I was to meet other men like this over the next few years: older guys with massive stereos in their bedrooms in their mum's house. And it was strange. The music tended to be strange. Strange and rather special. The pot that was invariably smoked on such occasions enhanced the experience precisely because of the style of music. Much of it was head music. Music I would never have got to listen to otherwise.

I'll never forget hearing Can's *Tago Mago* that night. Can were one of the key bands in the late '60s and early '70s German scene. Over time I have come to think of Can as being as important in my personal music world as The Velvet Underground. This was the first time I'd heard them.

There is one track, 'Halleluhwah', that takes up a whole side of this double live album. It runs for eighteen minutes, of which the entire middle section seems to be a hypnotic, studio-assisted drum solo. You would think only a machine could play like that. But I could never make that record sound as good again, despite the various remastered CD reissues. Much later, I finally found out why. I was in Austin, Texas, in the late 2000s, for the annual SXSW music conference and festival and was looking through a big exhibition of music posters. It was called Flatstock and ran alongside SXSW. Artists and small poster distributors set up stalls and sold their work. And then I heard it: Can's *Tago Mago* playing far away in the distance, yet sounding different, better, the way it had that night back in 1978. I zigzagged through the stalls and eventually found a guy with a turntable and big set of speakers. And there it was — except this was an American pressing on United Artists Records. Obviously, it was a vastly superior cut to the many different versions I'd heard over the years, on vinyl and CD. I guessed the poorer versions must have originated directly from the German version on the band's own label, Spoon Records, while somehow the American licensee had mastered a superior version.

In the shop, Del had a rule that we could play any music we liked except during lunchtimes, when it had to be more mainstream or commercial. He owned the business and he wanted to sell records, so it seemed reasonable. Commercial to us might have been different to Del's interpretation, but we were into the spirit of it. So we would play Steely Dan, 10cc, or even Supertramp and ELO, while he would have preferred Abba or Boney M. We would tap our toes to Abba but we couldn't bring ourselves to play it in the shop. Everyone, including Del, hated David Soul. Occasionally when it was quiet we would pull out one of his records and all give it a good stomping.

Record company reps would come in on a Monday morning to take the weekly order. This was exciting because we got to peruse the new releases. Even if some weren't to one's taste, there was still a sense of anticipation. We were actually rather keen to hear the new Abba album. How many hundred were we going to buy? Everyone wanted to hear and talk about that week's new releases. If there were promo copies spare, we would check them out more thoroughly later. Often we would be given things we were interested in to take home.

With my staff discount I could afford to buy records for the first time. In my first week I bought an import of Captain Beefheart's *Clear Spot* album. I still play it now. Beefheart was under pressure to deliver a commercial record and this is what he gave us; while relatively gentle, it still reeks of his wayward blues weirdness. I was on my way to building a sizeable collection of my own. Not that I was ever an obsessive collector.

I found myself discovering and enjoying all sorts of music, without ever feeling any of it represented my actual circumstances or generation. Everything we were listening to in the shop came from overseas and was generally appreciated by an older album-buying crowd. I became a fan of Brian Eno, Robert Wyatt and The Beach Boys and I still love that stuff. The more mainstream pop material that was played on commercial radio and dominated the singles chart appealed to younger listeners. The music my friends and I most strongly connected with on an emotional level was years old and from places so far away and alien that they were hard to imagine. It felt as if there was a void that needed filling.

CHAPTER 4

SAVED BY PUNK

In 1977 I was in my final (seventh-form) year at school —
traditionally an easy time working towards bursary exams at the
end of the year, which would provide the funding for university
study. I had no idea what I wanted to do and life was increasingly
centred around my part-time work at the Record Factory. I hung
out with the friends I met through the shop rather than at school.
I partied with these older, more sophisticated characters rather
than my schoolmates. I developed fun but bad habits. There was
little focus and I was drifting.

One day, Neil, the truest fan of progressive rock and jazz
fusion, took me aside to announce what the next big thing in
music was going to be. I knew he had listened to the Ramones
imports in bewilderment and greeted the first Television album
with bafflement, but perhaps he had heard the word and put two
and two together and seen how it was all going to play out. Yes, he
was telling me confidently, the next big thing to blow up big time
in music was going to be ... space music!

At the time, Neil would have defined space music as an extreme
form of progressive rock mixed with jazz fusion, Krautrock,

virtuoso playing and lots of solo noodling. A male-dominated form with ambitions to be taken as seriously as classical music, but with some electronic twiddling to make it modern and otherworldly.

Pink Floyd and 1969/1970–era Miles Davis were part of this, but not at its indefinable core. Jean Michel Jarre's monster 1976 success *Oxygène* was an example, though too popular to be typical. Perhaps German exponents Klaus Schulze and Tangerine Dream best encompassed the idea. Space music was an amorphous concept that many of its practitioners had no wish to be identified with. The pot must have been stronger than usual that summer, and I guess it made sense to Neil in and out of his head that the music he adored would become a dominant, commercially successful genre.

Within two weeks of Neil's bold prophecy, he was as devastated as I was exhilarated. Word was slowly filtering through from the UK that something was up. None of us really knew exactly what it was. Then in March 1977 *Radio with Pictures* ran a Dylan Taite special on the punk scene developing in London. The highlight was a grainy clip of the Sex Pistols performing 'Anarchy in the UK'.

It doesn't look like much now, especially if you view the original version rather than the doctored official version, but it represented a huge break with everything that had come before. The mix of anti-authoritarian lyrics pumped up with supercharged rock music, the radically dishevelled op-shop look, the working-class whine and hunched, sneering charisma of Johnny Rotten … it was all new. Many, if not most, hated what they saw; a few were excited and exhilarated. I was mesmerised.

The Sex Pistols represented a reaction to what had been accepted musically and successful commercially: middle-of-the-road pop pap, manufactured and cheesy disco, and pompous progressive rock, which held the 'high ground'. The stars were spending their wealth in excessive and ostentatious displays of egomania, while for most people times were hard. There was no work, no petrol and a nuclear apocalypse hung over everyone's head.

Punk offered instant nihilistic fun and escape. It wasn't about the future, it was about right now. Punks dressed for fun and to shock: self-cut spiky hair, Day-Glo colours, safety pins, bondage gear, bin liners, fishnets and, briefly, the swastika. Part of the fun for punks was outraging the rest of society — the mums and dads, hippies, police, news media, teachers, politicians and the monarchy. And they succeeded.

No one thought about the future possibilities or potential of this new music, or the lifestyle evolving around it, because there was patently 'No Future'. We would all be dead at twenty-one. This disaffection had multiple sources, from poverty and hopelessness to social repressiveness and simple dissatisfaction with current musical forms. I fitted the demographic, straightened my trousers and stuck an aesthetically 'just right'–sized safety pin in my narrow lapel.

The punk explosion of the late 1970s was a genuine music revolution. If the Sex Pistols gatecrashing the UK music market was cynically and expertly engineered, its impact on the collective musical consciousness and mainstream culture was still immediate and lasting. On the back of two perfect singles, 'Anarchy in the UK' and 'God Save the Queen', the grip of the dull, moribund, pretentious or banal on the culture was broken.

The old styles weren't swept away completely, but a new dynamic was established and began to build, grow, mutate and fragment. Other UK groups such as Wire, Buzzocks, The Fall and The Clash were inspired by the Sex Pistols to form, or adapt to the new style. Existing US bands, such as Television, Richard Hell and the Voidoids, Patti Smith and Suicide from New York, Ohio bands Devo and Pere Ubu, and other outsider art bands, were all loosely grouped in the new movement.

The Sex Pistols' career careened downwards due to mismanagement, artistic limitations and the Sid Vicious farce and calamity. The new bands learned to write songs and play their instruments on the job. Some never deviated from the original punk template and the likes of The Exploited and the Angelic Upstarts still tour the world today.

You might say the direct descendants of the Sex Pistols were the one-dimensional boot or 'oi' bands. All matching boots, straight jeans and black leather jackets with some short hair on top. Sort of dark matter with white faces. For others, the sudden inspiration of joining in and starting from scratch, with the new experiences of writing, playing and performing, resulted in a multitude of new sounds that would contribute to the post-punk renaissance, which was punk's true achievement. A bit like the universe just after the Big Bang, but with better music and clothes. It was art at its unpretentious, challenging, fresh and dynamic best. It was about ideas.

Old-style musicians could only scratch their balding heads and wait for the fad to pass. Some saw the commercial opportunities, got haircuts and jumped on the bandwagon. The Vibrators and the Stranglers re-imagined and redesigned themselves. Record companies started to sign a new style of act to feed the growing audience. It seemed anyone with the right look and a semblance of talent could get a deal in the ensuing frenzy.

What set the Pistols apart were Johnny Rotten's lyrics and vocal delivery. Without the two heavy-hitting singles, *Never Mind the Bollocks* was a very average album. Malcolm McLaren ruthlessly exploited the Sex Pistols' name with the *The Great Rock 'n' Roll Swindle* film and soundtrack, the Ronnie Biggs connection and later with the sad Sid Vicious releases. But the good that came out of it was what Johnny Rotten, or rather John Lydon, did next with Public Image. It was an exercise in challenging, modern art rock. Not progressive, but post punk.

In New Zealand, punk was a slow-motion revolution. We saw some of it coming, with a few of the key groups (Television, Patti Smith, Ramones) having records in the shops. But once it took hold it was like ditching your complete record collection and starting all over again. Okay, there were exceptions, and everyone knew what they were. Inexplicably, Neil Young was one. Yet there was a yawning gap and an enormous appetite to be fed, without much to listen to. Sometimes it felt like anything would do. There was a scramble through everything unfamiliar to see if it met the new criteria. Flaming Groovies, yes. Graham Parker, um, maybe. Brinsley Schwarz, no. Pretty much anything that wasn't progressive rock would do, but sensibilities refined as time passed. You had to be on your toes if ridicule was to be avoided.

We needed guidance and the UK music press of the *NME*, *Melody Maker* and *Sounds* was crucial. The writing was very good and what it was about was obviously important. Alas, they arrived by ship three months late and often covered groups and records that were virtually impossible to find or listen to in New Zealand.

It was unusual to subscribe to an overseas publication, but I must have just got hold of a credit card so I subscribed to the *NME*. It was a fantastic publication at the time, located at the centre of the new music universe. Hard to believe now, but Julie Burchill and Tony Parsons were exciting, on-the-ball young writers back then. Suddenly, it was all being expressed to me by airmail. I was up to date about new releases and what the critics were rating, and looking at the ads, and getting together with friends and ordering packages of singles and albums we knew would never be released in New Zealand.

Radio with Pictures was very important. Music videos were still new and novel, and this television show compiled the best that didn't fit the more commercial music programmes, such as *Ready to Roll* and *Shazam*, which had more mainstream slots and played charting material. It screened late on Sunday nights and was presented by radio DJ Barry Jenkin. Self-styled 'Dr Rock', Barry became a punk convert and would slip a clip or two into the line-up. Enough of the material was the real deal and made staying up late worthwhile. Video recorders were not yet available, so you had to be there. Miss it and you may never have seen Buzzcocks again.

There was always something depressing about the end of *Radio with Pictures*, though, because it was soon followed by the 'Goodnight Kiwi', signalling the end of the night's broadcasts. Eleven o'clock and time for bed. There wasn't anything else to do. Often we'd watch the TV static for a couple of hours in solitary protest. Or perhaps we simply couldn't move.

It wasn't always just about the music. Image, what was worn, how to scowl, and how to hold a bass guitar — it was all important. Those murky, inky poses in the *NME* were confirmed and animated. Punk was a style that was cheap to replicate. Op-shop suits and safety pins were easy to find and haberdashers must have wondered what was going on. Straight jeans were impossible to buy. You needed to be on good terms with a mother or sister who could do a decent job of taking in a flared pair. If all else failed a bin liner would do, even if it ran the risk of looking like a costume and therefore lacking authenticity.

It wasn't a tidal wave of change. Solitary school kids were turning up at the shop, wearing a badge or two, wanting to know what was happening. A customer might hear something in a record store and have an epiphany. Between those I knew through the Record Factory and the crowd that frequented the University Bookshop, there would have been no more than twenty people in the Christchurch punk 'scene'. I mean the people who were really into it before everyone's haircuts and clothes changed forever.

Mum and Dad were mystified by what was going on. The radio was tuned to either the classical music Concert Programme or National Radio. None of my brothers or sisters were allowed to play their records on Dad's stereo system in the living room. There were no stereos in any of the bedrooms until I was older. My second-to-oldest brother John was thrown out of home for wearing a Western-style string tie in 1964. None of us was allowed to wear jeans until I managed to slip home in a pair and encountered no resistance. Mum and Dad had been worn down by my older brothers and sister.

For me, National Radio was good for Philip Liner's early evening, easy listening 'Music for Pleasure', featuring the likes of 1001 Strings, Mantovani and Les Baxter. And, of course, there was 'The Goon Show'. Absurd and strange and just right for a seventeen-year-old boy, it conveniently played in the other room while we sat down for lunch on a Saturday.

My parents were already alarmed enough by the time they heard what I was listening to in my bedroom on a newly acquired rebuilt old stereo. I was playing Wire's brilliant first album and my mother knew it was 'worse' than the usual rubbish other teenagers listened to. 'Why must you play this ugly music, why can't you listen to something nice like other people?' I knew I was on the right track.

* * *

New Zealand cities were dingy places in the 1970s and Christchurch was the dingiest. Air pollution from coal-fuelled home fires hung over the city in the cold winter months. Most cars were second-hand and clapped out, like mine. Virtually all the live music was in bars and virtually all of it was terrible old-school shit.

In 1976, when I was sixteen, I crept into the upstairs bar of the Gresham Hotel on Cashel Street one Friday night after work and before closing time. Some friends had told me about a band worth seeing. It was hard not to notice the mixture of freaks in the audience: working-class punks, art-school kids, sailors, transvestites, men kissing men, and little old me. Some I knew from the shop. Everyone was very drunk. I had some catching up to do and there wasn't much time.

The Gresham had a terrible reputation as a dive, but I came to love bars like this. There was a special buzz to be had on a Friday night, with an hour to squeeze in some music, a bit of socialising and as much as you could possibly drink, all the while being hopelessly underage. I was never refused service or asked my age by police patrols through hundreds of pub visits before I turned twenty.

The Gresham wasn't a regular music venue, but the band, the Detroit Hemorroids, offered a little hope. Nicky Carter, Jane Walker, Alister Parker and Paul Kean might have been in their early twenties but Olly Scott looked older. They played pre-punk but quality covers and made it fun and exciting.

I realised there was more to life than listening to records or watching music clips on television. It was really all about the uniquely exciting dynamics of a band performing in front of an appreciative live audience. This was what I had been looking for — being able to take part in an extroverted, interactive musical activity. I knew I was never going to be in a band — I'd have had to learn an instrument. But this was different and more energising than just listening. I was going to be a part of the audience. Bands needed us. I was as drunk as everyone else and it was late. Ten o'clock and time to go home. But I'd be back.

* * *

I'd done enough to pass my end-of-year exams and get a bursary to study at the University of Canterbury. The 1977–78 Christmas holidays were the usual blazing hot, dry Canterbury summer, made more uncomfortable than previously because of what I was wearing: tight straight jeans and a black leather jacket over another dark layer or two. At least the sunglasses worked well.

Not that I was outside all that much with my holiday job at the Record Factory. It was just as well I'd bought a car because I now had to travel each day to the university, on the very opposite side of town. I lived in the poor east and, of course, the university was situated in the affluent west. I was excited. Like a lot of high-school students I felt I had been treading water in my seventh-form year but now I was joining a whole new world.

Perhaps I would find some direction, develop an idea of what I wanted to do with my life. I had no idea, other than that I was going to drift through university and get the degree I knew I was capable of.

My first day was a severe culture shock. My fellow students were different. They weren't from my part of town. Absolutely no one from Aranui went to university. Nor were there many from Shirley, or like the sorts of people I hung out with at the Record Factory. No, these people were from another social world completely. And they knew why they were there, to complete law or business degrees.

Orientation was a bit of a nightmare. There were some good live shows, despite the inevitably terrible acoustics you get in student union halls. The children of the well-to-do seemed to behave in the most terrible recreational ways: chunder miles and duelling yard glasses. There would have been plenty of like-minded and good people to get to know, but I was overwhelmed. If I was drifting, I was going to be drifting away from them and there.

Before long I started to spend time in the University Bookshop instead of at lectures. While most of their business was in text and academic books, they stocked plenty of other interesting publications, a lot of which they imported directly. I found the underground comic selection particularly rewarding.

Paul Smith, the friend I'd met on my first day at the Record Factory, had dropped out and was working at the University Bookshop by then. The ever-friendly Tony Peake ran the record department upstairs. If Christchurch had a face of punk, then Tony was it. The hair and clothing were just so, and always evolving. He curated an excellent selection of punk and reggae, among other styles, and a cup of tea and a natter made him well worth a visit. He was knowledgeable about jazz and art, with Andy Warhol being especially significant to him — not untypical of older people interested in punk and the new music at this time.

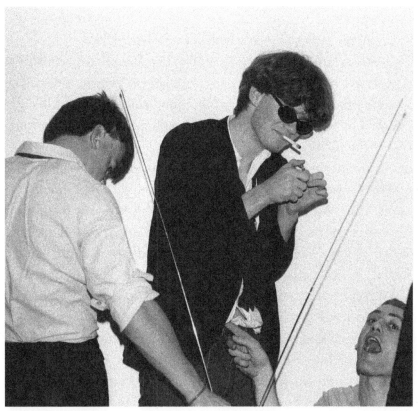
Left to right: Paul Smith, me and Tony Peake, Christchurch 1981 (photo by Robin Neate)

Imported records were hard to find. You needed a special licence and because it was part of an academic institution the bookshop had one. Tony had records you could find no other way.

I had a new girlfriend, too. I had met her at the Record Factory and we were spending more time together. She looked a lot younger than me, which made going to see bands in pubs difficult. But there was an occasional venue called Club da Rox in a large upstairs room on the corner of Colombo Street and a lane called Mollett Street. Only a fool would go to a place with a totally naff name like Club da Rox, so everyone called it Mollett Street. It was a red-brick-walled place with no liquor licence and bands played every second Sunday night. You could take alcohol in if you were discreet. I liked a drink. For someone like me, interested in live punk-style music, this was the place to be. In fact, it was virtually the only venue available for new live music.

I was aware of a few local bands. The Vauxhalls were still at school and had long hair, apart from singer Johnny Velox, who was very punk, wore plastic wraparound sunglasses and liked to put on a bit of a show. They were a work in progress, performing covers (including the famous TV jingle for Gingernuts biscuits) and a smattering of their own songs, which really needed work, and they never really developed as they should have. Johnny (real name Mike Williams) was always being kept at home to study for his exams, so they faded away. They were important, though, as they acted as a glue for the younger and older punks who wanted something other than bandwagon jumpers.

Vauxhalls guitarist Mark Brooks then joined up with Tony Peake to form the Newtones. Tony had been the singer in the early Christchurch punk band The Vandals, which also featured Alan Park, but he hadn't found the mix of competent older musicans and playing mainly covers all that satisfying. The Newtones should have been a success. A New Wave three-piece with lots of effects, controlled from the desk by Fred Krammer, they self-released a couple of seven-inch singles. Unfortunately you couldn't get past the average songwriting and singing, and the instrumental monotony, which the effects seemed to emphasise rather than embellish.

The Doomed were older musicians trying to keep up and play the new music. Dick Driver was their supposedly working-class singer and all-round oik. It was such a shameless put-on it made you realise that there was indeed something going on precisely because this lot were expending so much energy trying to be part of it.

Bill Direen's Vacuum were clearly a significant and important band during this period, as was his former band mate, songwriter, singer and guitarist Steven Cogle. He fronted the Victor Dimisich Band and shared some of the Vacuum players. Like them he trucked rather than rocked, hammered rather than rolled. Steven was solid and bushy-bearded. He had presence and a strong, distinctive, soaring singing voice. It was as though they had emerged from a wormhole all the way from the 1960s US garage-band scene, as was represented at the time on the popular hard-to-find but influential *Nuggets* and *Pebbles* collections.

Another band around town at this time was The Androidss, a motley collection of oddballs playing covers. Their showstopper was a cover of Iggy Pop's 'The Passenger' and I have found it difficult to listen to the orginal ever since. These guys really lived on the edge — on the edge of town, in a big old house out by Templeton Hospital for the disabled. They liked to throw parties. I never liked to stay too long. I'd slip out the back door when the vibe started to get too weird. You could pick that something was going to go off, you just couldn't be sure how it would manifest itself. The copious amounts of drink and the sheer volume and variety of drugs should have killed someone early on; as it was, damage was still done and in some cases teeth fell out and speech became permanently slurred.

The identical Marsden twins, Steve and Eric, were especially troublesome. One was more unpredictable than the other, but I could never tell them apart. I was fond of the Spencer brothers. Mark was arty and liked to wear make-up while he played away on his keyboards; Neil was thoroughly old Christchurch working class. I think he struggled with playing the bass, but he was always a solid friend in a prickly situation. He was as tough as nails.

Hanging out with The Androidss could be a bit hairy. They were a very wild, no-holds-barred outfit. To my mind, the odd man out in this band of oddments was guitarist Mark Wilson. He had been in the Basket Cases and seemed to be the band's musical backbone.

It wasn't just on the party scene that The Androidss created mayhem. David Bowie came to Christchurch in November 1978 to play the QEII Stadium and Paul Smith and I went along with our girlfriends. I was never a fan of the early Spiders from Mars material, but I had rather liked the recent Brian Eno–produced albums *Low* and *Heroes*. The song and video for 'Heroes' had reignited interest in Bowie and the concert was a huge event. We somehow managed to push our way close to the front of the stage, just behind where the Androidss had set up. They loved David Bowie and covered his songs live and were really cranked up for the show. Bowie had been in the press a few years earlier for giving coke-induced Nazi salutes in public and The Androidss thought they should acknowledge that foolishness with some of their own. Bowie announced that if he 'saw another right fist raised' the show was off. 'Crawl back to where you came from,' he said, and I thought about the inevitable party back at their place afterwards and shuddered. The salutes stopped and that's when the swinging chain appeared — perhaps the arms dropped because of the swinging chain. I'm not sure if it was the Androidss or some even crazier character doing the swinging, but it was terrifying, if brief. Luckily everything then settled down and the music finally became the rightful focus of the evening.

In 1981, the Androidss finally got to record a couple of their originals for Ripper Records. Doug Hood helped them record 'Getting Jumpy' and 'Auckland Tonight'. Andrew Shaw made a zippy video for 'Auckland Tonight' and they had a hit at number nineteen on the charts. But it was their swansong, and the band was over by the end of the year.

Ripper Records was owned by posh and booming radio voice Bryan Staff. Bryan had set up in 1979 with the seminal but patchy punk compilation *AK79* and later hit the big time with Phil Judd's Swingers and their 'Counting the Beat' hit. Ripper had the makings of a great independent record label, but the lack of any consistent taste soon manifested itself with a number of dud releases, including Marilyn Waring's cover of John Lennon's 'Working Class Hero'. The trouble was that Bryan's background was radio and he didn't really understand the music business, let alone music. A pity really, as the good things he released were undone by some appalling A&R decisions.

In Auckland, The Suburban Reptiles were fascinating and important, but ultimately musically unfulfilling. There were other good bands, too, but none that was a complete package, that really stopped you in your tracks. The one exception came out of Dunedin.

CHAPTER 5

CHRiS KNoX

In 1978 Paul Smith and I drove south to Dunedin to see a band I'd heard good things about. The reports must have been exceedingly favourable to prompt a five-hour drive in a clapped-out Morris 1100 that was barely powerful enough to climb anything resembling a hill. Whatever stimulated me to get down there and along to the Old Beneficiaries Hall in the town centre, nothing could have prepared me for the life-changing experience of seeing The Enemy for the very first time.

I had never visited Dunedin before. Dad was born above a butcher's shop on Cumberland Street in 1915 and refused to set foot in the town, so we always drove straight through at, at least for a fully laden underpowered car, high speed. Whereas Christchurch seemed grey, spread out and open to the sky, Dunedin felt darker and claustrophobic due to its surrounding hills and harbour. It was grimy, but it had a charm and the people were nice. They liked to drink too.

The Enemy were a revelation. Original songs performed by a very proficient band fronted by a charismatic lunatic. It was punk rock music all right, but not as I knew it. This was a different monster, untroubled by the affectations that had quickly congealed around the movement. The major point of difference was their original material. It wasn't played all that fast compared with what other punk bands were attempting to do. The Enemy played slower but the sound was bigger. They weren't ponderous, just determinedly grinding. They were the real deal and by far the best band I had ever seen live.

There was no collective fashion statement, just an assorted mix of everyday clothing. The guitar player was very good. The drummer knew his stuff and looked genuinely menacing — bell-bottoms over work boots and a Speight's T-shirt completed the South Dunedin working-class look to grim perfection. The bass player had long hair and also wore flares, which no one was going to take issue with. The singer, well, the singer was Chris Knox.

As I'd learn later, Chris was the adopted only child of Fred and June Knox. Born in 1952, he'd grown up in a comfortable middle-class household in Invercargill. Fred was an accountant and stockbroker and a keen Freemason who eventually rose to the top

The Enemy at the Old Beneficiaries Hall, Dunedin, 1978, with me on the dancefloor (photo by Jeff Batts)

of that organisation in New Zealand as the Grand Supreme Ruler. The Knoxes loved Chris and gave him everything he could want for, but I got the feeling they weren't all that sure what he was about.

A rather bolshie, sharp-witted child of reserved parents, he was largely left to his own devices. Spoilt and overfed, a bit fat and a bit short on friends, he lived in his own world of comics and music. He was open to all kinds of music, but especially The Beatles. He was academically able, but Chris's real interests were in what parents of that generation would have thought of as 'trash'. That's certainly what my parents thought of the comics, pop music and clothing consumed by the youth of the 1950s and 1960s. But that trash is now what we regard as popular culture, of course. Chris obsessively soaked it all up and developed the passions he would build his life around.

Chris had arrived in Dunedin from Invercargill in the early 1970s to attend university. I can't imagine university was ever going to be for him. Academic life would have been too rigid, too dull and too irrelevant. But it did get him out of Invercargill. Dunedin was a deeply conservative Presbyterian city that had been gradually declining for a long time, having once been the economic capital of New Zealand over a century earlier. Fortunately it was a university town and so maintained some connection with the rest of the civilised world. There was a bohemian set that flourished there and who supported bookshops and record shops and live music. Chris may have dropped out of university pretty quickly, meaning he had a succession of dead-end jobs (including grave digging, no pun intended), but he was free to read, draw and listen to music.

He was not a passive listener. Everything was analysed, approved of or rejected. He had a reputation as a heckler at live shows. He wasn't interested in rehashed covers, he wanted to hear bands playing their own music. If he could be a harsh critic, he was also willing to embrace and encourage those he thought were making the right sort of effort.

Punk had arrived at just the right time. Not afraid to overstate his own musical abilities, Chris had pulled together The Enemy with Mick Dawson, Mike Dooley and Alec Bathgate. He found his forte in the process, as a songwriter and collaborator, as a very fine singer, and as an over-the-top front man.

The Enemy were like nothing I had ever seen or heard before. Punk, yes, but with lots of other influences from the 1960s and 1970s mixed in. All sorts of strange things, from The Beatles, The Kinks, The Stooges, The Velvet Underground and even The Doors. In a funny anti-matter kind of way they were rather glam rock. Perhaps they were an unglamorous punk glam rock band. But while there may have been some theatrics from Chris, they were never Rocky Horror. They weren't like anything, really, from any other place or time. And I had never met anyone like Chris Knox before.

The audience at the Old Beneficiaries Hall wasn't big, but it was a volatile mixture of punks and surfers and other misfits, bouncing around under a framed portrait of the Queen. A fire hose was turned on and I found myself out the front door, where the evening's most bothersome punter (who had only one arm) was now lying beaten unconscious in the gutter.

I had the car and we careered through the centre of Dunedin with too many people on the inside and some sitting on the bonnet. The whisky bottle was in danger of becoming jammed in the steering wheel. Better there than stuck under the brake pedal while hurtling downhill, I suppose. As I said, the Morris lacked power and was especially ill equipped for the steep Dunedin hills. Everyone on the bonnet was happy to jump off and push.

It seemed my friend Paul and I were staying at The Enemy's house on Lachlan Avenue. Chris, Mike the drummer and band friend Doug Hood lived here. I'm not sure where Mick the bass player lived. Alec the guitarist was an art-school student, had a nice long-standing girlfriend, washed himself and his clothing, and liked to eat regular meals, so he lived elsewhere. The house was a rented, dilapidated affair. The wall of Chris's room was parting company with the rest of the house. There was a dead kitten in a preserving jar in the kitchen. Thank god there was no microwave. The drummer's appointment with the district court for assault was pinned to the wall.

There was plenty of lively chat until the beer and whisky ran out. I said I'd really enjoyed the show and asked for my money back so I could buy enough petrol to get back to Christchurch the next day. I passed out in an old worn-out and uncomfortable armchair rather than put my head down on the sofa — I knew who had been sitting there on a regular basis. I chose not to use the bathroom. We drove back to Christchurch the next day to tell everyone about this band we had seen in Dunedin. Nothing would be the same again.

The Enemy showed up in Christchurch soon enough. Every band wants to play to an audience and there was a good paying one in Christchurch. I knew the songs a little better now and I knew this band was the real deal. Everything else shrank by comparison, looked tame or fake or both.

I was also getting to know the characters in the band better, just by watching. Mick was eccentric and funny. Mike was quietly intimidating. Alec was a power-guitar genius, and a nice, reflective guy with it. Doug Hood was with them, sorting the sound and everything else, and was an easy-going, friendly guy. He got things done and was good with people. Someone with the band had to be. I soon came to understand that the scary thing about Chris was not any real physical menace, but what could and would come out of his mouth. He was intelligent, opinionated, outrageous, brave, sometimes plain stupid, and highly capable of creating extreme embarrassment and unease in those around him.

The Enemy were ambitious and wanted to connect with whatever was happening musically. So they drove their van — called 'Nothing' — north and relocated to Auckland where the perceived audience was that much bigger. But Auckland has never really delivered on the promise its size implies. It's so spread out; it's more a conurbation of loosely connected villages. The vast tracts of suburbia were just as provincial in outlook as the actual provinces themselves.

The Enemy frightened everyone in Auckland and made the boot boys look a bit lightweight. Squat, freaky Chris was probably the only one in the band who even thought about how he looked. Having been an overweight child had made him self-conscious, but he'd learned that being confidently confrontational was an effective defence mechanism. The Enemy's disregard for trend was actually an extreme form of street fashion before anyone in New Zealand knew what that was. The punk look in London had been quickly simplified, commodified and absorbed into the mainstream. The Enemy, with their everyday Dunedin duds and Chris's reverse mohawk, were anti-fashion. Everyone noticed, and that was the point. At the same time, there was no point.

The move to Auckland was a disappointment. They were warmly received but the audience didn't seem much bigger than the one they had left, plus it was full of idiotic boot people. Mick didn't like Auckland and headed back to Dunedin, which effectively finished the band. The others stayed and settled, Alec and Doug with the girlfriends who had travelled north with them.

The remaining members of The Enemy then recruited Jane Walker and Paul Kean (from Christchurch band Detroit Hemorroids) to play keyboards and bass in a new band called Toy Love. They added a certain Christchurch musical sensibility, as well as Jane's female influence. Her keyboards gave the band another musical dimension, too.

It was at this time that Chris met his match in Barbara Ward. Barbara is the one who helped Chris grow up and get a better perspective on the world. Having been born in Invercargill in 1952 could manifest itself in unsavoury ways, especially when it came to his views on women and sex. As his partner and soon-to-be mother of his children, Barbara was the sensible one in the family. She put Chris right on a number of fundamental issues, including women and meat. Chris was open to her guidance and became a passionate feminist and vegetarian. He even learned how to cook.

While The Enemy were punk rock, Toy Love were New Wave. They were still strange and peculiar, but also a bit poppy and much more accessible. They were to have a serious crack at crossover success. Definitions of the two significant and vaguely overlapping musical genres that grew out of punk are difficult, but crucially important to the way I view all the fantastic music that came out of that original big bang. Bands I would call New Wave included Blondie, the B52s and even the likes of Toni Basil. They were commercially driven and looking for mainstream appeal in their colourful straight trousers, skinny leather ties and bright shirts. While there was some great New Wave music, the post-punk movement was at the more serious and arty end of the same spectrum. I would describe Television, Wire, Pere Ubu, Talking Heads, Public Image, The Clean and Tall Dwarfs as post-punk bands. It was a blurry, ever-changing and subjective thing, but in my mind Toy Love were always a New Wave band. They had the musical intelligence and integrity of post punk but the naked ambition and overriding pop sensibilities of the New Wave.

Toy Love recorded one great double-A-side single, 'Rebel'/'Squeeze', and briefly became the biggest band in New Zealand. It's one of the best ever New Zealand singles — two poppy, knowing rock songs that defined the time and place perfectly. I saw them play a few times when they passed through Christchurch on tour. They were very good and certainly a better band than The Enemy, but it wasn't the same for me. In fact, seeing them live could be a loathsome experience. They attracted the psychopathic to their shows, really scary people, violent thugs that made your average boot boy look like what he actually was, a bit lightweight. My girlfriend was seriously harassed on the dance floor and I found it hard to keep on being a real fan.

Chris always felt the need to put on a show. Toy Love scaring the locals, Sydney, 1979 (photo by Carol Tippet)

The singles that came out after 'Rebel'/'Squeeze' didn't do it for me either. There was less excitement and less sense of direction in their recorded output. But live, my own misgivings aside, they were the biggest band in the land. Everyone noticed them and their predictably unpredictable, outrageous front man.

Everyone noticing was the point. Chris was hopelessly addicted to showing off. He was the weird kid whose mouth got him into and out of trouble. He was sure of his own ability as a performer, but he also understood that he needed the band. It was always a collaborative, democratic undertaking. In his natural element on stage, however, the boredom of being in a band and on the road would play out in all manner of ways. There were often props — bandages, watermelons, aluminium foil or a broken bottle. If the audience wanted a show then he was going to give it to them, sometimes with self-mutilation and blood. The spectacle of an insecure show-off putting on a show was in some ways a little passé. Post punk had shown that good music was enough, but New Wave was still very much about pleasing a crowd. Chris didn't need to do it. The band was good enough, the songs were good enough, and Chris could sing very well. The self-harming theatrics were in danger of detracting from the whole.

And the band was treading water. They had largely exhausted New Zealand and were clued up enough to understand the self-limiting nature of the local music business. They knew they had to make a move if they were going to stay together and keep making music. They backed themselves and knew that if they could get to London they had a chance of a real career. In 1979 there was no known route to the UK and into the music scene there. So Toy Love had to accept a deal that took them to Sydney first, with the 'promise' of the UK later.

Australia was a disaster. The rules for a new band in town were that you played around the traps and gradually built an audience. You paid your dues and moved up the pecking order until you could have a crack at proper success. The time it took was measurable in years, so it helped to have a thick skin and play towards the dumber demographics of the rock audience. Toy Love were a bit too mouthy and disrespectful for their open-armed hosts. The people who ran the venues, booked the bands and even those who wrote about the music didn't like them much. It was more about their attitude than the actual music.

They got as far as making an album they weren't all that happy with, and came back to New Zealand ground down and exhausted. The challenges of mindlessly playing out a predictable future of paying dues and living by the accepted record industry wisdoms were just too much. It was the end of Toy Love.

A big part of the band's legacy was how *not* to go about things in the music business. Their advice, based on experience, was to not go to Australia, not sign with a commercial record company, not bother recording in a fancy studio. Find another way of doing it. Quite what that might actually involve they weren't too sure. But their friends and fans in bands back in Dunedin took notice.

CHAPTER 6

THE CLEAN

So, early in 1981, I stepped into the record company side of the music business. I took note of Toy Love's disastrous experiences and saw myself as part of a worldwide proliferation of small, artist-centric labels that generally wanted to do things differently from the old-style record companies.

I travelled up to the PolyGram pressing plant in Wellington to try to get a handle on the whole record-pressing process. I wanted to put some faces to the names I was mainly writing to and occasionally phoning. My contact, Ziggy, was an enthusiastic, long-haired metal guy who, like a lot of Miramar locals, was a big softball fan. So, after an obligatory softball chat, he took me on a tour of the plant. From the cutting room to the making of the stampers to the pressing of the records, it all seemed like a horridly dirty and inexact process.

I had studied how records were made and I understood the process in theory. Now I seriously wondered how any of it could possibly work and result in music coming out of a set of speakers. It seemed like an impossibly haphazard process: filthy heavy-metal electro-plating rooms producing stampers; a large room with large, noisy metal pressing machines; and glassed-in booths where weary-looking women checked freshly pressed records for faults. I couldn't see how this car-wrecking environment could produce music. And it wasn't long before I began experiencing the pressing problems and faults that were to become a particular bugbear for Flying Nun.

Meanwhile, back in Christchurch, things were happening. A Dunedin band called The Clean came through town to play the Gladstone in an early-in-the-week slot from Monday 27 to Wednesday 29 April. I had seen them play support for The Enemy at the Old Beneficiaries Hall in Dunedin three years earlier. While I had been intrigued by their ramshackle performance, they couldn't compete with the bulldozer that was The Enemy that night. But things had changed.

After a few years living in different cities doing different things, with different bass players and different bands, brothers Hamish and David Kilgour had returned to Dunedin and found stability with Robert Scott on bass. They had flourished, they

Doug Hood singing with The Clean at the Old Beneficiaries Hall, Dunedin, 1978 (photo by Jeff Batts)

all wrote songs, there was a real variety to their material. The playing and singing could be delightfully unconventional but it was direct and inspired. They could be poppy or militantly post punk or genuinely psychedelic. Like The Enemy, they really did have it. They were the real thing.

I approached them after the show. In fact, I approached them as soon as they'd finished playing and were still on the stage. Want to put a record out? They said they were keen. Let's keep in touch and see.

After sitting on that for a day or so I decided I had to do more than just wait and see. I booked a flight to see them in Auckland, where they'd been headed when they stopped to play in Christchurch. Propeller was based in Auckland and I knew The Clean were good enough to attract attention from any alert or able record label. I badly needed to reiterate my interest and head off any potential suitors. This record label life was already getting exciting, if not just a little stressful.

I had never been to Auckland before. Whereas Christchurch is dominated by an ancient volcano that is largely no longer there, Auckland is set amongst a field of fifty or so volcanic molehills (or 'maunga', as we know them now), set around an isthmus that separates two attractive harbours. The city itself is a conurbation of small hamlets that have sprawled together to create what would be called a 'primate city' in any other country. It's New Zealand's biggest city and its commercial centre. Unlike in monocultural Christchurch, there was a large Polynesian population, at the time living mainly in the shabby inner suburbs of Parnell and Ponsonby. The heat and humidity were shocking and I immediately started sweating nonstop.

I was staying with a friend in genteel Devonport and I somehow managed to track down The Clean, who invited me to visit them that evening at the house they were staying at in Ponsonby. My friend agreed to drive me but she wouldn't stop on Ponsonby Road to let me out. Word was it was too dangerous because of the King Cobras (or KCs), an inner-city Polynesian gang. The KCs seemed to have it in for punks, no doubt due to an initially justified hatred of boot boys that had come to include all punks and new-wavers. They all looked the same, after all.

The upshot was that I had to jump out of a moving car, although my friend kindly cut her speed. The Three Lamps end of Ponsonby Road was unnervingly quiet. The junk shops were all closed and apart from the odd passing car there was no one about. The silence was broken by an occasional shout or scream in the distance. When I found the house, the door was answered by a polite and neatly dressed young man who introduced himself as Martin Phillipps.

Martin was travelling with The Clean and occasionally playing keyboards with them. I learned the house was being rented to The Androidss — there was no getting away from those guys. I didn't know what they had been up to, but the KCs apparently liked to launch attacks on the property by smashing all the windows. I was paranoid for the rest of the evening, but when The Clean returned from dinner we decided they would record a single at Nightshift Studio in Christchurch on their way back to Dunedin.

I had the chance to catch the band play a show at a place called The Reverb Room. A great name for a venue but the reality was alarming. The Edinburgh Castle Hotel on Symonds Street was one of those old-style pubs where people went to drink themselves to oblivion. The Reverb Room was upstairs. The stairs were completely open to the public bar below. I thought I knew my way around public bars, and perhaps I did in Christchurch. But I was in big-city, multicultural Auckland now and suddenly I knew I didn't.

Looking down from those stairs was like looking into a seething pit of broken humanity. Broken but still enraged and manically threatening. I was suddenly sweating again and it wasn't just the humidity or from the exertion of walking up those stairs. I knew the whole of the downstairs bar could smell that sweat. Somehow they could smell it over the terrible stench of hundreds of gallons of stale spilt beer. I made a mental note to leave well before closing time so that I didn't get beaten to a pulp.

The Reverb Room itself was a very plain space, the main decorative element being sturdy metal grilles fastened to the insides of the windows. I guess this was to keep the flying glass jugs from breaking the windowpanes. The crowd was noticeably smarter and more fashion conscious than I was accustomed to, and contrasted nicely with the timeless looks on display downstairs. Upstairs it was art students and miscellaneous groovers. It was ideal. Painful as they sometimes are, early adopters are vital indicators of a band on the rise. The Prime Movers played support and were proficient enough, but the early adopters were not there for them. Perhaps sensing this, drummer Chris Matthews would shortly leave the band and go on to greater things, connecting with Flying Nun in the future with Children's Hour, This Kind of Punishment and the Headless Chickens.

It was a flat live environment. The room was the wrong shape and configuration for enjoying a band or moving around, the sound system was average, the acoustics poor. But The Clean had long experience of playing halls in Dunedin with lousy acoustics and substandard sound systems. They knew how to uncomplainingly shine in such a situation and they put on a good show.

We had agreed to spend $50 recording a song called 'Tally Ho!'. It was a completely arbitrary amount, plucked out of thin air, as none of us had any idea how much time or money was involved. The band told Arnie at Nightshift they had $50 and they wanted to record a song and that was it. I guess we got what we paid for.

We chose 'Tally Ho!' because it was poppy and fun and maybe we thought this might translate into commercial success. Martin Phillipps played keyboards. It's a wonderful song, but not a single commercial radio station was ever going to play it, not even once.

The B-side, 'Platypus', was recorded live at the Gladstone. We sent the master tape off to the pressing plant.

The plan was for my friend Paul Smith to design the sleeve. When I started Flying Nun the idea was that Paul would be my partner and produce the artwork for covers. But events moved quickly and it became obvious the bands wanted to do their own art, or at least control the cover designs, and this seemed right. Paul did, however, get to design a generic Flying Nun seven-inch cover. It was black with a circular hole so the disc's label could be seen, with the label name and details in silver. Paul also designed the first Flying Nun poster, which was supposedly for both the Pin Group and The Clean's new singles but was really announcing the arrival of the new label.

The Clean seemed happy to go with Paul's generic cover for 'Tally Ho!' but insisted on an insert. Maybe The Pin Group getting their own cover had set a precedent. As it turned out, it was the first and last time the generic Flying Nun sleeve was ever used.

There's no denying the 'Tally Ho!' recording was primitive and didn't represent the band's live sound, but the response was positive. Reviews were supportive, and while, as expected, commercial radio didn't play it, student radio up and down the country did. The band reached their potential core audience

Early versions of The Clean 'Tally Ho' record labels by Paul Smith

Records

THE CLEAN   YING1 (FN 002)

THE PIN GROUP   FN 001

PO BOX 3000   CHRISTCHURCH

Paul Smith's 1981 poster for the first Pin Group and Clean singles

right then and built on it over the next year. That groundswell generated demand from retailers around the country and pushed the single into the national top twenty chart at number nineteen. It was there for one week. It felt like an absolute triumph.

The success meant people took us a little more seriously as a label. Jim Wilson was the promoter of shows at the Gladstone and the Hillsborough and had art student John Halvorsen doing basic artwork for posters. Knowing John played, he asked him to quickly form a band to fill a vacant night. The Gordons is what John came up with, featuring Alister Parker (guitar) and Brent McLachlan (drums). They were the sort of band that sprang from relative isolation, despite Alister previously playing in a covers band and in The Basket Cases with Jane Walker and Paul Kean. Their sound was singular and uncompromising: brutal, sparse and modern, and away ahead of its time. Well played, precise and clear. They were a bit aloof from the scene, but everyone was in awe of them.

The Gordons weren't at all a blues-derived heavy metal band, more skull-crunching guitar art rock — spare, intense and driven. And extremely loud. Not just unusually loud for the times but unquestionably loud for any era. I witnessed punters pushing over tables trying to get to the doors and away from the noise at their first Gladstone show. And that was after the initial minutes of excruciating high-pitch feedback, before the first song started properly. They were so inspiring on so many levels.

Brent McLachlan was and still is a friendly, warm, commonsense kind of guy, while John could be very friendly but a little shy. Alister could be a whole lot of things all at once. They were outsiders making outsider music. True to their independence and self-containment, they had self-released a single called 'Future Shock' a year earlier. It made a stir among fans of New Zealand post punk but little impression beyond, despite television's *Radio with Pictures* show making and screening a video.

Unfortunately, the boot boys loved them and this ultimately brought about the demise of the band. The violence and aggravation the boot boys brought to live shows wore them down. But before they broke up they recorded an impressive self-titled album. They needed help to press and distribute it, and I was able to help with both.

After our whiff of success with The Clean, shops outside the four main centres of Auckland, Wellington, Christchurch and Dunedin became interested in stocking our records. There were sales to be had. And the fact that we were now carrying a full-priced Gordons album made it even more attractive and kept the back catalogue moving along. Ramshackle as it was, Flying Nun now had the makings of its own distribution network, and an enduring relationship between the label and record retailers would soon develop.

The Clean relocated north from Dunedin after the 'Tally Ho!' release. The Kilgours' mother had moved to Christchurch and David and Hamish followed. It was a difficult time of alienation and attempted adjustment. Christchurch can take some getting used to, even for those born there. The topography and weather are peculiar: the flat plain and the alarming winds. But this was when I got to know and like the band as people.

Before moving to Dunedin in their teens, Hamish and David Kilgour had lived in small South Island towns such as Ranfurly and Cheviot, the kinds of places people tend to come from rather than go to. Drummer and singer Hamish, the darker older brother, is socially aware and concerned, and some of his militant, agitprop views are well expressed in many of his Clean compositions. David, the taller, blonder younger brother, likes to surf most days, which is surely rare in independent music circles. Friendly and polite, he's also a bit harder to get to know, a touch introverted, maybe, but quietly determined and uncompromising about his music. He is an exceptional, self-taught, unorthodox guitarist. His delightfully mangled integration of rhythm and lead is a highlight of much of the band's material.

The Kilgours played as The Clean with a number of other musicians, on and off, from their first gig in 1978. It became their mission to find a bass player, and the search dragged on from Dunedin to Auckland and back again to Dunedin where they eventually found their man.

Robert Scott was from the town of Mosgiel just outside Dunedin. The amiable and easy-going son of a mathematician, he wrote songs, sang and played confident and steady bass. It was what the band desperately needed. Robert was to be the rhythmic anchor that held the charmingly loose and scattered drumming together with the inspired, intuitively free-flowing and soaring guitar.

Three-piece bands cannot operate without a gifted bass player acting as the glue between the other instruments, as well as providing additional musicality to fill the extra space where a rhythm guitar or keyboard might normally lurk.

Robert's temperament was also very important. Hamish and David were close but had very different personalities. While they worked extremely well together, there could be tensions. Robert was a calming, disarming influence, a naturally sunny, happy guy who wasn't afraid to pull out his Donald Duck impersonation to cool a heated moment on stage or in the studio. (You can hear the calming duck dialogue between 'Fish' and 'Flowers' on the *Great Sounds Great* twelve-inch EP or the *Anthology* CD.)

* * *

Chris Knox had settled down in Auckland with Barbara and started a family. With a small inheritance he bought a second-hand Teac four-track tape-recording machine and started experimenting. He had no band and no intention of working, so he had the time to fiddle about. The four-track was simple but still required some application and technical expertise to use. Its limitations meant any sophistication in recording was possible only with careful planning and operation.

Chris teamed up with ex–band mate Alec Bathgate. They had always got on well. Despite different appearances, backgrounds and lifestyles, they shared a common view of the music they wanted to make. Mucking about in Chris's living room they came up with some recordings and released an EP, *Three Songs*, on Furtive Records (an offshoot of Propeller) in 1981. They called themselves Tall Dwarfs.

Having made this quirky statement of intent, Chris put together some simple homemade films to go with the songs. A film fan and lover of animation, he applied the same DIY, find-out-by-doing ethos he applied to making music. The video for one of the songs, 'Nothing's Going to Happen', was made with scraps of film donated by TVNZ and employed stop-motion animation techniques to turn everyday objects and settings (including a top twenty music countdown on a TV screen) into something altogether weirder and funnier. Barbara and flatmates Doug Hood and Carol Tippet supported Chris's film apprenticeship, and the result was a pioneering video that showed another side of his talents.

Three Songs sold very well, largely due to the residual interest in Toy Love. It was a basic recording but hinted at the possibilities of a whole new world and way of doing things. Tall Dwarfs brought a host of ideas to their songwriting. Some of it was conventionally structured and some of it was closer to improvised 'noise'. Either way, recording on basic equipment and retaining more control over the process freed the band from the tyranny of the studio. It wasn't just a cost-saving exercise, it was artistically liberating.

It was around this time that I got to know Chris a bit better. I had always been a bit wary of his sharp tongue and knew when it was time to quietly slip away, usually later in the evening after a few drinks. Chris was always sure of himself, confident in his ability to win an argument even if he wasn't right. Over time, as we worked together, we became better friends. He mellowed and became a little more generous to those around him. He didn't stop kicking, but the kicks were a bit better aimed as he aged.

* * *

Once settled in Christchurch, The Clean got out and played more shows on the back of 'Tally Ho!' and more people came out to see them. The band wanted to record again, this time using Chris Knox's four-track. They were all old friends, including with Doug Hood, who had been The Clean's original singer the night I had seen them at the Old Beneficiaries Hall. Doug had left the band to travel with The Enemy and then Toy Love as soundman and fixer.

Being the practical one, Doug Hood rang to say it would cost $750 to record a new Clean EP over three days. It was a lot of money but ultimately a bargain, considering the cost of tape, extra gear, venue hire and people's time.

The Bond Street building, the Legion of Frontiersmen Field Headquarters (which we renamed Frontear). It was here that The Clean recorded *Boodle Boodle Boodle* (photo by Jonathan Ganley).

They set up in a small hall on Bond Street on the edge of Auckland's Grey Lynn, right next to the bridge over the northwestern motorway. The five songs were very simply and well recorded. They were nicely varied in style and pace. In many ways it was a perfect EP. 'Billy Two' kicked off side one with a propulsive acoustic guitar strum, whiny David vocals, oblique lyrics and a nice big chorus, with some swirly backwards guitar to keep everything a bit strange. Short, concise and winning. 'Thumbs Off' is a bit plodding but its inclusion was a welcome contrast to the other material and has historical importance as the recorded debut of Robert's unique and world-famous seemingly off-key singing style. 'Anything Could Happen' is another good example of the band's well-paced 'pop' songs.

Side two opens with 'Sad Eyed Lady', which sounds more edgy and post-punk. Finally, 'Point That Thing Somewhere Else' is a five-and-a-half-minute drone-rock epic. The song dates back to the earliest days of the band and had been co-written by the Kilgour brothers and co-founding member Peter Gutteridge.

I knew The Clean were a very good band, but this convinced me they were so much more. Now I knew they were special, as good as anything on offer anywhere.

Part of what made these songs work so well was the integration of ideas and musical references within The Clean's sound. They were obviously a post-punk band, inspired to form in the big bang of punk. They drew on immediate punk and post-punk influences like The Enemy and Toy Love from Dunedin and contemporaries from the UK and the US. But what The Clean shared with many other Dunedin bands was a keen awareness of what came before. Sixties psychedelia, The Beatles, The Velvet Underground, The Stooges, US garage bands, Bob Dylan, Big Star and much more were all thrown into a stew that had a depth most other bands could not match. Picking up a few ideas from a fashionable overseas band was no substitute for the long simmering of ideas, sounds, styles and nuances from many different scenes and periods that The Clean had now distilled.

OPPOSITE PAGE: Carol Tippet took the photo. LEFT: Chris Knox based his drawing on it for The Clean's *Boodle Boodle Boodle* cover.

Television New Zealand chose to make a video for 'Anything Could Happen'. The result, directed by children's TV host Andrew Shaw, was remarkably good, fronted by a Dylanesque David Kilgour and shot around Christchurch landmarks like the Square and the Bexley dump.

Chris Knox put the now-famous front cover together, basing the black-on-white drawing of the band fully clothed and sodden in a bath on a Carol Tippet photograph. The back cover was a collage of drawings by the band members themselves. And, of course, there was a comic, with contributions from the band and friends (including Martin Phillipps and Chris Knox). Unfortunately, the sequence was muddled and the pages appear out of order, but no one seemed to mind. The EP's title was mysterious: *Boodle Boodle Boodle*. What did that mean?

Money, maybe. The money spent on the recording, or the money to be made on the 10,000 copies sold in EP form in New Zealand alone. Whatever, *Boodle Boodle Boodle*, released in November 1981, was very successful. The reviews were glowing. Student radio thrashed it. Record shops bought it in batches of a hundred and were constantly running out of stock. It went to number three on the singles chart in December 1981 and came back to the same spot in the new year. It stayed in the top forty for twenty-six weeks.

The Clean were hot property, playing to more and more people at more and bigger shows. They were very much the darling band of the moment. As for Flying Nun, there was a little money sloshing around now, as well as the confidence to want to do something more with it.

CHAPTER 7

FOUR-TRACK

Thanks largely to the success of The Clean, Flying Nun enjoyed a spectacular first seven months of business through to March 1982. The label had released some really good records, important records that did well and had charted. We had sold a phenomenal number of The Clean's *Boodle Boodle Boodle*. But I didn't see Flying Nun as a business with a long-term future at this stage.

I was still working at the Record Factory during the day and spending my lunch breaks at the post office trying to get all the mail-order packages away. I was living in a house opposite the beach in Sumner, twenty minutes out of Christchurch. I had an office there and worked late most nights when I wasn't in town at a gig. I never once stood on the sand of that beach.

Yet while I didn't see it as a full-time concern, that is what Flying Nun was steadily evolving into. The company was capitalised with $300 when I set it up. Initially, I was selling singles that did not have much margin, being relatively cheap to buy but comparatively expensive to make. Then the *Boodle* EP, with a little more margin, sold an awful lot of copies. With no office expenses or wages to pay, overheads were low. There was some spare cash and a real feeling of optimism. The sense that anything could happen was heightened with naive recklessness as Doug Hood and Chris Knox aligned themselves and their projects with the label, dictating developments in the new year.

Between the release of 'Tally Ho!' and *Boodle* there was a loose collection of releases, including the two Pin Group singles, various Bill Direen seven-inch EP projects and the Gordons album. The loose distribution system that built itself on these releases revolved around friends holding stock and dealing with the shops in the four main centres.

Roy Colbert in Dunedin had his second-hand record shop, succinctly named Records Records, and it was a bit of a hub for the hip of Dunedin. Roy was exceptionally knowledgeable about music, wrote about it (and cricket) for the Dunedin *Star*, had been a fan of the long-haired bands of the early '70s and then seen the light with the rise of The Enemy. With the transmutation of The Enemy into Toy Love, Roy's shop became the focus for the post-punk kids inspired to have a go themselves. It became the place to meet, talk about music, form a band and commit to learning an instrument … probably in that order.

Doug Hood had put me in touch with his Toy Love friend and roadie Ian Dalziel, who was now living in Wellington. He was willing to help get our records into the shops there. It seemed important to have someone on the ground looking after and over things. Wellington always felt different to the rest of New Zealand. The extreme weather gave it a worn, blasted look: peeling paint, bleached bare boards and rusty roofing iron. The people who lived there didn't look in much better shape.

With a large civil service population, there was a quasi-intellectual thing going on alongside the self-employed juggling busker scene that radiated out in multicoloured circus rainbows from the bucket fountain in Cuba Mall. Faded-black-clad skinheads still stumbled the streets, there were serious metallers in the Hutt, office workers listened and danced to Latin music, and older disenchanted rock fans now tapped their fingers to country music.

All sorts and oddballs, but there was a large enough number of the sane and musically astute to buy good quantities of our records as well. Ian also had a job, so he formed a collective of volunteers who dealt directly with the shops. It seemed convoluted but it worked. When Ian moved to Auckland to work at music magazine *Rip It Up*, Chris Lipscombe took over, followed by Kevin Jenkins, before our distribution became more mainstream later in the decade. All through the 1980s the label depended on good people like these who volunteered their time to help glue covers, sleeve records or coordinate orders and deliveries to shops. Their motivation came from wanting to help with something that was culturally important to them. Nothing much would have happened without their involvement.

In Auckland I discovered the practical Doug Hood also now had a job with musical equipment hiring outfit Live Sound. He suggested the non-working, stay-at-home Chris Knox could do the rounds of the shops in Auckland. The big record stores were doing enough business to pay the high rentals in the middle of things. All the key shops were reasonably central, on Queen Street and in nearby Newmarket. Chris didn't like to drive but he could slip on his jandals and catch a bus, so it was easy enough and the shopkeepers loved to see him. It was probably the only chance most of them ever got to see a mouthy rock-star-troublemaker-legend up close. And here he was, every week, delivering our records.

I looked after the Christchurch shops and all the main regional outlets by phone and post. There was a reasonable number of them in those days, too, with every decent-sized town having a record shop or two, and the smaller ones usually having a larger general retailer with a record department next to the whiteware.

The major nationwide chain was EMI. (In Dunedin the EMI stores would increasingly be staffed and run by Flying Nun band members. They too were important meeting places and sold huge numbers of our records.) EMI was strong everywhere that mattered except Auckland. It seemed to be this Wellington-based corporation's blind spot. Otherwise, they had the best locations in each town and really motored through the sales.

Being British they had impeccable internal bookkeeping systems that meant I could ring up on the due date and be paid in full for the previous month's sales. It was a phone call I would soon be making every month, and our cash flow came to pivot on those substantial payments.

Retailers came to recognise Flying Nun as The Clean's record label, which had also released or distributed some other interesting Christchurch and Dunedin artists that seemed to share some sort of blurred southern aesthetic. They were interested not simply because they were sympathetic to the music but because they could see the value in stocking it. No doubt there were a couple of local oddballs who had read about these records in *Rip It Up*, but almost without exception retailers were curious, friendly and supportive.

I guess we also had that underdog appeal. Compared with the big and wealthy multinational record companies, Flying Nun was a small ragtag local outfit that had quickly proved (with The Clean in particular) it could shift big commercial quantities of its new releases.

In that first little-over-half-year of business to March 1982 we turned over roughly $11,000, mainly in singles sales, with some *Boodle* sales at year's end. We were selling the seven-inch singles to shops for $2 wholesale, sold at $2.99 retail, and the *Boodle* EP for $3.25, retailing at $4.99. While margins were low, in a sense this economy helped create a house style — a philosophical and practical approach that defined how the label and its associated artists went about things, as well as the general sound of the recordings that were released.

Key to all this was the manner of the recording itself. Chris Knox's four-track produced a quality that was clear and direct rather than flashy and elaborate. As a process it was relatively simple and unfussy. The machine came with two sets of sympathetic ears, Chris's and Doug's. It was cheap. For The Clean, the simple technology suited their level of know-how and produced recordings that matched their growing audience's expectations. It was a step up from the primitive Nightshift Studio experience, but not a leap into the unfathomable of a major commercial twenty-four-track studio.

I knew we couldn't afford to use 'proper' studios. They were not just expensive, but also time-consuming to use in order to get a result. The cost of that result would likely never be recouped from record sales because of the limited size of the New Zealand market. The notion of selling New Zealand music overseas was a daydream at that stage.

Staff at such recording establishments were generally not at all sympathetic to music made outside of the commercial rock pop 'mainstream' — defined by what was successful overseas. They fretted about quality control and production values, whereas we were concerned with maintaining and projecting the spirit of the music. The technicians tended to dress and behave appallingly and they reeked of condescension. No one from our neck of the woods was comfortable with letting their hard-saved money, let alone their treasured songs, anywhere near these yesterday's characters. Relations tended to be frosty.

The punk and post-punk experience had already shifted the emphasis away from the high-end technology that had grown around music in the 1970s. Expensive state-of-the-art sound and lighting gave way to the short, sharp and direct. Songs were stripped back and delivered in a more forthright, honest manner. Decades later the word 'authentic' would be used to describe it. The Clean were always authentic, in that they had developed in an organic way and were their own people, honest about their music and free of pretension.

The received wisdom was that you needed the full studio treatment not only to satisfy your fans but also the radio programmers. They were the gatekeepers to the airwaves, airplays, sales and chart success. The fact those programmers were highly unlikely to play anything that hadn't already made the US or UK charts didn't deter countless hopefuls from throwing their money at expensive studios. You might even say the industry was based on the dreams of wannabes rather than the success of the few that actually made it.

* * *

Late in 1981, Chris and Doug stopped over on their way to Dunedin to discuss bringing the four-track down to Christchurch. The idea soon became a bit grand and ambitious — slightly crazed in a way that became a hallmark of Flying Nun and that helped make it what it became. Not little and modest and boring but big and sprawling and out of control. It was the music business, after all. Wasn't this how it was meant to be played?

It was the first time we had got together for a decent chat. I think we met upstairs in the Lounge Bar of the United Services Hotel on the corner of Colombo Street and the Square. I liked the rough public bar downstairs for the pure danger, but the upstairs bar with its visiting farmers and their wives became my informal town office. They liked me there. It probably had something to do with the extra business I was generating for them. It became a bit of a pattern, this meeting in bars.

Chris and Doug probably mistook my ranting lunacy for enthusiasm. We bounced some ideas around about what we might do for the next Clean recording. Chris was keen to record a new Tall Dwarfs record and to release it on Flying Nun. This was fantastic news. I was a fan and recognised there were sales to be had and I knew that none of this worked without sales.

For Chris, becoming a partner and father had meant the end of the traditional rock lifestyle. The home recordings and film-making suited his new existence in Grey Lynn. There was an element of cautious control — no huge gambles or disruptions, just a steady creativity. It all suited the collaborative Flying Nun ethos very well and the label was the perfect home for Tall Dwarfs. No conventional record company would have allowed the level of creative indulgence Chris and Alec enjoyed, nor reaped the benefits.

It became the model for the productive years to follow. As well as writing and recording and dealing with the shops, Chris was finding other artists for Flying Nun, liaising over cover art and attending cutting sessions in Wellington. What success the label enjoyed owed a lot to this eccentric business setup. No one was going to get rich, but some great records would get made.

Doug Hood (in the mirror), the Teac four-track and Chris Knox (photo by Alec Bathgate)

CHAPTER 8

DUNEDiN

The guys in The Clean had been telling me about the other bands I should be checking out. While I was working with a number of Christchurch bands it was pretty obvious that something special was happening in Dunedin. I began driving down for the odd weekend to see if I could find out what it was.

The four-and-a-half hour drive each way in a less than dependable car had to fit around work at the Record Factory. I would head down on Friday night for a show on the Saturday and a party or two afterwards. I often stayed at Roy Colbert's place and the trip was always worth it. The music was good, there was always something new, and I made friends with so many people I had so much in common with. A shared interest in music and whisky goes a long way.

There seemed to be a lack of regular venues, but the music was exciting. It was a small but real scene — different to what was happening in Christchurch, not as dark but also '60s influenced, more engaging and accessible. The bands were really rather good. I could see the potential and I knew if they made records I could sell them.

My thinking turned to the idea of recording and packaging together the best of these young Dunedin bands. A number of local compilations had done the usual 'twelve tracks by twelve different artists' thing, with some sort of overarching title and cover concept. You were presented with a collection of self-contained songs, but they were in isolation and without context — it was hard to get a real feel for the bands involved.

I liked the idea of giving individual bands enough room on a compilation to shine properly and so I came up with another approach — albeit one that made no short-term sense economically — a double 45-rpm twelve-inch EP with a gatefold sleeve, showcasing four bands, each of whom would have a whole side of the EP and their own side of the cover. It would be called the *Dunedin Double*.

Chris and Doug came down to Christchurch in late February and set up the four-track in Paul Kean's house on Longfellow Street in Sydenham. The initial plan had grown a bit. On top of bringing four younger Dunedin bands north to play and record, both The Clean and Tall Dwarfs were to record EPs.

David, Hamish and Robert more or less suggested the line-up of the acts they thought worth recording, mostly young bands that had very limited opportunities to play live in their native Dunedin. The pub venues weren't interested in independently minded bands like The Clean, let alone their younger underage friends. This was the reason The Clean had their own PA, which they towed around the country on a trailer, so they could play halls.

Early on, the young Dunedin bands didn't really have much of an audience beyond their own friends, and that was the extent of the scene. It was very small but very concentrated and creative, and eventually found a suitably small home when the Empire Tavern opened its doors as a regular live venue. But Christchurch was different, with more venues and a much bigger, keenly interested audience.

I had seen The Verlaines when they had travelled north with The Clean early in the year to play a Gladstone show. Led by the charismatic, white silk scarf–wearing singer-songwriter-guitarist Graeme Downes, they were an intense, angular band unlike anything I had heard before. Graeme was studying classical music at Otago University and had been directly inspired by The Clean to form a band to play his carefully and intricately structured songs. He was serious, focused and intense about his music, but always interested in a little whisky to help the conversation along. We became rather good friends.

More than a few people were talking up a band put together by Martin Phillipps. They were called The Chills. We had already met when he toured with The Clean and played on 'Tally Ho!'. He had struck me as smart and confident, a quietly ambitious young man. Having earlier played with another Dunedin combo, The Same, he had a bit of previous experience. He was serious about songwriting and the songs he wrote were very good — complex and quirky yet accessible and poppy. The Chills was such a good name, and Martin was properly connected and endorsed by The Clean, so they were in.

I had acquired a couple of cassettes by a three-piece called The Stones. Very basic live recordings made at parties, one was called 'Live at Altamont' as there had been a stabbing; the other was 'Gimme Smelter', a humorous reference to the historically controversial proposal to raise the levels of Lake Manapouri in Fiordland to feed the proposed Aramoana aluminium smelter with cheap hydro-electricity.

The Stones were a big rollicking roller of a band with a belligerent attitude and a snotty view of life. Bass player Jeff Batts and guitarist Wayne Elsey were such raucous personalities that, by necessity, drummer Graeme Anderson was the civilising influence in the band. Musically the least conventional of the four bands, perhaps the simplest and at the same time most interesting, they often played large, grooved improvisations rather than songs with traditional structures.

Who else? David Kilgour recommended I check out Sneaky Feelings. Based on later interviews, I think David may have liked them partly because they *weren't* influenced by The Clean. He has commented and complained about Dunedin bands lifting his guitar sound and even some of Hamish's drumming style, and here he found a band that shared his interest in other influences rather than wanting to pay homage to him and his band. David was shy and sensitive to what was essentially flattery and it made him feel awkward.

Sneaky Feelings were in many ways the most musically conventional. They seemed the likeliest to have a mainstream career, with radio play and all the other impossibilities, but the songs were very good. I especially liked the magnificently fraught ones by David Pine.

We all liked David; he was a great guy and very talented. The others were a little shy and standoffish. The other main songwriter, singer and guitarist, Matthew Bannister, and the drummer, Martin Durrant, were smart and talented as well. But there was a determination to succeed that didn't sit well with the relaxed 'anti-stardom' vibe that generally existed in post-punk circles. Bassist Kathryn Tyrie seemed plain awkward, and then her playing got awkward when her arm ended up in a sling. She eventually left to be replaced by the much sunnier John Kelcher.

Mainstream success seemed so unlikely back then that few were willing to risk being perceived as uncool by declaring their ambition. Given the apparent inevitability of failure, it was best to feign indifference: you cared a great deal about the music you were making but you weren't going to sell out to The Man. Partially because there was no Man to sell out to. So there was a clubby, friendly atmosphere among the bands. They got on and helped each other out, offered each other encouragement and avoided hierarchical attitudes. Sneaky Feelings let their ambition hang out a bit and were perceived to be outside the inner group as a result.

So The Stones were raucous, The Chills were psychedelic and poppy and The Verlaines were serious and deliberate. Sneaky Feelings always seemed slightly out on a limb. David Pine was a smart, social, good-natured sort with a natural charm that would take him on to a career in the Ministry of Foreign Affairs, culminating in postings to a number of South-East Asian countries. But the others in the band wanted something more conventionally recorded so they could have a crack at radio play. The recording of the *Dunedin Double* set up a battle of wits with Chris Knox that was to hang over the band's relationship with the label and prove difficult to resolve.

The Christchurch music pubs welcomed the bands because local promoter Jim Wilson saw the potential. Originally from Dunedin, Jim had a long history of putting on shows. He was an astute promoter who had spotted the rise of The Enemy and had booked Toy Love into the key Christchurch venues he oversaw — the Gladstone in town and a bigger, suburban barn, the Hillsborough.

He had heard the fuss about The Clean when they started to gel as a band when Robert Scott joined and had travelled to Dunedin to see them play, subsequently booking them into the Gladstone in 1981. By 1982 he also oversaw the Star & Garter on Oxford Terrace near the Barbadoes Street intersection, and was more than happy to book in The Clean, Tall Dwarfs and the other Dunedin bands while they were in town recording.

The idea was to keep everyone busy and earning money while they made the records, and to make sure everyone's playing was as sharp and practised as possible. Playing live developed a band more than working away in a practice room. So each band played two or three nights at the Star & Garter. It was a relatively modern tavern with a pleasant atmosphere.

The Star & Garter was relaxed, and just over the road the river drifted past. A routine was settled on. The Chills and The Stones paired up and played five gigs in eight days, all the while

Me in one of my favourite places, the lounge bar of the Gladstone Hotel, Christchurch, in 1982 (photo by Jane Walker)

recording three and four songs, respectively. The Clean and Tall Dwarfs played the next weekend, and The Verlaines and Sneaky Feelings were there for a couple of midweek dates after that. It proved to be an ideal environment for anyone wanting to check out these new Dunedin bands. The sizeable and knowledgeable audience in Christchurch was willing to pay to see quality live music. Those who came were impressed and the word soon spread.

All the bands also played at the University of Canterbury, and The Clean and The Chills were offered up to the agricultural students at Lincoln College, just outside Christchurch. For many years university orientation gigs were irresistible and much-relied-on annual money-spinners for all of our higher-profile bands. National tours were often built around them. By the early 1990s there would be twenty Flying Nun–associated bands playing more than fifty individual orientation events up and down the country each year. Mostly the venues weren't ideal spaces for music. Both Auckland and Canterbury were brutalist concrete student-union function-room bunkers with terrible acoustics. The huge audiences of drunken young students weren't always receptive, and Lincoln College, with its inebriated horde of toga-wearing hayseeds, was the worst.

* * *

During the recording of the *Dunedin Double* I hung out and drank too much whisky. There seemed to be a ready supply of Takaka heads from Golden Bay and that stuff was far too strong for my delicate psyche. There always seemed to be pot about, but most of it would have been New Zealand Green of various strengths — pretty innocuous stuff that encouraged merely chatter, giggling and an appetite. The stronger stuff, available seasonally, would blow your head off; the effect was to stun, incapacitate and make one ill, especially if too much alcohol had been consumed previously.

The marijuana I saw seemed to be passed around among an informal network of friends; money changed hands but it was all very casual. We had all heard stories about the incredibly strong imported 'Buddha Sticks' available in previous years, but that predated my interest, and it was a few more years before we became aware of the connection between them, organised crime, Mr Asia and murder.

There might have been other drugs but I really didn't encounter much. I'd seen a friend of a friend in a terrible overdosed and near-death state several years previously, so I knew to keep well away from heroin. People talked about speed but I never actually saw any. I assumed working people kept it for when they were operating heavy machinery and driving long distances.

The police were a constant hazard nonetheless. After the Springbok rugby tour there was an uneasy tension when they were about, visiting live music bars looking for underage drinkers to charge and convict. They were the same cops who would have been anonymously slamming protesters' faces with long batons the previous winter. They all wore moustaches but that was the least of it. There was a sense they were against us, not there to protect us, but to protect the interests of an older status quo that had as much relevance now as flares.

It added to a general feeling that we were living in a dysfunctional state. Aligned with Prime Minister Robert Muldoon and his 'law and order' politics, the police had adopted a polarising, brutalising stance. Now they were on the lookout for marijuana, and anyone who didn't conform was fair game — as was anyone caught underage in a pub.

So for me it was a bit of pot occasionally, although in time I became recreationally addicted and would have a puff or so every night. Anything to calm me down and release me from the gradually increasing stresses of learning to run a record company by running a record company. Eventually, as the worry grew greater and the pot got stronger, I found the original effect reversed. It no longer made me laugh and unwind. Instead, it amplified the latent psychotic and paranoid aspects of my personality. But all that was to come, and anyway, pot was never my primary form of release.

What I really liked to do was drink. I was a shy young man and drink made me sociable. I found I could be sociable behind a counter in a record shop but not at a gig after work, and especially not with girls. Drink loosened me up to be chatty and, depending on how many the other person had had, possibly funny. The trouble back then was that the beer wasn't very good. I was neither a Lion Brown nor a DB man. There was nothing appetising or sophisticated about that stuff. And I found it didn't really make you drunk or even properly tipsy. Hopeless.

I liked the other brown drink an awful lot more. Whisky was the drink for me. And what this meant in the early 1980s was blended whisky like Johnnie Walker or Famous Grouse. No one seemed to know about single malts and if we had and been able to afford them, they would have been adulterated with the ginger ale I habitually mixed them with.

No, I liked the industrially produced stuff. You knew what you were getting and how much you could drink to get what kind of result: chatty, surly, incoherent, staggering, collapsed, unconscious or dead. I liked a drink, so my experience tended towards the end of that scale, though luckily I tended to stop at unconscious.

I wasn't alone in my young functioning-alcoholic lifestyle. Drinking, like smoking, was more tolerated then than it is now. You could be tipsy from lunchtime on and you could smoke in shops, pubs and other people's houses. Still, I was pleasant and functional enough to be amiable and constructively conversational.

I had no real technical expertise or any real creative reason to sit in on the *Dunedin Double* sessions, so I simply got to know the bands. My ideal kind of job really. I was a sort of ugly cheerleader in black who became increasingly incoherent as the evening wore on, but I did cement a number of important relationships with the bands and with Chris and Doug. It was time well spent.

The Dunedin bands were almost all nice, smart people, music fans who were carefully ambitious and enjoyed the process of learning how to record. It was a real opportunity to get their careers under way and learn how the recording process works as full and equal participants. They were serious and taking it all in, but they were also into the joys of downtime entertainment. It was hard work but great fun and so exciting.

* * *

After the recordings were completed the immediate concern was to get the cover art organised. I recall there was some excitement during this period for Manchester's Factory label and the Peter Saville design element in their releases. I always liked a bit of design, but after 'Tally Ho!' we were never going to have a conventional design programme at Flying Nun. Our bands wanted to control the sleeve and label designs themselves — and rightly so, whatever the outcome.

Each band had one side of the cover to design. Originally there were two print runs so that each band would have a turn on the outside as well as the inside of the gatefold. Fortunately, I put my foot down and said no to colour printing, or this project would have sunk us.

The Stones' cover was a montage of photos of them behaving badly. The Verlaines' side was more meditative, with musical notes and staves tastefully blended together with a drawing of Paul Verlaine.

There is lots of information on The Chills' cover. Some of it is cryptic and the rest is in code, such as the stylised joint in the corner, which I bet Mum and Dad didn't notice at all. Martin Phillipps is there, tilting his hat, so he was clearly the main Chill, but the overall effect is too cluttered to make a good cover. They were a band that needed to make records on their own, if only so they could have a back cover for all of the thank yous.

Sneaky Feelings organised themselves, found a proper photographer and chose a nice shot of the band with a very simple handwritten 'Sneaky Feelings' across the top. It looks very tasteful and well done.

So, collectively the *Dunedin Double* cover art was a bit of a ragbag of different ideas and styles, a bit like the music it packaged, but it did its job of introducing four new and quite different young Dunedin bands to the rest of New Zealand and, although we weren't thinking about it at the time, the world.

Band art often, albeit subconsciously, illustrates what a band is about. Tall Dwarfs always had rather mad record covers, but they were in control of the madness, letting it all out just as they did in their music, so many ideas just pouring out in the music and the art. But sometimes bands can unwittingly expose a bit too much of themselves through cover art. Or worse, develop some crazy idea that will only turn off the potential purchaser.

Somehow this never happened to us. At worst, even if it wasn't my cup of tea, a cover at least matched the band, the music and the potential audience well enough to do the job. Often the results were spectacular and beyond expectations. But I never knew what was coming, so it was always a surprise.

Proper grown-up record companies take the design out of the musicians' hands and give it to graphic artists, who often deliver bland commercial art that bears no relation to the artist they are supposed to be representing. Safe but horrible covers aimed solely at shifting units out there in the marketplace. So when The Clean made it clear that they wanted to control their own cover design I was happy to let them. They made good covers, and their gloriously naive, natural and fine aesthetic sense extended beyond their music and into the art they produced. With the genie out of the bottle, all the bands had to do their own thing, which is what created the house style, or lack of one.

Gradually my role became more defined. I was a facilitator rather than a record company director. I was happy for the bands to control the nature of their recordings and what they delivered. Unfortunately, this left Paul Smith's role diminished to the point of non-existence. I'm not sure that we ever talked about it properly. We simply drifted apart as my life took me away on this rather wild adventure.

Some of Paul's art was, however, included in a double-sided black-and-white collage poster I had printed up around the time of the release of the *Dunedin Double*. There was a general collective feel developing around the label and with the bands, and a collage seemed like a good way to incorporate lots of different art generated by the bands and associated artists. The idea was that this was the kind of non-specific poster that could stay on a record shop wall for some time. The inclusive nature of this type of collage was an idea we were to revisit in the future around the designs for 2006's twenty-fifth anniversary box set and 2011's *Tally Ho! Flying Nun's Greatest Bits* compilation.

While some of the bands may have later had mild reservations about the quality of their first recordings, overall the *Dunedin Double* was a great success. Commercially it could not have been better. There is not much margin in a double twelve-inch vinyl gatefold package that sells for less than a full-price album, but it was the right record that came along at the right time. It sold in truckloads, and we were constantly battling to keep it in stock. It effectively launched each of the bands and directly contributed to the creation of an enduring myth.

With all the amazing music coming out of Doug Hood and Chris Knox's four-track, Dunedin was suddenly on the musical map in a way it had never been before. The city had enjoyed strong music scenes in earlier times, but nothing that had entered the national consciousness like this. In fact, no one city's music scene had done this until now. Inevitably it was given a name.

David Kilgour originally coined the 'Dunedin Sound' tag and he came to greatly regret it. At Flying Nun we were happy to use the term as a kind of shorthand for the growing list of Dunedin-based artists we were recording and releasing. But David's throwaway line was never intended to become a catch-all description — largely because no one could agree on exactly what it meant.

The 'Dunedin Sound' was only ever a convenient label for something rather complex and difficult to describe. There wasn't really a single sound. There were sounds, and they were diverse, powered by the myriad influences and styles that mingled and surfaced within different bands. They may have shared Dunedin as a home and 1960s influences, played guitars, initially recorded on a single four-track machine and released their records through the same record company, but there was no single, simple, identifiable sound coming out of Dunedin.

There were, however, some commonalities, as Matthew Bannister pointed out in his fine book *Positively George Street*. Like guitar reverb, for example. Reverb is the persistence of a sound after it is produced. It is generated when the original sound is

Flying Nun collage poster, 1982, side 1. Contributing artists included Paul Smith, Ronnie van Hout, David and Hamish Kilgour, Robert Scott and Martin Phillipps. Note my handwritten note regarding upcoming releases at the top right.

Flying Nun collage poster, 1982, side 2. Contributing artists included Paul Smith, David and Hamish Kilgour, Robert Scott, John Halvorsen, Martin Phillipps and Chris Knox. A list of the then current catalogue can be seen towards the top left.

repeatedly reflected — a bit like a short, rapid echo. It can occur naturally, but it can also be created electronically or digitally. It especially suited David Kilgour's developing guitar style and it's said he began using it extensively to help fill out The Clean's sound when they were forced to play huge, bare wooden halls. Other Dunedin bands then realised how effective it could be in making them sound better, especially if they had just one guitarist and no supporting rhythm guitarist or keyboards. Reverb also has a tendency to dull and blur, which can help obscure mistakes.

Guitar drones and jangle were widely adopted by the Dunedin bands for much the same reasons: to make more noise, fill out space and disguise sometimes-limited musical expertise. Drones are often used in indigenous and ethnic music to provide a background to a melody — think didgeridoo or the bagpipes if you can. The Velvet Underground exploited the effect in the 1960s and it was later a feature of Sonic Youth's art-rock sound. When a folky guitar drone effect is electrified, it is called a jangle. Dunedin groups like The Verlaines, The Chills and The Stones adopted these effects as necessary and distinctive tools. Snapper took them to a fantastically simpilfied extreme, thereby forging a link with the likes of the New York pre-punk pioneers Suicide, as well as later bands such as Spacemen 3, Wooden Shjips and Moon Duo.

The Dunedin bands took songwriting very seriously. This was what everything was built on and they were serious and conscious writers who understood the process as a craft and an art. They soon became bored with simple song structures and started to experiment. Indeed, Graeme Downes, now a senior lecturer in music at Otago University, asserts that the key trait of the Dunedin Sound and its major legacy to music was its use of much freer song structures and non-traditional musical patterns. Beginning with The Clean, Dunedin bands adopted song structures that were loose and unconventional without collapsing into chaos. 'Tally Ho!', for example, broke all the rules by avoiding traditional verse-chorus-verse patterns and essentially consisting of one long chorus. Yet you will still hear it being played today in hipster café hangouts worldwide.

Mixing all these ingredients, along with some other factors, like vocal style, unflashy but steady drumming and common recording practices, produced a huge variety of material from the bands involved. You can hear the common underlying influences, but they are always mixed together differently and the resulting songs and recordings are likewise very different from each other. The *Dunedin Double* bands all sound quite distinct, for instance, and I think this is true of all the Dunedin bands that came after.

Nevertheless, the so-called Dunedin Sound had a real but subtle influence on music internationally. I see it most clearly in the UK 'shoegaze' groups of the late 1980s and early 1990s. Bands like My Bloody Valentine, Spacemen 3 and Ride, among others, shared many musical qualities with the Dunedin bands, as well as a healthy disregard for presentation while performing. Like the careers of key Flying Nun bands The Chills and Straitjacket Fits, shoegaze was stalled by the arrival of grunge and, to a lesser extent, Britpop in the early to mid-1990s, but its — and the Dunedin bands' — disregard for traditional song structures and a non–show business attitude to performance and recording continue to resonate throughout music internationally.

What was key at the time, however, was the small but powerful scene that exsisted in Dunedin, for without a real social base none of this would have happened or developed in the way it did. It initially whirled around a small group of contemporaries who were inspired by the Sex Pistols to form groups and play music, further inspired by The Enemy and Toy Love, and then crucially kicked into life by The Clean. Two key groups subsequently formed: Bored Games and The Same. They were made up of a small core group of musicians (and some others) who moved in and out of different line-ups built around singer-songwriters with strong visions, such as Martin Phillipps of The Chills, Graeme Downes of The Verlaines and Shayne Carter of The DoubleHappys, Straitjacket Fits and Dimmer.

There was a genuine sense of community in this scene. People played for each other and a few early punters. The aesthetic was op-shop chic — pickings have always been rich in the South Island. Bands and audiences dressed alike. The audience sometimes formed bands themselves, or learned how to do sound, or lights, or write about it all in fanzines like *Alley Oop* and *Garage*.

The lack of real live venues, apart from self-promoted hall gigs, reinforced the communal feeling. Parties were the main meeting places — Dunedin has always been good at parties. Drink was central to the social experience. Maybe it's a Scottish thing, but it suited my temperament just fine.

The other key gathering places were naturally the record shops. The EMI shop on George Street was managed by Lesley Paris (also the drummer in Look Blue Go Purple) and staffed by others from the local scene. People continued to hang out at Roy Colbert's fine second-hand shop on Stuart Street, checking out the bins for the reasonably priced, the rare and the wonderful, chatting with Roy and each other about music, and finding out where the parties were. It was us and them. And in those days there were still only a few of us and a lot of them.

I got down to Dunedin as often as I could. The Cook Tavern was occasionally allowing some Flying Nun bands back in to play, having banned The Enemy years before because of Chris Knox's arm-cutting performances. It was one of the only music pubs near the university and it was a terrible dive. Some remember it fondly, but mostly what I remember is the incredibly sticky bar top. There were also bands at the Oriental, which is where I saw the Netherworld Dancing Toys play to a packed audience on a Saturday night and had my interest piqued.

The scene finally found a base at the Empire. It was a pub on Princes Street on the other side of the Octagon, away from the university and its students. Built in 1879, it was part of the old

Many considered Roy Colbert to be a mentor to the young Dunedin bands of the late 1970s and early 1980s. Chris Knox certainly thought so when he drew this illustration for Flying Nun's tenth-anniversary trading card set.

centre of Dunedin, but was now rundown, empty and deserted. The building had three floors with a bar on each. The top bar was a small L-shaped room with the stage located around the corner at the far end of the L. Bands associated with Flying Nun first started playing there in 1981 and over the next year or so it gradually became the prime focus for independently minded live music in Dunedin.

The bands now had a regular home, although it has to be stressed just how few punters could be packed into this limited space. Still, this was to become the epicentre of original music in Dunedin for the next ten years. All the post–*Dunedin Double* bands played here. It's no exaggeration to say that without the Empire there would not have been another wave of Dunedin bands. Owners John and Maureen Simpson were pivotal in it happening. When they left in 1989 it was taken over by Norma O'Malley (Look Blue Go Purple and Chug) and Alf Danielson (Goblin Mix, Chug and Stephen).

Dunedin became a bit of a second home for me. I had a lot of friends there, and it never occurred to me that I wouldn't just fit in. I never felt like I was treated differently — as the 'record company guy'. Perhaps I was naive. But in the South Island we were all a little naive, so I was in the right company. Anyone who was a bit sharp or flash, probably down from Auckland, stood out very obviously for their speech, their clothing, even their body language. Conversation tended to dry up pretty quickly. Definitely no party invites for them. It was a bit of a club.

When I was in Dunedin for a weekend I had some regular haunts. If there was a morning meeting before the pubs opened I would go to Stewart's in the Octagon. It was a downstairs cellar crammed with all sorts of eccentric Dunedin life. It had real coffee, made with one of the first espresso machines to come to New Zealand, though typical of all things that came to Dunedin it seemed different. Instead of producing coffee as the rest of the civilised world came to know it, Stewart's turned out coffee that tasted like it was bulk brewed in industrial quantities and strength — which was how the locals drank it, possibly to wash down the huge quantities of cheese rolls they also consumed.

Later on I would be in the upstairs London Bar or in the back bar of the Robbie Burns, both on George Street and both good meeting places. I always seemed to be in the cosy Robbie Burns at closing time, too. If you wanted something more exotic than a pub pie to eat there was always The Governor's, which at this time was co-run by David Pine of Sneaky Feelings. It was unlicensed so the time I spent there was necessarily limited.

There was also undoubtedly an element of historical serendipity at work here. Dunedin had been the first real economic capital of New Zealand, built from gold-rush prosperity. Hard-working Scottish immigrants constructed a small, southern replica of Edinburgh, complete with some grand Presbyterian churches and a statue of Robbie Burns in the heart of the city. When the money drifted north after the gold ran out the city stayed still. Buildings were left empty rather than knocked down or redeveloped, which over time preserved its charm. The university and the annual influx of students saved it from becoming a ghost town and added to a bohemian, creative culture that now thrives inside its stony walls. It's not too big, it has a centre, and is easy to get around. More than anything, though, it is isolated, way down State Highway 1, with its airport a long way out of town, and flights in and out are very expensive. It was within this self-contained little world that the vibrant Dunedin music scene was created and nurtured for over a decade from the late 1970s.

CHAPTER 9

GREAT SoUNDS GREAT

Chris Knox really didn't like Christchurch very much. He enjoyed working with the young Dunedin bands, but the major reason for him coming down and spending three weeks working rather hard on the *Dunedin Double* was so that he could also record a new Tall Dwarfs EP with Alec Bathgate.

Louis Likes His Daily Dip was the outcome and it represented a huge leap in recording quality over the *Three Songs* EP. The material sparkles, from the surreal and improvised 'Louis the First' through to the melodic pop of 'Maybe' and 'Clover', finishing with Tall Dwarfs climactic showstopper, 'Song of the Silents'. It's a neatly linked collection of varied but compatible material, inventively recorded.

The record came with an informative insert about how all the songs were recorded, and the whole thing was wrapped in a shiny full-colour cover. It's a beautiful product, featuring a small sculpture by Barbara Ward of Louis sitting in a bath of orange jelly in the shelter of a giant glass hand. I still don't know what the rather sunburnt-looking Louis is, but the idea that he is a mutant yam has always stuck with me.

The image looks great set against a black background with the title seemingly scratched into it. The back cover is a collage of freaks and crazies, cuttings from magazines with different heads, eyes, hair, mouths or animals substituted on different figures. Chris and Alec lurk down in the left-hand corner, Alec looking like a 1960s fop and Chris inexplicably wearing a yellow and black Australian ski outfit.

It was one of our first colour covers. I was persuaded to do it because of how little Tall Dwarfs cost to record — and because The Clean had asked for one, because their sales justified it. I hate to think how much those covers cost. Having the film and plates made was at least $1000 — before we even started printing. Of course, I didn't know how much it added to the unit cost until after we'd printed both The Clean and Tall Dwarfs covers. By the time the bill arrived the cat was out of the bag. After this it was an argument we'd have with every band over every cover — colour or not, or some sort of compromise.

Louis Likes His Daily Dip was a perfect EP's worth of great material, and the start of a run of great records from Tall Dwarfs, who added another dimension to the label. They possessed something different to the other bands out of Christchurch and Dunedin, something unconventional, if not downright odd. And there was an audience and a market for the music they were making, consisting of the old Toy Love fans who could handle the abrupt change in direction, and a new, younger bunch of kids who had no idea who Toy Love were but liked this stuff.

At the time I felt *Louis* was a very important record for Flying Nun. It represented a further broadening of what we were making available, a confident embracing of the difference that was so much a part of the post-punk revolution, and which articulated the label's new confidence and wider outlook.

The Clean, however, found it hard going after the huge success of *Boodle*. These weren't guys looking to capitalise on their success in either personal or material ways. They were a bit uneasy with it

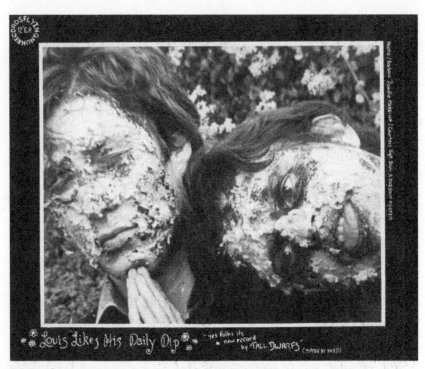

Tall Dwarfs' *Louis Likes His Daily Dip* poster, 1982. Barbara Ward took the photo and Alec Bathgate did the design.

all. They played more gigs up and down the country but found the attention a bit much. Robert Scott is a laid-back, friendly soul who will happily talk to anybody. David Kilgour was still very young and naturally shy, and really disliked the attention that came with being the focus or de facto front person of the band. Hamish was older and more assured. He had strongly held beliefs about what was right and wrong and wasn't afraid to talk about them. He was the nominal leader in a band that very consciously did not have a leader. Everything was shared and equal and that was one of their many strengths. They found out they did not like the conventional trappings of fame and success by becoming famous and successful.

The band's sense of discombobulation was probably compounded by the move to Christchurch. Dunedin is hilly but compact and walkable. Christchurch is much bigger and sprawls across a flat plain. Dunedin's heritage is Scottish, and

Christchurch is very English. Dunedin is a university town and Christchurch banished its university to the suburbs in the 1960s. I know they all found it hard to make the adjustment.

All the same, I was very excited about The Clean setting up for another recording. They used the same equipment and personnel as they had with *Boodle* and, with everyone a little more experienced, it ran smoothly. They recorded another outstanding EP's worth of songs. It was a big ambitious recording, bristling with determination, optimism and considerable momentum. In a knowingly unconventional gesture the opening song, 'Fish', is one of two full-blown psychedelic instrumentals recorded.

The EP is a juggernaut and a real statement by the band: this is what we do and you can like it or lump it. To help make it all a little harder, the band came up with an excellently catchy title — *Great Sounds Great, Good Sounds Good, So-so Sounds So-so, Bad Sounds Bad and Rotten Sounds Rotten*. I loved it, but *Great Sounds Great* soon became good enough for me.

I liked the cover too. They wanted colour and had sold so many *Boodle* EPs I couldn't and wouldn't argue. The new design was subdued and I'm not sure it came out the way the band initially intended. It depicts the three of them lying down next to each other, with a light box throwing an orangey glow over them. There's a swirly paisley graphic with the band's name and the title attached. The overall effect is psychedelic: muted, warm colours, yet a little dark and mysterious.

Simon Morris at TVNZ made a rather good video of the most upbeat and accessible song, 'Beatnik', in a Christchurch coffee house. I imagined the setting had some genuine folksy connection with the 1960s that perhaps Simon maybe knew about. The video featured many of Christchurch's post-punk characters, including Michael Higgins from RDU (Canterbury University's student radio station), Paul Kean, Jay Clarkson and artist Ronnie van Hout, as well as a few unfortunate ring-ins. I missed the shoot. I must have been tired and emotional or asleep somewhere. Or

I might have been out and about looking for something stronger than coffee.

I felt the instrumental, 'Fish', should have been the featured song, but TVNZ were making and broadcasting the clip so obviously had the final say. It did the job. The sense of the band doing their own thing worked well against — and with — the flippant, jokey elements in the video treatment.

Great Sounds Great also did well and charted in the top five. The *Dunedin Double* and Tall Dwarfs sold extremely well. All of these releases gobbled up space on student radio and in the music press. We were starting to get fan mail from overseas in response to the sample copies we had sent various foreign music magazines. After just over a year, Flying Nun was well established, selling really good volumes of its releases and, most importantly, had a strong roster of young bands at the start of their careers.

In fact, we had become less a little, niche record label and more a large, sprawling and rather eccentric record company.

CHAPTER 10

TOTALLY WiRED

We all loved The Fall. They were one of the original English punk bands inspired by the Sex Pistols' visit to Manchester and quickly grew into something much more interesting, a band on an altogether different trajectory.

They were a markedly regional band. Proud to remain ale-swilling northern outsiders rather than join the homogenous lager-sipping London mainstream. Do-it-yourself provincials playing non-brand instruments and making unfamiliar sounds, including big, angry, angular bass riffs that crunched on top of each other like some damaged, badly constructed, repetitive live loop. I liked them a lot, more for individual songs and singles than the dense, rambling albums that veered a little close to the edge of some parallel universe of uneasy listening. 'Totally Wired': yep, I could relate to that, including the occasional sleepless night.

The label was busy. I was still working my day job as a record shop manager and running an increasingly successful independent record business on the side, overseeing national distribution for lots of great releases, all of them well received by the music press, student radio and retail, and some even making the charts.

But I wasn't sure where my own destiny lay. I had been to Dunedin and more recently to Auckland, New Zealand's biggest city, and knew how terribly small New Zealand really was. Three million people, or just a little more than the population of greater Manchester at the time — and significantly further away from London, the centre of the musical universe. Was there a future running a successful record company in New Zealand?

I needed a sense of the wider music world and The Fall was my entrée. Not through the main entrance but rather through a dimly lit side door down a dark alley. I didn't seek out that side door; I stumbled through it accidentally, then made the odd wrong turn once inside. The music business was badly signposted in those days, especially if you were from the other side of the world.

But the post-punk idea was enabling. I was doing my thing with Flying Nun. Chris Knox was involved as an artist, a producer and a kind of anti-mentor to younger artists, as well as being our sales contact for shops in Auckland. Doug Hood had a day job with Live Sound, but also had the energy, practical intelligence and nous to embark on a career in live music promotion. He was going to bring the sorts of overseas acts he and his friends liked to New Zealand and he called the business Looney Tours. The Birthday Party were the first act he toured, followed by The Fall in 1982.

The Fall *wanted* to come to New Zealand. They had scraped onto the local chart at some stage, not realising this meant little more than that a few fans had purchased their latest release over the same couple of days. A similar chart position in a more populous country like the United Kingdom would have been the result of multiple factors at work, a solid sales base generating attention, in turn generating more sales. Nevertheless, there was a perception that The Fall were big in New Zealand. And perhaps they were.

'Happy Fall Guitarist' was the headline on the front page of the Christchurch *Press* when they arrived in August 1982. And he really did look happy to be there to play a show at Canterbury

University — a show I missed because I fell asleep in my car in the car park, only to wake up alone, cold and deserted. It must have been that lack of sleep catching up with me.

I caught up with The Fall the next night when they played to a half-full Christchurch Town Hall. Perhaps they did have more fans than I thought, because I couldn't remember selling that many of their records at the shop. I followed the band to Auckland and discovered them ensconced at Chris and Barbara's house in Grey Lynn.

Chris had gone out to the airport to meet them. I think there must have been too much grovelling in the van on the way back because guitarist Karl Burns had punched Chris in the face (something many had felt like doing over the years but few had followed through with). Karl didn't realise he was being slobbered over by a national-treasure-in-the-making and lashed out in the only way his hard northern hands knew how. Chris was laughing it off and the band were sulking around the house, sort of relaxing with beer and morose northern chat. There where two distinct camps: the band, and Mark E Smith and his girlfriend, Kay Carroll, who claimed to be a witch.

I had never met a real live witch before. Growing up in Christchurch we often came upon their burnt remains in the Square or by the village ducking pond, but live ones were hard to come by. This one came with the band. I knew that Mark E Smith was from Prestwich in greater Manchester, where for a time Kay Carroll worked in the local psychiatric hospital, the biggest in Europe. I knew they enjoyed the play on the 'wich' in Prestwich, and had released the *Live at the Witch Trials* album. The next album would be called *The Hex Induction Hour*. Carroll had the kind of personality you could imagine being an asset working in an old-fashioned mental institution, but her expectation of being seriously accepted as a witch struck me as remarkably crazed.

But these were interesting people playing highly original music, trying to make a career of it, and trying to get on with each other on the opposite side of the world from their industrial hometown. Mark E Smith was a little aloof but carried the burden of being the star attraction, which is how he liked it, I think. It was his show and he was running it, with the witch doing the unsavoury bits.

This was the classic Fall line-up: Karl Burns, Marc Riley, the Hanley brothers Steve and Paul, Craig Scanlon and, not to be left out of the onstage fun, Kay Carroll on backing vocals. After a few beers the band lightened up and we came to like them a lot and felt friendly enough to warn the witch off Ponsonby Road after dark. Of course, the real loose cannon in the room was Chris Knox. I turned to see Chris gleefully licking Mark E Smith's impassive face and quietly slipped out the back door. Totally wired.

Auckland post-punk fans were very excited about The Fall playing at Mainstreet. This was the usual stopping place for medium-sized overseas bands. I remember a distinct lack of ventilation and sweat dripping off the ceiling on particularly hot and packed nights. In the madness surrounding The Fall in Auckland, Doug had presented as the voice of reasoned sanity and convinced Mark E Smith they could make a decent recording of the show on the Teac four-track. So the whole show was recorded and when the Ampex tape ran out, the two long encores were recorded on that much-maligned format, the cassette.

And it sounded really good. They played very well, including the 'hits' and some new material that would appear on studio albums in the near future. Noted by many observers was the absence of their most recognised and appreciated song, 'Totally Wired', on the extended set list that night.

Somehow Chris then convinced Mark E Smith that Flying Nun should turn the whole thing into a record and release it. 'Really?' I said to Chris. 'Yes, really, it's all agreed.' I worried that making a record with a high-profile overseas band was drifting away from our main business, and everything felt a little hazier than usual. But I was a positive, optimistic young man who knew we could sell a few of those records in New Zealand and make some money to pump into some of the other projects we had on the go. We were selling singles and twelve-inch EPs but not releasing many full-priced albums, and that's where the margin was — and with it a future. So yes, we were doing this. 'They agreed right, the witch and all?' 'Yeah, just do it is what they said.'

The sixty minutes of the main set sounded pretty good, but the quality of the cassette-recorded encores of unreleased material (which would turn up on *Hex Induction Hour*) was a little inferior. It was ninety minutes of music though and Chris, being the fan-nerd he was, decided all of it had to be released. The main part of the show would just about fit onto two sides of a 33⅓-rpm twelve-inch album, and the thirty minutes of encore could be best crammed onto an additional 45-rpm twelve-inch EP.

Big commercial live albums up to this point were usually ropey affairs. Try listening to Neil Diamond's *Hot August Night* or even *Frampton Comes Alive* and you'll get the idea. Added audience atmosphere could sound very fake. These were huge-selling records of very average recordings, with the faults amplified because of their double length. Record companies loved them, though, because they were relatively cheap to make and they could sell them for a whole lot more.

What could be exciting about a live record was the faithful recording of a performance, 'faults' and all — the capturing of a unique performance in a particular room at a particular time. Chris wanted to faithfully document the Fall show and oversaw the recording with some help from Doug (who was probably doing the band's live sound). He did an excellent job with the means available. You couldn't really tell it was recorded in a sauna in hell (without the groovy lighting). The half-capacity audience of around 600 seemed to like it and cheered along when they were supposed to.

I felt a little uneasy when I saw Chris's artwork for the album cover. If we were going to sell a 'double' album, with double the pressing costs, for the same price as a single album, the cover would have to be simple — a single black-and-white sleeve. That wasn't the problem, though.

The cover was very much Chris's work, including the album title: *Fall in a Hole*. Few would have argued that Mainstreet didn't qualify as a hole, but the thing that threw me was the newspaper clipping that dominated the front cover. It was the 'Happy Fall Guitarist' picture and headline from the Christchurch *Press*. Not a photo of undisputed main man Mark E Smith, but the member of the band he had most recently fallen out with, Marc Riley. Mark E had reportedly whacked each member of the band after a poor performance in Sydney, just before arriving in New Zealand, and Marc had had the nerve to punch him back. His days in the band were numbered.

The rest of the art featured 'Fall' in one of Chris's hand-drawn fonts, consisting of arms and hands to form the letters. The 'plug' for the 'hole' was hand drawn and the back cover was a montage of Carol Tippet photos. The song titles and recording details were all in Chris's artistically neat handwriting but it seemed to have a new catalogue number: not the 'Live 1' and 'Live 2' as printed on the record labels, but 'Mark 1 + 2'. I guess the joke was irresistible.

It all added to the general sense that this did not look or feel like a proper Fall release. Surely if the band were serious they would have provided some sort of art, even if we had to build a cover around it.

I played it and really enjoyed it, and never listened to it again until I wrote this. The Fall made dense records. Whereas the singles are delightful, thick slices of post-punk weirdness, the albums seem to come as uncut loaves. It's simply all too much. I haven't really listened to any of their subsequent albums since. But Chris was so much the obsessive that he wanted it all there, squeezed onto two groaning discs. He was so into the band he assumed everyone else would share his fascination. Many did. There were enough obsessive Fall fans around the world to be very interested in this record.

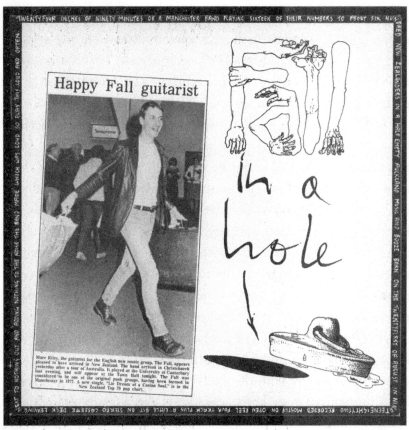

The *Fall in a Hole* record cover by Chris Knox

It took a long time to appear. Recorded in August 1982 and released in December 1983 is one heck of a slow turnaround. I really can't remember why it took so long. Perhaps Chris took a while to put the artwork together. There were always delays at the pressing plant, but surely this was an absolute priority for us. Perhaps we were just too busy with the other twenty-three records by New Zealand artists we put out that year.

The test pressings finally came through in late 1983. We had never ordered test pressings before. The pressing plant had discouraged it, despite it potentially being a way to iron out our manufacturing problems. Our unconventional recordings could confuse a cutting engineer, resulting in never-ending subjective debates followed by further expensive test pressings. Instead, I encouraged the bands to have someone attend cutting sessions and develop a relationship with the engineers. Chris Knox always travelled to Wellington for his cutting and often oversaw the cutting of other material while he was there.

A lot of pressings still came through with faults, especially those not overseen at the cutting stage by Chris or other band members. The record might be cut at the wrong speed, or there might be a track missing. The spindle hole might not actually be in the middle. The bass might be too loud or not loud enough. We listened with the band and tried to make a pragmatic decision about whether we could live with what we had. I would say that no one was happy much of the time, there were serious concerns roughly 40 per cent of the time, and we asked for re-cuts or repressings on about 20 per cent of our initial pressings.

So Chris had insisted on a test pressing for The Fall. He now knew the engineers and he knew the process and it was worth the effort — especially with the *Fall in a Hole* cutting, as there was a lot of music to fit onto four sides of vinyl and a trade-off in quality versus quantity. Chris understood the issues and resolved them to his satisfaction. The test pressings confirmed that everything had gone to plan. Just in time for Christmas.

The sell-in to shops was very good despite the initial buzz having abated and the band having released two excellent and one so-so studio albums in the interim. I was even happier when Sounds Unlimited rang to say they had some export interest. Sounds Unlimited was a very good record shop in Newmarket, Auckland. We liked the people there and they were unusual in that they actively exported finished records around the world. They sold New Zealand pressings into the Pacific Islands and hard-to-get New Zealand–only releases of international acts into Europe and the US.

Fall in a Hole was just such a New Zealand–only release. There was an international audience for this record. 'Can we export this?' I asked Chris. 'It shouldn't be a problem.' And I really didn't want it to be, because there is no sale like an export sale in December.

We pressed more for the export orders. There was more and more interest from around the world and we were having trouble keeping up with stock. Financially it was looking good. Sounds Unlimited was a well-run company and a prompt-paying customer. And there would be all these Fall fans around the world who would now know there was an interesting record label in New Zealand called Flying Nun. It irked a little that they would know it for a non–New Zealand artist's release, but never mind. I was already fantasising about a summer holiday.

I was at the office fiddling with the Christmas decorations I'd bought with the anticipated income from the Fall export sales when the phone rang. I've never liked telephones. It was a music publisher ringing from Australia. I'd never had a phone call from Australia, let alone from a music publisher. What do they do again?

It was about this *Fall in a Hole* album ... The words unauthorised, illegal, bootleg, lawsuit, conviction, fine and prison were all mentioned or imagined.

Mark E Smith had already seen a copy in the UK and was not amused. Of course he wasn't. It was a recording made by a bunch of crazy fans far, far away on the other side of the world sixteen months earlier. Yes, he vaguely remembered agreeing to let this tiny record label release it, but here it was all of a sudden selling as a rather expensive import and he hadn't heard anything more about it and certainly hadn't seen or heard a test pressing as would be normal practice. And what's more, it didn't look like a Fall album. And worst of all, it had ostracised ex-member Marc Riley on the cover.

Mark didn't have to be furious with us. He had his music publisher to do it for him out of Australia. So my first contact with the overseas music business was an angry, demanding one. Desist from export, press no more copies, and give us all the income from all of the sales.

I feebly restated the agreed understanding but soon caved in to their demands. It was bruising and sobering. Through ignorance we had done wrong. The international music business won, and rightly so. We paid up and it didn't kill Flying Nun. But it did slow things down for a while, and it made me much more wary. I had never had to endure such a hardball conversation about money before. The threat of legal action was bad enough, but worse, I felt, was the fear of the loss of reputation. I wasn't going to be called a bootlegger.

We had acted unthinkingly and poorly. We had not kept in touch. In an interview much later, Chris shed some light on how everything had broken down thirty years earlier. He'd had the test pressings but couldn't afford to post them to The Fall — something that could so easily have been done by our office in Christchurch or with money forwarded to Chris. There had been poor communication and assumptions made that everything was fine. 'She'll be right, it's all fine, nothing to worry about.' A loud and clear alarm bell we were unable to hear.

CHAPTER 11

AFTER THE CLEAN

It was near the end of 1982 and The Clean had just come back to Christchurch after playing some North Island dates. David came to see me in the second and smaller Record Factory shop that I was now managing. Located underneath the United Services Hotel at 719 Colombo Street, between the Square and Hereford Street, it was a small store with a big turnover and I was cramped behind the counter. I wasn't expecting what David was there to tell me.

The Clean had decided to break up. They weren't enjoying the band experience, too much pressure had come with their success and they had had enough. It was very much the Kilgour brothers' decision. Spending more time working together, touring extensively with the added stress of alternative stardom, had culminated in a brotherly stress-out. They had had enough and were ending it. The band was over. I was taken by surprise, but I knew David well enough to know that he was adamant that this was it. It was over.

It felt like it was already the end of an era, too, if not the end of everything. I didn't have much more than a few short-term plans based around a small number of bands and their immediate recording projects. But, still, it felt a bit premature.

There were no contracts, so thinking and planning was inevitably ad hoc. Even with a contract no band was going to keep going if their hearts weren't in it. The music business is built on the energy and work of creative personalities so it's naturally disruptive and volatile. Given that, you could argue that short-term thinking was a flexible and sensible approach: any money and time expended on any band was a punt that could go spectacularly wrong at any time for reasons totally outside your control, or indeed theirs.

All the things that interfere with normal human relationships can derail a band, plus a few others peculiar to the music business; the hothouse social environment of being in a group, drug and alcohol issues, madness or just plain old artistic differences — take your pick.

So The Clean were breaking up just as they had hit the top of their game. They released their magnificently rollicking swansong 'Getting Older' as a seven-inch single, to a surprisingly lukewarm reception, and then they were done. Given that they were Flying Nun's biggest band, the news did make the venture feel a little vulnerable — but not for too long. It was quickly apparent that there was plenty more to be working on, especially the next projects from the bands featured on the *Dunedin Double*, bands themselves mostly inspired by The Clean. Then there were the groups that would form out of the old Clean itself.

Despite the causes of The Clean's demise, David and Hamish immediately decided to work together again as The Great Unwashed. It wasn't that they didn't want to work with Robert, simply that they wanted to make music away from the high profile of the old band. So they made some lo-fi recordings on a four-track machine and released them as the *Clean Out of Our Minds* album in 1983.

The intention was to make it as obvious as possible that this was not a Clean project, but in reality they merely reinforced the link in the process. The album is a diverse collection of material, much of it laid-back and charming. 'Obscurity Blues' is representative of the overall sound, and the band made a video for this back in Dunedin. It was filmed partly outside in some truly godforsaken southerly storm and then inside the cosy warmth of Roy Colbert's music room, where the brothers and friends relax and read and ponder.

The Kilgours then decided to recruit original Clean band member Peter Gutteridge to record a double seven-inch single. Of the five tracks, three were excellent compositions by Peter: 'Can't Find Water', 'Born in the Wrong Time' and 'Boat with No Ocean'. Greg Rood, then a trainee director with TVNZ, shot a video in a day. Peter lived in Dunedin and couldn't manage to make it to Christchurch for the shoot, so artist, photographer and Axemen drummer Stuart Page stood in for him — wearing a Peter Gutteridge mask and an Axemen T-shirt.

The video was a big success. As a bonus, the Jackson Pollock–inspired backdrop — a plastic curtain splattered with black and white paint — was cut up and sewn into record sleeves. It was an intensive, manual process: three separate pieces of stiff, heavy-duty plastic were stitched together on a specialised commercial sewing machine, one at a time. Demand quickly outran our ability to make them, and eventually the huge plastic curtain was all used up. But it made a wonderful cover that with time would shrink to encase the enclosed discs in a plastic tomb.

The music was great, too, and represented a real progression from the Kilgours' Clean material. Combined with the fantastic packaging, it made for a surefire hit. Naturally, the double-single format ensured we could never make any money on it, even if the cover cost nothing to make. So there was then a delay while the release was re-cut as a twelve-inch, with a new cover designed by Ronnie van Hout (a simple handmade screenprint hand-painted with watercolour washes). Again, the process meant we couldn't keep up with demand so we eventually settled for a conventionally printed cover. It was typical of the idealism of a project not quite matching the commercial reality, which in this case was the very real consumer demand.

With Peter in Dunedin and unable to get to Christchurch regularly to practise or perform, the Kilgours recruited Ross Humphries from The Pin Group to play bass. It became the line-up that would play through to the end of 1984 before breaking up. David eventually went back to live in Dunedin, where the surfing was better. Hamish worked at the Flying Nun office until he felt the need for a job with better career prospects. He was a little older and in a settled relationship and no doubt needed something with a more tangible future than the ongoing chaos of Flying Nun.

* * *

Bill Direen was very much at the forefront of music for me in the late 1970s and early 1980s. I had seen Bill play with Steven Cogle and Peter Stapleton as the Vacuum around town at Mollett Street and the Gladstone and they were a superb band. Influenced by The Velvet Underground, The 13th Floor Elevators and American garage bands of the late 1960s, they were also very much doing their own thing — dark, intense and imperious. They were a big part of my decision to start Flying Nun in 1981.

Cogle and Stapleton left soon enough, and both went on to work in a number of very good Christchurch bands such as the Victor Dimisich Band, The Pin Group, The Terminals and Scorched Earth Policy. Bill kept making great records without ever settling on a steady band, or a name or a long-term plan.

One of the best projects I would work on in the early 1990s was a multi-CD compilation of some of Bill's post-Vacuum music. The first CD, *Max Quitz*, featured the *Six Impossible Things*, *High Thirties Piano*, *Soloman's Ball*, *Schwimmen in der See* and *Above Ground* material from the late '70s and early '80s, originally released as seven-inch singles and EPs, many on or distributed by Flying Nun. It's fantastic stuff and captures Bill in some his best collaborations, especially with Alan Meek and Malcolm Grant, and for me conjures up the Christchurch of the time. The songs are well arranged, played and sung, with a perfect degree of articulate artfulness filtering through them. The band was sometimes known as The Builders (or the Bilders, Die Bilders, Bilder Bergers and so on) but not always. I think they won a Battle of the Bands competition as The Urbs before returning to The Builders after some confusion from Herbs fans on an Auckland visit.

The second CD was a reissue of The Builders' first album *Beatin Hearts*, recorded with Doug Hood and Terry King at Progressive Studio, along with some gentler material made with Chris Knox in his living room in mid-1982. (Recording was originally meant to have taken place while Chris and Doug were in Christchurch with the four-track earlier in the year but was delayed to coincide with Bill and his band visiting Auckland.)

Chris and Doug had seen Bill play in the old university quadrangle in the Christchurch Arts Centre on an earlier trip south (you can see us all on the cover of the *Soloman's Ball* second seven-inch pressing). We were all big fans and felt he had a future in music on a par with The Clean or any of the younger Dunedin bands. *Beatin Hearts* is a *tour de force* with so many great songs: 'Moderation', '1,000,000 Hearts', 'Bedrock Bay', 'Dirty and Disgusting', 'Alien', 'Accident', a brilliant version of Denis Glover's poem 'The Magpies', 'Magazine', 'Kicks' and more. All of it pulls together cohesively to form one of the genuinely great New Zealand albums, a masterpiece.

This formidable recording was Flying Nun's first proper album release, coming out in January 1983. We were by then starting to feel a bit grown up. *Beatin Hearts* sold well enough, though not in the quantities that The Clean or the other Dunedin bands did. The music was excellent and totally timeless to my ears, but didn't seem to have as broad an appeal. Perhaps it was a bit too grown

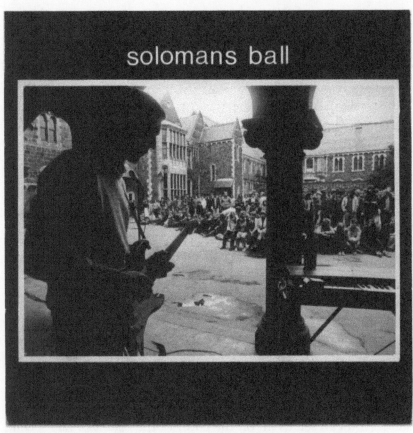

solomans ball

The cover of the 1982 seven-inch EP *Soloman's Ball* showed The Builders playing
the Christchurch Arts Centre (the old city-based site of the University of Canterbury).
Doug Hood, Chris Knox and an Android can be seen in the crowd on the right-hand side.

up for some of the younger record-buying kids who were into the
Dunedin bands, who were themselves noticeably younger than
Bill and his band.

I was pretty matey with Bill during this period. We would go to
Lancaster Park together to see the odd rugby test match. It was a
tricky time to be looking a bit bohemian, the assumption being you
were anti the Springbok tour. Wearing a beret and wraparound
sunglasses on the embankment definitely aroused suspicion. Bill
couldn't resist shouting, 'What about the tour then?' during a lull
in play. It was greeted by an ominous silence that was finally broken
by a distant wry laugh that was just sufficient to ease the tension.

Rugby games in those days were not exactly family affairs. The crowd was harder and tougher, like the game itself. And it was no place to be stoned. With Bill's ability to ratchet up the atmosphere, paranoia was never far away.

Over time I came to feel that Bill deliberately made things difficult. He seemed to have a habit of sabotaging the relationships that his collaborations were built on. Maybe Bill had become bored with me and his part in the Flying Nun setup. I certainly now had a sense of indecision and changeability on his part. There was a constant change of band line-ups and band names that was confusing and distracting. I'm not sure he could ever settle on the little things when he still wasn't sure if he was a musician or a writer or a dramatist — or all three all at once. The music was still very good, but his focus drifted from the mid-1980s on, as his other interests in literature and drama began to dominate his attention.

Though Bill was slipping away to do his own ever-diversifying thing on his own South Indies label, I was still keen on the bands that had grown out of, and reflected, that period of Christchurch music, the stuff that had been given impetus by punk. So I was very pleased when the Victor Dimisich Band re-formed to record an excellent EP, which of course Flying Nun released.

The great voice of Steven Cogle and drumming of Peter Stapleton went on to become The Terminals and we released a couple of their records in the '80s. They were in the tradition of '60s garage punk bands with Steven's stunning vocal delivery flying high over the driven beat and momentum of the band. Peter was in another, not dissimilar, Christchurch band, Scorched Earth Policy, who were always worthwhile live and made a couple of darkly entertaining EPs for the label.

* * *

Former Clean member Robert Scott must have wondered what was going on when the band broke up and the Kilgour brothers reappeared as The Great Unwashed. If he was dismayed when the Kilgours seemed to renounce everything they had achieved together as The Clean, he responded by simply getting on with things, playing with ex–Toy Lovers Paul Kean and Jane Walker. When Jane left, Robert's flatmate Kaye Woodward was recruited, along with ex-Builder Malcolm Grant, and The Bats were formed.

Singer, songwriter and guitarist Robert was a fan of Gram Parsons and the band started out with some country inflections. The rhythm section was accomplished and the melodies had charm. Early on, Robert's singing was a touch atonal and nasal, but it improved over time as the band developed.

The Bats approached me in 1984 with the *By Night* EP. I thought the recording was too rough and ready, but after some discussion we agreed to release it. By this stage I felt there had to be a general improvement in the sound quality of the recordings we were releasing, and I did worry about Robert's voice. But the buying public was forgiving and supported the band as they developed musically.

They made a major step up with the *Music for the Fireside* EP and, later, the *Daddy's Highway* album. While the band had improved considerably as musicians they didn't greatly alter what they were doing. Robert's voice now sat more comfortably in the mix, but they were still uniquely and undeniably The Bats. No one sounded anything like them, and they won over a sizeable audience largely on the back of their live shows.

* * *

By the end of 1983 and after two years of activity, Flying Nun was incredibly busy. Aside from the new core bands that emerged out of the *Dunedin Double*, there were all sorts of post-punk experiments by the likes of Fetus Productions, Marie and the Atom, They Were Expendable, Children's Hour, This Kind of Punishment and Skeptics. The Builders, the Victor Dimisich Band and the Gordons also all produced new material.

At the time the EP was the ideal format for a lot of our bands. It was senseless for them to record a single in isolation, and usually they didn't have the material for a full album. So the EP was the answer: four to six songs on a twelve-inch record, played at either 45 or 33⅓ rpm (depending on the number of tracks), with a whole cover for visual impact. The bulk of our output was dominated by the twelve-inch EP for quite some time.

A number of bands recorded rather good one-off EPs that stand now as invaluable documents of their best musical moments. I was particularly fond of Alpaca Brothers, Bored Games, Wreck Small Speakers on Expensive Stereos, The Orange and Children's Hour; their music might have vanished unrecorded had it not been for the cost-effective EP.

EPs were also important stepping stones for the likes of The Jean-Paul Sartre Experience, Straitjacket Fits, Snapper and The Chills (1985's *The Lost EP* pulled everything together for the band after a string of great stand-alone seven-inch singles).

Obviously it worked for the fans, too, otherwise these EPs wouldn't have sold so well and the musical landscape of 1980s New Zealand would have looked rather different. The record-buying public was willing to take a punt on a couple of EPs as an economical way of checking out and supporting an act without the investment of a full-priced album. In the ten years from 1981 to the end of 1990 Flying Nun released 184 records of which 17 per cent (or 31 titles) were seven-inch or twelve-inch singles, 42 per cent (78 titles) were twelve-inch EPs and 41 per cent (75 titles) were LPs.

The twelve-inch EP format worked well for Tall Dwarfs. *Louis Likes His Daily Dip* began a brilliant run of EPs over the next few years, and with *Canned Music* (1983) and *Slugbucket Hairybreath Monster* (1984) was collected with *Three Songs* for a compilation album, *Hello Cruel World*, for release on licence in the US and

Europe, and on CD in 1988. It's a brilliant compilation that the later albums never quite matched for either individual songs or overall coherence.

Of the EPs, *Slugbucket* was probably the high-water mark. All the songs were good, with a couple of showstoppers in 'The Brain That Wouldn't Die' (an homage to the B movie of the same name) and 'Crush'. It was available in three different-coloured covers with an insert. The record release show was held at the Windsor in Parnell. Despite barely working, primitive backing tracks and cardboard percussion, the Dwarfs were nevertheless immense. With Chris singing and playing some guitar, keyboards or Casiotone, and Alec pulling out all the stops on guitar, the whole set built to a crescendo. 'Crush' was the finale, with the duo joined on stage by This Kind of Punishment (Chris Matthews, Peter and Graeme Jefferies) and Mike Dooley for a twelve-minute rhythmic, percussive climax. Members of the audience joined in with drumsticks or pieces of the furniture. I stayed standing at the back. It was never a good idea to be too close to the stage when Chris was performing.

Remarkably, the numerous EPs and albums Tall Dwarfs released over the next decade and a half continued to be made with Chris living in Auckland and Alec in Christchurch. They would share material and eventually get together for the occasional recording session. They were all good records, made with gusto and imagination. The material spanned a huge range, from gentle, sweet, melodic love songs to crazy, full-on walls of guitar noise.

As always, however, musical fashion was shifting, and shifting away from what these two great talents were producing. There always has to be a next big thing. But Chris and Alec kept at it, acknowledged worldwide as DIY recording pioneers and beloved members of an international, independently minded musical movement.

* * *

Stuart Page's poster for the Flying Nun Recording Party at The Gladstone Hotel,
10 December 1983

In 1983, which was an especially good year for music, I managed to get involved with the Netherworld Dancing Toys. I seem to remember stumbling in on one of their gigs at the Oriental Hotel in Dunedin. I was always a sucker for a live show and I would have been in a party mood. I was also one for wild enthusiasms rather than anything considered and cautious. That was the basis of the label's origins, success and survival so far.

The Netherworlds were doing their thing that night — kind of a 'Jackie Wilson Said', Dexys Midnight Runners–type white boy soul with a brass section boil-up. Self-confidence and an undeniably propulsive force bulldozed everything before it. The large, squeezed-up crowd of students loved it. They had no choice.

Nick Sampson and Malcolm Black wrote the songs. There were a few superficial similarities with the best of the core Flying Nun bands of the time, but this band was moving in a different direction. They were hellbent on mainstream success and had the self-belief (matched with the necessary willingness to bend a little) to achieve it. Musically it wasn't really my thing, but they did it with conviction and I couldn't help noticing that others thought so too.

Unlike any other band I'd known so far, they were not just ambitious but had already organised themselves for the kind of success that is defined by radio play and sales based on that exposure. We did three records together in the twelve-inch EP format that worked so well for the other bands on the label. The songs and performances were good. The recording was basic but good enough. That was important, because the musical territory these guys were mining required a different approach.

The first EP went very well, achieving good sales in their hometown of Dunedin and charting at number ten nationally. It looked and sounded different to other Flying Nun releases, but still you knew it was one of ours because the speed wasn't printed on the label, leading to some confusion in choosing what speed to play the record — 45 rpm or 33⅓ rpm? It wasn't on the artwork for the label that the band provided, but I should have checked.

Their second release in 1983, 'The Trusted Ones', was a twelve-inch single and was accessible enough. It sold well but didn't make the charts or the radio. In hindsight, perhaps the song wasn't strong enough — something I should have been thinking and saying at the time rather than taking the longer indie music view, where things can develop slowly and you gradually build an audience. These guys needed chart and radio action and they needed it now.

The Netherworlds had emerged from a particular musical fashion and needed to capitalise and consolidate before things moved on. They had been working hard, touring up and down the country to big crowds, but couldn't convert that live following to record sales without radio play. Unfortunately, no commercial station was going to play something released on Flying Nun during the 1980s.

The third release, *Song and Dance*, released in 1984, was back to the EP format, with a three-song live side and a two-song studio side. The cover had a different look to the stylised graphic of the first two. It featured a quirky image of the Dunedin Orphans Club — it was a bring-it-back-and-reconnect-with-your-roots sort of record.

Like all Dunedin bands, the Netherworld Dancing Toys were very conscious of where they came from. You can see that in their later video of 'The Real You' — self-consciously of Dunedin and just a little sentimental (in the same way Sneaky Feelings' 'Husband House' was). *Song and Dance* did a bit better, with a number thirty-three chart entry, but our relationship was spent.

There was no 'Thanks to Roger' acknowledgment on the back of *Song and Dance*. Not that I noticed at the time — focus wasn't one of my strengths in the mid-'80s. And I was paying so much attention to my relationship with the Netherworlds that I was apparently the last person to know they had signed to Virgin Music. I found out when the Virgin sales rep came into the Record Factory one Monday morning and sold me their debut release.

She was very keen on the band. Apparently they were the next big thing.

She was right. The 'For Today' single was huge in 1985. They got the right song, took it into a decent studio, and arranged and produced it well with Annie Crummer's backing vocals, so that Virgin could take it to radio and be taken seriously. The song went on to win the APRA Silver Scroll for Song of the Year. Following it up was tricky, though, and the band found it was hard to gain attention offshore — as it was for everybody.

Maybe the omens were there from the start. The name Netherworld Dancing Toys is taken from the lyrics of 'Spin Me Round' on Roxy Music's *Manifesto* album. I am, predictably, a fan of early 1970s Roxy Music, but never warmed to this 1978 comeback album. I felt they'd become a band that had subsumed substance in favour of style. The Netherworlds were not at all like Roxy Music, musically or otherwise, but there was a hint we weren't on the same wavelength. If I'd been paying more attention, perhaps it could have all been better thought through.

But I appreciated the band's professionalism. They weren't just hard-nosed business guys, they were very loyal to each other and remain the only band I know that not only treated their sound and light guys (Tex and Ged) as equal partners, but featured them in photos and videos as well. I liked them all a great deal and I think they helped me better understand the music business.

* * *

In January 1984, the Netherworld Dancing Toys were the only Flying Nun–connected band to play the Sweetwaters Music Festival at Pukekawa, south of Auckland. Perhaps The Chills were unavailable to play and surely would have been included in the line-up if they had had a functioning band at this time. None of our other bands were deemed worthy of being asked.

That year's festival was headlined by a seemingly unstoppable top line-up of Talking Heads, The Pretenders, Simple Minds and Eurthymics. However, the numbers were down, and it was the last of the big multiple-day festivals for more than a decade before a disastrous attempt was made to resurrect the format.

Inexplicably, I travelled up for the event. Doug Hood had organised a shared Flying Nun/*Rip It Up* caravan. *Rip It Up*'s Murray Cammick and his full-time music writer Russell Brown were there to cover the event. Doug may have had a couple of bands playing that needed him to look after sound, but I went simply because I was at a bit of a loose end. We were set up in the civilised backstage area among the performers and the mainstream music industry they were mainly aligned with. Doug had thoughtfully brought along his own rather powerful PA, which he set up against the caravan with the speakers pointing outwards across this music-industry microcosom.

This was a different sort of event, on a much bigger scale, from my only other festival experience, at Punakaiki the previous year. That small two-day festival had been held in an acoustically pleasing bush-clad valley just inland from the famous Pancake Rocks, north of Greymouth on the West Coast. The focus was remarkably different from that at Sweetwaters. All the bands at Punakaiki were examples of New Zealand post punk: Nocturnal Projections, Not Really Anything, The Androidss, the Gordons, Look Blue Go Purple and The Chills. I went unprepared, not counting on cold and then rain at night. Look Blue Go Purple kindly let me into their tent and in return my chattering teeth no doubt kept them awake all night. The rain made the single road out impassable and the entire, now largely trapped audience watched The Chills destroy their van's engine by over-revving it as they tried to escape. A general sense of desperation took hold as everyone tried to get out of that now primeval, dank, dissolute place. While the bands must have thought I was foolish turning up without shelter or warm clothing, they could only have been impressed by my foresight in parking my car back on the main road.

Sweetwaters was a much grander affair. I seem to remember particularly good hash, and lots of it, along with a huge quantity of booze, beer and whisky. We had taken enough to last three days, but it was all gone after the first night — our caravan became a bit of a magnet for industry outsiders and Doug and I were free and generous hosts, as well as, soon, rather crazed. Luckily Murray Cammick was driving the couple of hours back into Auckland each night to file copy at the *Rip It Up* offices and was able to restock. Extra supplies were ordered to cover the remaining two days and by the next day they were also gone.

Being a social bunch, we decided to play a game of cricket in a small open space among the crowded caravans. A proper bat and ball were produced and we took turns batting and bowling. The hard ball made an incredibly loud noise when it struck the tin-sided caravans around us. Damage seemed inevitable, so too a not-to-be-returned ball. Undeterred, we played on with whatever came to hand, including fruit and, finally, a large cabbage.

I was having so much fun I only ventured out of the sanctuary of the backstage area once, towards the end of the event. I clambered up the giant hill in front of the main stage and zigzagged through the bodies on the ground and the glassy-eyed still standing. It was like a war zone out there and the casualties were enormous. I finally got near the top of the hill and looked back towards the stage just in time to see Simple Minds (I think, but it could have been anyone and at the time it didn't matter to me at all) work towards the end of their set. What I immediately noticed was how loud Doug's PA was when Simple Minds weren't playing. Iggy Pop and The Stooges' 'I Want to be Your Dog' was blasting out from behind the main stage at what must have been huge volume. I knew I needed to get back to where the real action was. So back to our caravan I stumbled.

There was a bit of trouble when I got there. The hard-rocking New Zealand trio The Narcs were, strangely, trying to get some sleep and had complained about the noise coming from our caravan. Warners were soon doing the same: they were hosting a barbecue for Talking Heads some way off and couldn't hear themselves think. They threatened to tip our caravan into the ditch that formed the festival perimeter — a perimeter constantly patrolled by police, who for some reason never managed to look through the open window and spot me with a large plastic coke bottle full of smoke in my mouth. I certainly was a bit of a mess by the end of that long weekend. Meanwhile, the Netherworld Dancing Toys, the only one of our bands in attendance and perhaps our least typical band, behaved impeccably and delivered the goods on the biggest stage in New Zealand music at this time.

With Hamish Kilgour in the Hereford Street office, 1982 (photo by Alec Bathgate)

CHAPTER 12

COMMERCIAL REALITY

By the end of 1982, the number of releases, sales and stock started to mount up and it was impossible to manage everything out of my home office in Sumner. The workload also meant I couldn't run the business part time. Long evenings were spent shuffling paper and making phone calls before exhaustion and inebriation took hold. I wanted to stay working at the Record Factory for the time being, so Hamish Kilgour organised a job creation scheme grant and came to work for the label in a very run-down room we'd found upstairs on Hereford Street next to Shand's Emporium, down towards the river. It was our first office and it cost next to nothing, but it had holes in the floor and we had to cover the walls in cardboard because the plaster had fallen off and it was permanently dusty. Which is why your very early Flying Nun purchases may have been covered in a very fine white powder.

It was busy, I was charting unknown waters, finding out what would work, and how, as I did it. As they say, you learn from your mistakes. Or perhaps, 'what does not kill you makes you stronger'. So there was stress and sometimes that stress demanded a whole lot of self-medication. I couldn't cook, and looking at photos of my old half-self it looks as if I didn't eat either. The kitchen was a mass of empty glassware waiting to be washed. The fridge was for storing beer and ginger ale.

There was plenty of space for touring bands to stay in my large flat in Sumner. It was an opportunity to get to know the people from Dunedin. I didn't see it as business or networking and many of us just became friends. We shared the same interests in music, drink and rugby, even if no one felt comfortable talking about the rugby any more.

Hamish was Flying Nun's first paid employee. Not paid enough; no one, including myself, ever was. But he showed the way: underpaid and overworked yet he really cared about what he was doing.

I would pop in at lunchtime and after work, while Hamish took care of the day-to-day business — checking the post, chasing orders, packing them up, sleeving records and spending a lot of time at the post office, clearing the mailbox and sending off shop orders and the few mail-order purchases that were starting to trickle in.

Initially, those orders were from backblock places, miles from any record shop. Later they came from fans in towns and cities who just liked to deal direct — to get their records in the post with a note from Hamish or a doodle on the corrugated cardboard package. We liked this aspect of the business and would slip in spare band or old touring posters whenever we could.

Fans and friends liked to call by for a chat. All would be co-opted into the endless tasks of glueing seven-inch picture sleeves together or putting records into covers. By early 1983 the single room was already too small. Hamish found us a space to share above Echo Records on High Street, a block or so away and still very central.

The shared nature of the space wasn't ideal and neither was the giant single-flight stairway. The couriers delivering 100-kilo cartons of records no longer found us an exotic alternative business oddity, more a damn nuisance. But it was a sunny and happy space and people shopping downstairs were always welcome to

Hamish and me at the High Street office, 1984 (photo by Stuart Page)

come up. It was great that they paid in cash, but the chat was just as important. Not that we knew it or that it had a name at the time, but there was an extended community building around the label and its activities.

What I knew about running a record company was based on some pretty basic observations made from my retail experience. The multinational record companies were based in Wellington or Auckland. I had had no connection with any overseas record company or label. There was no internet to find out how an arrangement with an artist might be structured. I thought it up out of thin air.

I still didn't see Flying Nun as a business with the financial stability to pay myself a wage. So the setup was a bit blurred, with lots of different people involved, working in various capacities, with a loose feeling of it all being cooperative. Ironically it was Hamish, the only paid employee, who gently promoted the cooperative idea. Back then you could say that word without embarrassment. But the truth was it was more anarchist than socialist.

I became aware that things were slightly awry one evening when a total stranger introduced himself as the owner of Flying Nun Records in the public bar of the United Services Hotel. It was a place for the unreliable, untrustworthy and delusional, but I was bemused all the same. It came only a week or so after a mutual friend referred to a peripheral helper as a co-owner. I accepted the idea that core characters like Hamish, Chris and Doug probably would become partners in the business at some stage, if stable circumstances allowed it. I wanted these key people to share in any benefits if and when they arrived, but I was in no hurry to have them share the obvious hazards.

The financial volatility was alarming because the growth in sales was exponential. The business was under-capitalised and I lacked the skills to understand and control the situation. The occasional acquaintance or total stranger claiming some sort of ownership steeled me to get a bit tougher and more decisive with those wanting to share in the feel-good atmosphere without any thought to the financial stress and risk that I was shouldering alone. I needed to toughen up and learn, which I then did, though perhaps not as quickly as needed.

As we sold more records, the stairs to the office seemed steeper and longer. We dragged the cartons of discs and sleeves and inserts up and carried down the made-up records to be shipped to Auckland, Wellington or Dunedin. Shipping records was a tangible measure of success. They were going somewhere to be sold or were already sold. I loved those mail-order customers whose purchases had already been paid for — they were so important in keeping the whole thing going.

There was a different satisfaction to be had in the promo runs for new releases. Copies went to *Rip It Up*, the country's only dedicated music magazine, newspapers' review sections and student radio. I might occasionally make a phone call to make sure they had received the goods and see what they thought. That was the extent of our promotional world.

The only real resistance was from Dunedin's *Otago Daily Times*, which refused to review EPs on the grounds they were not proper albums, despite so many of them being important releases by groups in their own town. But there were lots of smaller papers in the regions with quality music writers, all generating generally supportive reviews and forging an important link with music lovers outside the big cities.

All the handling of these records in the office — to be glued, inserted, counted, repacked and dispatched — made the business seem very tactile and real. We were taking ephemeral things like sound recordings and images for the covers and sending them away to factories in Wellington, from where these ideas came back as tangible things with a monetary value. I became rather obsessed with the process. There was Roger Shepherd, record company founder, and there was the more mundane Roger Shepherd, warehouse guy. We all worked on that side of things. It was the nuts and bolts of the business.

Soon I found myself obsessing over the nature of packing materials — double-wall corrugated cardboard with perfectly square cut cardboard dividers. I became good with a knife but never got used to using cellophane wrapping tape. The more you use it the more you hate it, trying to find the edge, having it stick together, trying to cut it with a knife or worse, in desperation, one's own teeth. No, my fondness was for the cardboard. Lots of people like to pop bubble wrap but I have deeper feelings for double- and triple-walled corrugated card. I try not to hoard it.

I thought it was my secret until a few years later when Dave Mulcahy from The Jean-Paul Sartre Experience presented me with a T-shirt he'd had made. It featured the logo of quality Australian cardboard manufacturer Visy Board. I felt outed but was thrilled to bits. I still have it and wear it for my visits to my storage lock-up, where I can spend hours amusing myself with all the cardboard.

We valued the packing because of what was inside. Records damage easily; the disc can run through the cover and split it if the packing isn't tight enough, or the records can warp and the covers bend if the packing is too loose. We took the trouble to do it right because we loved those records and we knew the eventual owner would feel the same. We weren't just selling music to customers, we were communicating with friends.

It was a time when the world seemed open to what the bands at Flying Nun were doing and anything was possible. The biggest problem was that no one had a clue about how to tap into that perceived goodwill effectively. Did a band need to relocate overseas? How did you finance that? What about an overseas manager? Should you stay on Flying Nun, who would sub-license your records to a third party in a foreign territory? How does the money work in those sorts of arrangements?

Often the answers weren't that attractive for the artists or for Flying Nun. There are still questions today about the best way to approach it. One might conclude there are no rules and there is no 'right' way. Each band or artist has to find the best way for them and their music to find their audience, which is ideally an international one. With The Clean, for example, we plugged away selling their records and sending promos to college radio and for review long after they broke up. They were surprised to discover that there was an international audience there for them when they finally went overseas in 1989 and were in turn emboldened by the interest to record the *Vehicle* album for Rough Trade in the UK.

It took a good deal of trial and error to find the answers, too. In that respect, along with The Chills and The Bats, Sneaky Feelings led the charge overseas and paid the price with an expensive battering. Their *Send You* album, recorded and released in 1983, was a masterpiece. It had a typically professional-looking cover that reinforced their difference from David Pine's friends in the other bands. Good music is good music, and I thought the cover was great, but the band struggled to be fashionable. They were named after an Elvis Costello song from his *My Aim is True* album, but it always sounded a bit clunky as a band name to me.

But Sneaky Feelings made up in ambition what they lacked in perceived hipness. Their sound wasn't best suited to four-track treatment on the *Dunedin Double* and they were one of the first bands to look beyond inexpensive methods towards what a proper studio could offer them. The aim was to produce something that would be played on commercial radio and give them a crack at mainstream success. Alas, commercial radio at that time was never going to play something by a Dunedin band, no matter how good the song or the recording or the marketing. The band was endearingly blind to this unsavoury reality, so they never stopped trying and they made some very good records in the process.

When I think about it now, being on Flying Nun was probably a hindrance for a band when it came to commercial radio. There was a lot of fuss at the time about mainstream radio's lack of support for local music and the big stick of compulsory quotas was being bandied about. Radio hated us, with the perception being that everything we did was poorly recorded and rather strange.

Many, including Chris Knox, were now talking a great deal about what a scandal it was that radio was not playing New Zealand music, but I couldn't see that changing anything for us. They were going to play what suited them, which was whatever best fitted the demographics of selling advertising. With a quota for New Zealand music, any benefit would be reaped by middle-of-the-road artists before any of our acts enjoyed primetime airplay. In fact I was concerned that a quota could strengthen the mainstream that we had effectively helped weaken with our left-field success over the previous years. I decided to keep my mouth shut on the subject. There seemed little point in inflaming the situation.

The Netherworld Dancing Toys had had to move to Virgin Records and spend proper money in a studio before they generated radio play and a massive hit with 'For Today', and perhaps that would have been the better route for the Sneakys too. Flying Nun didn't experience real radio play and full-blown commercial success until The Chills released 'Heavenly Pop Hit' in 1990 and the Headless Chickens hit number one with 'George' in 1994.

The Sneakys did give it a real go with the 'Husband House' single in 1985. It sold well and charted at number sixteen on the national chart. The video, which looks a bit sentimental now, did a good job of building their audience, but it proved hard to follow up.

The Sneakys were one of those bands who could save money. They didn't just spend it in the studio, they used it to travel overseas. Jeremy Freeman was from Dunedin and had experience in the marketing world (jeans or cola I think), and was managing them. We all plugged away trying to keep up with the travel to the UK and Germany, the gigs and the record releases they were promoting.

If their relationship with Flying Nun was chaotic in New Zealand, imagine how impossible it all became on the other side of the world, with a third party involved. They were one of the first Flying Nun bands to travel to Europe and it was very much a trip into the unknown, without the support or connections that, say, The Chills or The Bats had. It was an adventure, but must have been frustratingly hard for them.

The releases that followed 'Husband House', *Sentimental Education* and *Hard Love Stories*, were fine albums, but lacked the obvious singles that might have generated the radio play they craved. I thought the excellent 'Trouble with Kay' might have got them there, but no. Lots of little things conspired against them. They never became fashionable in the way The Chills or Straitjacket Fits did. They became increasingly stranded in a no-man's-land where it doesn't matter how good the music is, the audience simply isn't looking your way. Fashion is cruel.

Matthew Bannister would later write about his experiences with Sneaky Feelings in his excellent book *Positively George Street*, which was subtitled 'A personal history of Sneaky Feelings and the Dunedin Sound'. He did a fine job, writing well and self-knowingly about being a bit of an outsider in that scene, and he was especially frank about his relationship with Flying Nun and me. He also included a scathing portrayal of Chris Knox, with whom he had a fraught relationship. Chris had been generous to all of the *Dunedin Double* bands with advice and assistance, coming along to and being supportive at gigs and often putting the bands up at his house. But the annoying side of his personality really got to Matthew and it is this tension that Matthew developed into the central drama of his book. I thought Chris should rise above it all, but instead he reacted angrily, in a way that I think revealed a rarely exposed, underlying insecurity.

* * *

Whether I liked it or not, Flying Nun was growing into a proper business. The first year's turnover of $11,000 had ballooned to around $85,000 in 1983. I had no general business experience and it was only thanks to Hamish, who went out and did a basic business accounting course, that we even had monthly creditor and debtor listings. Up till then debts had been tallied on the back of an envelope, with bills stuffed randomly in a drawer to be paid according to what was sitting on top at any given time.

Specialised record industry considerations such as royalty calculations followed no known precedent for the simple reason that I didn't know what the industry norms were. Music publishing, which represents the income of songwriters as opposed to performers, was completely misunderstood. It didn't matter so much at the beginning because the performers on the records were generally the songwriters, but it later became an issue. There was no one to talk to and get advice from and very few in the industry knew how it worked; it was a closed shop.

I was still at the record shop. My canny boss Del Richards had had the foresight to sell his four Record Factory shops to EMI, and I was now the regional manager of six shops dotted around Christchurch. I learned a bit more about retail nuts and bolts from EMI, always mindful that retail was really about the interface with the customer. And while the customer came first, the customer wasn't necessarily always right. Some were just plain trouble.

Around this time Gary Cope had started dropping by the office at lunchtimes. He worked as an accountant for his brother's accountancy firm and offered to help out. The bulk of his day job was spent with farming accounts but he had the experience to handle those aspects of our books that were simply another burden for Hamish and me. Gary was a godsend. But the best thing was that he was such an avid fan of the music. He loved all of the new music coming out of the UK and the US, and was a huge fan of what was happening locally.

When Hamish decided to leave, Gary seemed an obvious choice to take over his role as the lowly paid full-time worker. His stabilising influence gave me some space to think. There was plenty to be done at Flying Nun. If I was going to be there full time I had to back my ability to generate the sales to cover my basic wage. So I made the leap. In 1986 I became a full-time employee of my own record company.

What really sealed the decision was my realising that interest from overseas was continuing to grow. The trickle of mail-order enquiries had become a torrent. All sorts of fanzines, music magazines and radio shows wanted to hear our music, write about and broadcast it. The more samples we posted out, the more mail orders flooded back. John Peel had first played one of our records in May 1984, 'Duane Eddy' and 'Neck of the Woods' by The Great Unwashed, followed in June by Children's Hour's 'Washed Away' and The Chills' 'Pink Frost'. This created initial interest that soon led to a run of features and 'Single of the Week' reviews in the UK music weeklies, especially once The Chills arrived in London later in 1985 (with The Bats and Sneaky Feelings not far behind).' This was soon followed by small record label interest, then by independent distributors, and even the occasional A&R guy at one of the bigger overseas companies. There was clearly plenty of scope for increasing international sales as we made more contacts, fed the growing publicity and built arrangements with overseas distributors.

It would have all been academic if the music hadn't been coming through. Fortunately it was. Along with the *Dunedin Double* groups and Tall Dwarfs there were all sorts of talented new artists emerging. Music was thriving — not just in Dunedin, where it was getting very exciting, but also in Auckland and Christchurch. Now I was working full time at Flying Nun I was spending a lot of time in Dunedin and Auckland. There were good things happening.

* * *

By the mid-'80s business was very good, entirely because sales were very good. With fewer new releases in 1984 there was a small increase to $90,000 in sales, and then a big step up in the number of new releases and turnover to $165,000 in 1985. But the growth in sales was putting a big stress on cash flow — not that I knew enough to put a name on it at the time. Under-capitalisation was another concept I would eventually become familiar with. I didn't need to know about 'insolvency' until quite some time later.

What I did understand from my fifth-form economics was supply and demand. Demand was huge and I was having trouble keeping up the supply. Much of the inefficiency and chaos around this time could be put down to being owed more money than we were owing, but not being able to collect it fast enough to finance bigger recording budgets or bigger pressing runs to meet that demand.

The newer bands were still best suited to making EPs, but the more established bands were now looking to make albums. Increasingly they had the material and expertise, and had developed enough of an audience to support these bigger projects with sales. Albums with more songs were more expensive to make but they had a greater turnover value and margin than the shorter formats. We needed to be making albums and we needed the extra margin that albums generated.

I kept imagining the multinationals would start chasing some of our more successful or accessible acts, as none of the bands was formally signed to Flying Nun. But the majors never came looking. The fact the bands were so far away in Dunedin probably helped. And they probably thought that if any of the other artists were half as prickly as Chris Knox then it was all too hard.

But the major record companies did want to do some business. PolyGram probably had the best idea of how much we were selling because they owned the pressing plant. They became very persistent about wanting to be our distributor. The deal offered was a distribution service for a fee of 12 per cent — which was ridiculously generous at the time. They would help with the manufacturing, which would make a huge difference to our planning and general organisation, but I was very reluctant to surrender our independence at any level. The deal seemed too good to be true, which made me wary. I knew our relationship with retailers was one of our strengths and I didn't want a major record company's sales team getting between the label and the shopkeepers.

There was a bit of a strange vibe around PolyGram at this time. They'd had some massive success with the likes of Dire Straits, but were also undertaking a series of huge deletion sales — effectively dumping tens of thousands of overstocked records, sold cheaply to clear, so with no royalties paid on them. A lot of attractive titles were included in those deletions.

It wasn't hard to get the feeling that PolyGram were short of cash. I'd later read the excellent music business book *Hit Men* by Fredric Dannen, which detailed PolyGram's near ruin through its involvement in Casablanca Records in the early 1980s. It's a not untypical story of ego, drugs, madness and enormous amounts of lost cash. I later couldn't help wondering if I was witnessing part of a worldwide strategy for survival by raising cash by any means possible. Or perhaps PolyGram simply knew the CD was on its way in and it was time to shift all of that vinyl and generate a few dollars while it still could.

Either way, ultimately I knew instinctively that being distributed by a major wouldn't be good for Flying Nun at this time. We had an underdog reputation that translated into increased support and sales with our end customers via our special relationship with retail. Whereas I could sell ten copies of a release to a store in Timaru, I knew in all likelihood PolyGram would sell one. And would a bigger store in Auckland buy ten copies from them rather than a hundred from us? Ninety per cent of our sales at that stage were through New Zealand record shops and I could be risking our sales base collapsing through this kind of deal. It could have been all over within a year or so; fewer sales, fewer releases and the more important bands drifting away to other record companies — including PolyGram perhaps.

The lack of proper contracts with the bands would have made that easy, and it was very much a feature of how the company was run throughout the first decade or so. It was hardly unique to Flying Nun, with many independent labels operating this way internationally. It worked both ways — a band could leave at any time, and the label was free of any long-term obligation to the band. But even a normal record company contract that locks a band into a deal for, say, five albums will always still allow the company to get out by not picking up the option on the next record. Standard music-industry contracts have always been very one-sided.

At Flying Nun, arrangements were made on a pragmatic record-by-record basis: how much to spend on recording, where and when to release, and how. There was an element of discussion and compromise about money, but it seemed to work. The bands made some great records, and no one ever did leave to sign up with someone else — except the Netherworld Dancing Toys, of course, but if we had talked about it I think it would have been mutually agreed.

I preferred royalty arrangements to profit splits. I wasn't sure there would ever have been profits to split anyway, so paying a flat royalty seemed fair. As I had no idea how this would work, the rate was very low in the early days. But it was still probably more than a conventional deal with a major would have paid.

Early on, the recording costs were not recoupable against those royalties. This was fine for smaller-budget recordings, but simply couldn't work when the recording costs quite naturally crept up as bands became more ambitious. Then the tab would be picked up by the band, or was advanced against future royalties, which was a more conventional arrangement. But without contracts the label was taking the gamble the artists would stay beyond the next recording and release. Usually they did.

Gary beat our royalty accounting into shape at a time when it was still all done manually. There were no computer programmes to do it for us, and anyway we still didn't even have our first computer. Royalty accounting is a very specialised skill. Most accountants flounder and those who master it are prone to breakdown and dysfunction. Gary built Flying Nun its own manual system that tracked the date and number of pressings along with cover print runs, monthly sales from each of the main centres and New Zealand and overseas mail orders as well as export sales. It worked, but it didn't mean we could pay royalties on time. Money tended to go to those who needed it for further recording or overseas touring. That didn't mean royalties weren't paid, just that priority was given to those who needed it the most. Artists, like many of our trade creditors, were understanding, and their support made survival and growth possible.

It was yet more of that ongoing self-educational process, trying to find out what kind of arrangement would work best in any given situation. Certainly, a contract would have been beneficial in the case of The Fall's live album, but you live and learn. Gradually we worked out how it all worked and we grew into a proper record company in the process.

CHAPTER 13

OUT OF THE DOLEDRUMS

It was mid-1982 and The Chills had come to stay at my place. Martin Phillipps and various Chills, I'm not sure which ones exactly. They were a band on the way up, ambitious and keen to take advantage of the groundswell of interest in them as the next big thing. They just needed to get some recording done and some records out. There had been some bad luck and they needed to regroup and get things moving. For some reason it was never straightforward.

I don't know who the ringleaders were, but I knew something was up when I returned home after they had left. The glassware was washed, dried and put away. Significantly, there was a pot I didn't even know I had soaking in the sink. It was badly burned and coated with some evil-looking substance that gave off an extremely unpleasant odour I was now starting to gag on.

Acting decisively, I poured my first oversized whisky of the day and opened the fridge for the ginger ale. But there was no ginger ale, just large symmetrical chunks of succulent green cactus, and lots of it.

My guests had been out the day before in the band van, cruising the old people's villages and clusters of small state retirement homes. Sure enough, some old duffer had a giant San Pedro growing magnificently against the sunny side of their home, as yet (and remarkably) unspotted or harvested by the local Christchurch drug crazies. The band returned that night, tied the cactus to the towbar, wrenched the huge whole thing out of the ground, manhandled it into the back of the van, and made their getaway before any of the elderly locals could get their slippers on.

They had cooked up a mass and consumed it in one of two possible ways. It was revolting stuff but most people drank it mixed with (or followed by) anything handy and palatable. This explained the absence of my ginger ale. Vomiting was still largely inevitable, but I guess enough of the active ingredient was retained or absorbed to deliver the desired hallucinogenic result.

The other way of consuming the stuff without the unfortunate side effects was anally. Some people swore by this method, despite enema kits being relatively scarce. You needed help, of course, so it was undoubtedly a chance to find out who your real friends were. I fleetingly thought about giving it a go, but that slab of succulent green in the fridge reminded me of a human limb and I knew it would not be a happy experience.

I drank the whisky neat.

* * *

I'd first spotted Martin Phillipps when he played keyboards with The Clean in Christchurch in 1981. He repeated his live performance of 'Tally Ho!' on the recording as well. I didn't actually meet Martin until that night I followed the band to Auckland and he opened the door of The Androidss' house on Ponsonby Road. He'd told me then he had his own band called The Chills and was only helping out with his friends The Clean. He clearly didn't want me to make any assumptions. I had just been pushed out of a moving vehicle so I probably looked prone to confusion. I was then twenty-one and he was still about eighteen.

Despite different upbringings we shared similar interests and tastes. His father, Donald, was a Methodist minister, which explained why Martin had been born in the unglamorous parish of Milton in South Otago. He was a caring, liberal kind of guy who collected copies of the *Wisden Cricketers' Almanack* and played the cello. Martin's mother, Barbara, was the no-nonsense, can-do, practical one.

Like my own family, the Phillipps were keen on music, except they played while we only listened. Martin's family supported his musical enthusiasm while mine seemed to consider working in 'pop' or 'rock' as little better than male prostitution or drug dealing. Eventually I would see their point.

Martin's family would remain involved with his musical interests and explorations, whereas I kept my work and play in the music world quite separate from my family after I left home. It seemed simpler that way. I knew it was all too hard to explain. I had made a break and was out on my own. Martin stayed closer to his family, and their support was important, if not crucial, for him.

He was a very likeable young man. Softly and considerately spoken, he had a sense of humour that displayed a quirky, offbeat intelligence. Not overly expressive or flamboyant, he was still always nattily dressed. His smile was genuinely engaging. Whereas The Clean were a complete unit, Martin seemed more of a lone operator. When first I met him, he was taking a break from his own band while his keyboard-playing sister, Rachel, concentrated on school exams, and bass player Jane Dodd was away for a spot of overseas experience. This would become something of a pattern: though it was Martin's band, he needed to work with others to make it happen, yet their lives tended to get in the way.

Martin's first band, The Same, had been a young punk-inspired combo that played when and where they could and had supported Toy Love. The Same had gradually shed members to The Stones and The Verlaines, and transmuted into The Chills.

Jane Dodd and Rachel Phillipps had been joined by original Clean bass player Peter Gutteridge and drummer Alan Haig. So its beginnings were somewhat involved, and it got more complicated from there on. Peter left early due to musical differences with Martin: he was interested in noise and drones and went on to co-write 'Point That Thing' and 'I'm in Love with These Times' with The Clean before forming his own long-lived band, Snapper.

When Martin returned to Dunedin from the 1981 Clean tour he was energised and decisive about building a new band around Fraser Batts (The Same), Alan Haig and Terry Moore (Bored Games). They were very good players, forming one of the classic Chills line-ups, and were up for the challenge of making the project work musically and as a group. This was the band I saw in late 1981 and wanted to work with, which eventually led to their inclusion on the *Dunedin Double*.

In many ways The Chills had the most to lose by recording on a limited budget on DIY equipment. Their songs and sound were the most ambitious, and needed extra time, care and technology to be properly realised as recordings. The three songs they contributed to the *Dunedin Double* — 'Kaleidoscope World', 'Satin Doll' and 'Frantic Drift' — sound a little thin these days. But they were complex, even eccentric, but light and accessible enough to satisfy their fans and make new friends. Of the four *Dunedin Double* bands, The Chills were the ones most obviously marked for success — proper crossover commercial success, with gold records and everything.

The cover says a lot about the band at the time — fussy with lyrics, band photos, graphics, exhaustive credits (a Chills constant) and their own take on Egyptian hieroglyphics. They knew their songs were at the poppier end of the indie spectrum and wanted people to know there was more to them, with a 'these are some of our more light-hearted songs, see us live' note on the sleeve. They rightly backed themselves as musicians and they could play from the start.

Like the other *Dunedin Double* bands, The Chills were finding a receptive audience on the back of The Clean's success. An audience that liked the idea of indie rock music from New Zealand had been revealed and it was open to all sorts of different sounds. The irony was that the press picked up the 'Dunedin Sound' tag when in truth it was very much about Dunedin sounds, plural.

The Chills' *Dunedin Double* songs might have sounded thin, but their ambition was undeniable. The self-conscious variety of the material and the complexity of the songs themselves caught people's imaginations far more than any concerns about the sound. They would follow the band and watch them grow and develop through thick and thin.

When new drummer Martyn Bull became sick with leukaemia the band went into hiatus as he fought for his life. Tragically he died in July 1983. The loss was keenly felt by all in the Dunedin scene. Martin Phillipps took it hard — young people aren't meant to die, and Martyn had been only twenty-two. The Chills were put on hold while Martin tried to see a clear way forward.

When he did it was with a name change to A Wrinkle in Time — not a great name for a cutting-edge pop band and I have to admit to having expressed some exasperation. Fortunately, common sense eventually saw The Chills' name reclaimed. Good band names are hard to come by and The Chills is a very good one. It was also the band Martyn Bull had been in, part of an important, ongoing enterprise, not simply a band with potential and a couple of good records that ended when he did. Surely that's what Martyn would have wanted — for The Chills' name to be retained.

Martyn had also been part of the recording of two key singles. The 'Rolling Moon' release helped maintain some momentum while he was ill. 'Pink Frost' was finally released in June 1984. It's a different kind of song to previous Martin Phillipps efforts, spare and sparse, atmospheric but driven along by Martyn Bull's propulsive drumming. I always felt 'Pink Frost' represented a direction the band could have explored further. A more experimental approach that was less about the song in a traditional way and more about sound in a modern way. An approach that wasn't so hung up on precision playing, expensive studio recordings and hit singles, but was more about feel and groove and a bit of noise. That was what was starting to happen in the indie world overseas, with cutting-edge but commercially successful noise merchants like Sonic Youth and Dinosaur Jr in the USA and The Jesus and Mary Chain and My Bloody Valentine in the UK.

The Chills wrote and played songs that needed a great deal of attention in the studio and the consequent expense meant they had no real choice other than to have a crack at commercial mainstream success. They were an intelligent pop band. Martin knew he needed a variety of material to demonstrate what they were, and he very effectively delivered it.

From early on, like Sneaky Feelings, The Chills had wanted to go overseas. Traditionally, musicians who felt they'd outgrown New Zealand moved to Australia. Success in New Zealand was a self-limiting experience. How successful could you be before you and your audience became a touch too familiar with each other? You can only tour so many times and it's hard to make a decent living. A few bands had got beyond Australia: Split Enz to the UK in 1976 and then back to Australia, Dragon to the US before settling on the more manageable and familiar in Australia. Hello Sailor had given it a go in Los Angeles before coming back almost broken.

The Chills wanted to get to London. Martin believed they were good enough. No one knew what was really involved, but a few Australian bands like The Birthday Party and The Go-Betweens had managed it and achieved critical success and solid sales (if not radio play and *Top of the Pops*). If you could generate a degree of interest in a band in the UK weekly music press, it could help open up interest in Europe, with its paying touring circuits, and in the USA, with its even bigger market and budgets.

But first, money was needed. It's hard now to conceive just how difficult such an undertaking was. It was a daunting trip into the unknown. Before the internet, connections and arrangements had to be made using the painfully slow postal service or the very expensive telephone. Split Enz's overseas stay had almost destroyed them. One of them, Mike Chunn, later said The Chills would never get as far as Auckland International Airport — he understood first-hand how hard it was and thought The Chills were too amateur and lacking in production values. Yet there had been changes in the music world after punk that now made such a trip more feasible.

Doug Hood was a key influence here. He would eschew the description of manager, but that is what he effectively was. Being Auckland-based, he couldn't directly motivate or help Martin with his ongoing personnel issues in Dunedin, but he did put together a number of tours that generated the cash that eventually allowed the band to travel to London.

I have my doubts, though, whether Doug's March 1984 Flying Nun Looney Tour helped the finances much. Four bands on the same bill must have been too expensive to produce to make much profit, but Doug was a smart operator and successfully sold the idea to the university orientation committees.

The tour showcased four of our bands from around the country: The Chills and The DoubleHappys from Dunedin, Jay Clarkson's The Expendables from Christchurch, and Children's Hour from Auckland. It was an update of the old 1960s band package concept but with a subversive left-of-centre slant. A statement of intent — here we are, all together with Flying Nun, and here's your chance to see us all on the same night; this is serious now, so pay attention or you'll be left in the dust with your worn-out Citizen Band and Dragon albums. From that point of view, the tour was a huge success. It reflected the diverse nature of the bands on the label and introduced some new bands to their natural audience.

The DoubleHappys were Shayne Carter, formerly of young, seminal Dunedin pop punks Bored Games; drummer John Collie; and Wayne Elsey from The Stones (Wayne needed some respite from fellow Stone Jeff Batt's contrarian intensity). The DoubleHappys were doubly charismatic. They were the exciting newcomers.

Jay Clarkson had been in Christchurch band The Playthings. Her band The Expendables played smart, angular material that was high in mood and tension. Children's Hour were kind of Auckland's *enfants terribles*, a confident, noisy band whom trouble had a habit of following around. The Chills were the undisputed headliners. All were supported by a crew that included Doug, Rex Visible, Andrew Frengly and David Merritt. I am not sure what David did on that tour but he settled in Christchurch afterwards and became one of the Flying Nun help committee.

This was the beginning of the Looney Tours operation and its long and significant career in live promotions, touring hundreds of bands into and around New Zealand, including The Clash, The Go-Betweens, Hoodoo Gurus and Eric Clapton, and later looking after Auckland's Big Day Out. Doug managed it all and always aimed to benefit the local bands he liked and championed.

The Chills were the chief beneficiaries in 1984 and 1985, and I know Doug went out on a limb personally and financially to support and promote them. They would get beyond Auckland International Airport because Doug was there to make sure it happened and he so much wanted it to happen. He would even go to London with them to help the transition into the much bigger and more brutal world of the international music business.

Doug also made sure recordings were started and eventually finished. Chills records never seemed to be finished in one go. Repeated visits to the studio were needed, as time and money ran out. But enough was released in time to keep some sort of momentum rolling. The Chills' audience, too, was forgiving with the delays and line-up changes and general prevarications because they believed in the band. The Chills were going to have a shot, go all the way.

Two more releases, the 'Doledrums' seven-inch single in 1984 and *The Lost EP* in 1985, sold well around the Martin Phillipps, Alan Haig, Peter Allison and Martin Kean line-up. 'Doledrums' is a lightweight but effective song about the joys of being on the dole (which could be a lifestyle choice back then, not the state of absolute last resort it is now). *The Lost EP* was a much more ambitious effort — a twelve-inch in the Flying Nun style, without an obvious single, just a little collection of songs, a mini album to be going on with. It was recorded between July 1984 and February 1985, with Doug Hood's and Chris Knox's input, at Terry King's Progressive Studio and with Phil Yule at Mascot.

This Chills' line-up was hard at work touring and saving towards getting to London. So it came as a bit of a shock for the well-liked Martin Kean to be told he wasn't up to scratch as a bass player and was out of the band. The whole of Dunedin seemed to know about it before Martin was told. In the end he would go on to play bass for high-profile Anglo-French electro-rockers Stereolab. Not so much not good enough; more not right enough for The Chills.

This would become a constant issue for the band, with various members failing to gel or play in the required manner. It was very much Martin Phillipps's band: a blueprint had to be followed, rather than sounds and songs being allowed to flower organically in a collaborative manner. Martin would say that band members having more say in how they played resulted in more generic sounds and diluted The Chills' sound. Whatever the reason, it meant the band seldom held together long enough to have a proper run at establishing a collective career. There was a tension, in that Martin wanted a proper democratically functioning band but also needed to have the final say in everything musically and on the business side. I know many of the stronger key talents and personalities involved in the band found it impossible to understand where they fitted in, and left in frustration. And these were players with whom Martin needed to collaborate if he was to successfully realise his dreams. Perhaps he should have had more help from management to communicate and negotiate with his band members. But Doug wasn't officially The Chills' manager, so it wasn't his responsibility, and the air of uncertainty endured.

Martin Kean did receive the strangest farewell, however, co-writing 'Dream by Dream' on *The Lost EP*. It's an ambitious four-part suite about his leaving the band, expressed from both Martins' perspectives. Phillipps obviously felt terribly guilty about it and the song is a kind of joint catharsis, an exorcism of the bad vibes. The ending is truly cringe-worthy, with a *Waltons*-like round of 'good nights', including what appears to be a God-like voice (Chris Knox is my guess) intoning 'Good night, Chills'.

Despite all this *The Lost EP* charted at number four, the band's highest placing yet, up from number twelve for 'Doledrums'. The market now clearly preferred the twelve-inch format when it came to New Zealand music.

Luckily for The Chills, the formidable Terry Moore was available to step back into the bass spot. It seemed obvious that Martin Phillipps wouldn't have let Martin Kean go without having someone lined up and ready to travel to London with the band. Terry was very much an asset, a strong personality and an excellent bass player — as you can hear on 'I Love My Leather Jacket', which the band recorded when they got to London.

I was getting to know Martin Phillipps a bit better now. Quietly spoken and serious about his music, interested in comics and a little fixated on childhood things — books and toys and TV programmes. Martin analysed everything carefully and publicly. He was an obsessive record collector and once noted that my collection was heavy on recent releases and light on older material. It was a criticism.

I had a lot of records but I didn't collect. I was given samples of new releases at the shop and more arrived in the post from overseas record labels. I didn't collect because I was frantically busy and spent most of my rare spare time drinking in an effort to relax. I was really keen on music, but I didn't have the time for hunting down the harder-to-find material that would have transformed me into a completely cool person. Before the internet, you needed a lot of time to find that cool-inducing material, and hours could be wasted in second-hand shops. Being in a touring band was perfect for this. You just had to be careful you didn't spend all the money you were making on records. Bands everywhere still do this, even ones from overseas, sometimes even looking for those rare Flying Nun discs that will make them look cool when they get home.

Boredom can be a feature of band life. Being in the studio is boring unless you have a specific job to do. The rest of the time is spent watching others do their jobs, often over and over again. Being on tour is boring — the travel can quickly become a grind and there's a lot of waiting: waiting at the soundcheck, waiting for the gig to start, waiting for the promoter to show with the money. It's usually impossible to use the downtime to write songs. Cheap thrills become significant: drink, drugs and sex. Obsessing at a local record shop seems like a healthy pursuit by comparison.

I only went on tour once, with The Go-Betweens around the North Island. Doug Hood was promoting their tour and Roger Grierson was their manager, before he became a bigwig in the Australian music business. He was a young New Zealand–born, Australian-based man with taste — good enough taste to be managing The Go-Betweens. We were all stuffed into a van together. Robert Forster remains the only touring musician I have ever seen actually reading a book.

I always felt things would be going well if The Chills could achieve the level of success The Go-Betweens had had. They too had relocated to the UK, worked hard and made a living. As time went on the income increased, with growing publishing income from the catalogue and the occasional windfall from advertising and film. If the planets aligned, a hit single might even strike.

But I could see it was hard work: keeping the non-writing (and therefore non-publishing-income-earning) rhythm section happy and busy; being represented by an ever-changing patchwork of record companies and distributors; grinding away touring the world between recording, with only a couple of weeks off to write new songs. I lasted three days on that Go-Betweens tour of Wellington, Palmerston North, Hamilton and Auckland. I probably had alcohol poisoning by the second day and everyone wanted rid of me. I was gripped by a sort of cabin fever on wheels and became surly and unreasonable. I would never go on tour again — even with a decent book to read.

The Chills weren't that different from The Go-Betweens. Both were from the same part of the world and inhabited a part of the musical universe where quality song craft was taken seriously. Their audiences could be the same, too. One major difference was that the creative hub of The Go-Betweens was a duo, Robert Forster and Grant McLennan. It might not have always been easy, but ultimately they had each other for support.

So in 1985 The Chills began planning a trip to the UK. Doug had no desire to act as their manager internationally, but cared enough to want to help them set up properly. I was very excited that they were going. Mail-order sales had been steadily increasing and we fuelled the demand by posting review copies to what looked like the best music papers in Europe and the US. The reviews were positive and there was a swelling interest in Flying Nun, and in the Dunedin bands especially. As the mail-outs grew and the number of samples rose, so did the cost. But it was obviously the way forward and out of the confines of our small, isolated home market.

A small German distributor, Normal, was buying from us and on-selling to specialist record shops in Germany. It was a small label, importer and mail-order company based in the then West German capital of Bonn. The level of interest was small, but there was an eagerness to hear the music and it was relentlessly growing. We would write each other letters — mine handwritten, theirs typed. My German was nonexistent but their English was as good as mine.

Normal saw the potential and expressed an interest in pressing some of the records and releasing them in Germany. That really meant Europe-wide, including the UK, as they had a big import–export operation. Normal was sometimes difficult to deal with. Finding the right words to express the more extreme emotions of frustration and anger can be difficult when they need to be translated, and in such situations misunderstandings can escalate quickly around minor quibbles. I know this was a mutal problem.

I also went to London on my first overseas business trip in early 1985. I had some government trade-development money to help pay for it, so I was obliged to go to the very mainstream MIDEM music business conference in Cannes, France, in late January. I went on to London afterwards. I visited Rough Trade and met with a number of fans working there and was heartened that it was possible to get into that organisation and sell some records. We would start exporting finished records to them within the year. I also attempted to make contact with John Peel, and he kindly returned my call late the night before I departed. He said he really liked the music we were releasing, and it sounded like he really meant it. He was a nice man in what I already understood to be a crazy business. I also met with Alan McGee, owner of the new and much-hyped Creation Records. His orchestration of The Jesus and Mary Chain during this time had made him a major player and tastemaker in the London music world and Creation were the indie-world darlings. We met in a packed pub and, as the night progressed, I noticed that the jam of surrounding Englishmen thinned out as they gradually retreated from close proximity to the now drunk and raving Scotsman. He was hard to understand, but I enjoyed his enthusiasm. Creation agreed to release a Chills compilation. It would take us a good year to get the complicated art for the *Kaleidoscope World* cover together and have the record released, but it was a perfect way to kick off business in the UK, especially with The Chills soon to be heading over for a visit.

* * *

By 1985, we felt we had more than enough material for a multi-band compilation. We pulled a track listing together and it looked very strong, although finding a name proved to be torturous. We finally settled on *Tuatara*. It didn't feel too 'naff Kiwiana' at the time because naff Kiwiana didn't really exist yet. That would come later when we started to manufacture nationalistic pride in the things that made us New Zealanders. Music was a part of that, hand in hand with Buzzy Bee and the *Edmonds Cookery Book*. But at the time *Tuatara* sounded right and cool. In hindsight it must have been totally meaningless to the international audience it was directed at. An ancient, slow-moving, stay-at-home lizard from New Zealand that would live a long, uneventful life if the rats let it be — perfect!

We asked Lesley MacLean to design a full-colour gatefold sleeve. Lesley had been designing magnificent, bright posters for us and she produced another winner with *Tuatara*. Roy Colbert wrote the sleeve notes and it was ready to go. There were the usual production headaches, including the first run of covers coming back a dark browny purple rather than bright red. But overall it was a great compilation with a brilliant cover that captured the essence of what was happening with the label in those early years. There was a joyous variety of material that all sat together harmoniously.

Tuatara kicks off with The Clean. 'Tally Ho!' was the logical choice, but I still felt it was too roughly recorded. It's taken me thirty-odd years not to flinch whenever I hear the song in some hipster café or bar, or even the local supermarket. I always liked The Clean's instrumentals, though — sort of psychedelic surf

ABOVE: Partying
with Lesley
MacLean,
Christchurch, 1983
(photo by Stuart
Page) RIGHT: Lesley
MacLean's poster
design for the
Tuatara compilation
release, 1986

12 great bands
on 1 L.P.

Tuatara

a flying nun compilation

the clean

sneaky feelings

the gordons   tall dwarfs

the verlaines   the chills

the expendables   children's hour

the great unwashed   the bats

fetus productions

marie and the atom

also available on cassette

tunes that have a huge urgency. So I chose 'Fish' instead. In my mind it works as an overture or entry point to the alternative music world that *Tuatara* showcased.

The *Dunedin Double* bands are mostly there. The Chills with their eerily great 'Pink Frost', Sneaky Feelings' 'Throwing Stones', and The Verlaines' homage to decadence, good poetry and odd but proper chord sequences, 'Death and the Maiden'. There were also sounds from beyond Dunedin, with the unique noise and intense vision of the Gordons, youthful Auckland mayhem from Children's Hour, a modern semi-industrial take on things with Fetus Productions, Marie and the Atom's beautifully awkward 'Isol', and The Expendables' 'Man with No Desire'. And all ending on a note of normality and sanity from Tall Dwarfs with their showstopper, 'The Brain That Wouldn't Die'. Phew.

I was very happy about what we put together, but the strength of the compilation, the total lack of filler, meant plenty of very good material from the likes of The Stones, The Rip, The DoubleHappys, Scorched Earth Policy, Bill Direen and This Kind of Punishment (among others) missed out. Making friends, and all the time potentially making enemies, was the nature of the business, I discovered. Decisions were hard to make when they directly affected individuals you liked who were making music you loved.

We released *Tuatara* in Germany and New Zealand around the same time in 1985, including on CD. The reviews were great and the sales steady. We then released it in the UK and the US. It helped spread interest in the States and was perfect for mailing out to our new friends in college radio.

Compilations can be tricky things. They may fail as a collection of songs, represent too much that is unknown or out of context. But the strength of what was happening around Flying Nun meant we could put together a powerful set of material that represented who we were and piqued the interest of music fans around the world.

By then I knew that The Chills spending time in London would increase their profile, we would sell more Chills records and that would rub off on the label generally. *Tuatara* was helping too, but The Chills were the band spearheading international progress. More than Sneaky Feelings, The Chills were the band that best fitted where popular musical tastes were then at in the UK.

But I was also apprehensive. We had no contract and if a larger record company became interested in The Chills, our part in their future would be up in the air. By this stage the band was too big and too expensive for us to 'own' their world rights. And we weren't sufficiently knowledgeable or well resourced to contemplate running a band's international recording career from New Zealand. We were still having problems keeping up with what Chris was doing in Auckland, never mind managing overseas releases and all the work they would entail.

The Chills arrived in London in October 1985 and stayed until December. They played a number of gigs that generated the required positive music press and also recorded a John Peel Session, an important step in any group's career advancement, given the legendary BBC DJ's influence in the UK market. The band also managed to record 'I Love My Leather Jacket', a song about the jacket Martyn Bull had bequeathed Martin. This was a major progression in recording and Peter Cathro made a great video for the song, featuring the band enjoying the sights around London.

The Chills also linked up with expat New Zealander Craig Taylor, who managed That Petrol Emotion. Built around the O'Neill brothers from The Undertones, they were a band on the up in the UK indie scene, with global ambition. Crucially, Craig had experience in the London music world. Doug was impressed and described the laconic Taylor as dynamic — as most things about London appear to sleepy green New Zealanders. Craig was keen to work with Flying Nun, and The Chills making him their manager outside New Zealand seemed to be a way forward that suited both the band and the label. We would set up a side business in the UK, supported by Rough Trade distribution, and Craig would oversee it.

A feature article appeared in *Melody Maker* in February 1986, written by freelance music journalist Martin Aston. Martin loved The Chills and the other Flying Nun bands he had learned about through them so much that he became The Chills' and Flying Nun's (poorly paid) UK publicist. He was excellent at his job, getting music writers interested in the music and writing enthusiastically about it and generating press coverage that would be read all around the world.

If The Chills' exploratory trip was an overwhelming success, there were still problems. As often happens when a long-awaited overseas tour eventuates, half of the band found it all too much. The hard work getting there and the shock of new realities can be disheartening. Peter Allison and Alan Haig left at the end of the tour. The pause button was pushed. Terry Moore wasn't keen on sitting around, so he left six months later too, leaving Martin back in Dunedin, wondering how to capitalise on what had been achieved, and how to get a band together yet again.

CHAPTER 14

THE SQUARE iS NOT SQUARE

I moved the office again in 1985, to some rooms in the Dominion Building on the north side of the Square, on a short-term lease in a building earmarked for demolition. There were only a few other tenants, including a down-on-his-luck lawyer and a brush importer; otherwise it was just lots of locked, empty rooms waiting for the wrecking ball. Compared with the High Street space it was not at all sunny, but it was more secure and had a view across the Square towards the cathedral.

Unlike Dunedin's Octagon, which has eight sides and is indeed an octagon, the Square is not square. It is an irregular dodecahedron that looks like a square cross from above, with ChristChurch Cathedral in the middle of it. I didn't care for the Gothic Revival cathedral. It always struck me as a rough affair, built on the cheap with big blocky stones and lacking the finesse you saw in similarly inspired architecture in the UK, Europe or even Dunedin.

Until recently the cathedral had a mad assortment of architectural styles surrounding it on all twelve sides. There were the green-marble modernist Bank of New Zealand building on the far south side, opposite the old United Services Hotel; the red-brick Italian Renaissance–inspired Post Office with its clock tower; and the Regent Cinema with its huge dome that was rumoured to house a studio flat.

The tall, modern 1960s glass Government Life Building was next door to us, and further around the dark northerly side was the *Press* building, Warner's Hotel and the Dog House. The Dog House was the one place in town that was open late where you could buy badly made fish and chips or a burger. It was food only the drunk or demented would eat and there was always the risk of who you might run into there. Drunks, criminals and psychopaths all frequented the Dog House. Perhaps that's how it got its name.

By the mid-1980s traffic was restricted in and around the Square to prevent it being used as a stock car track on Friday and Saturday nights. The reconfiguration turned it into a soulless expanse of concrete piazza that became an arena for the elements. You slipped on its wet, windswept surface in the winter and were blinded by the bright Canterbury sun bouncing off the stark tiles in the summer. In time I learned to avoid a direct crossing and instead skirted its edges. Efforts to break up the bleakness with big concrete planters, or the police outpost, just re-emphasised the windswept openness of it all.

Inevitably, I got to know the Square well during the Dominion Building years. They were busy times in 1985 and 1986, with roughly thirty releases in each of those years. There was a lot of bustling back and forth to the main post office for mail-outs and faxes. The fax had revolutionised the business, greatly increasing the efficiency of receiving orders from distributors around the world, which did wonders for our sales.

We had a special A4 form printed up for mail-order customers. It seemed like a good idea now we were accepting credit card payments. We wanted to make it as easy as possible for our customers to write in the correct details, as this was quickly becoming the most popular form of payment. The days of the postal order (a sort of international money order you could buy over the post office counter) were numbered, but there were still customers who liked to send their orders by conventional mail.

All sorts of things came in the mail. One sunny day the police and New Zealand Customs raided us in a joint operation. There were ten or so burly chaps and a dog and they seemed pretty excited about busting what must have seemed like an obvious drug-distribution and money-laundering ring. They couldn't believe it had taken them so long to realise that a ratbag record company like mine, with its import–export distribution setup, was the perfect front.

I felt terrible. We were all caught in the act: Gary scratching through some dodgy-looking manual accounts; good-sort helper Ian Dalziel in one of the storage rooms making up orders for dispatch; the student from the local school, with us for the day on work experience, putting Crystal Zoom covers together; and me staring out of the window at the small but rapidly growing crowd staring back at me.

Just one out of the three rooms was actually an office with desks, phones, filing cabinets and people in it. The other two rooms and much of the hallway connecting them were for stock. Packed-up finished records, empty seven- and twelve-inch covers, inserts, records without covers, posters, master tapes and corrugated cardboard for packing, stacked to the ceiling. There was a system. We knew it backwards. The Great Unwashed's *Clean Out of Our Minds* was over by the door, The Stones' *Another Disc, Another Dollar* was on the floor by the window, and, oh my God, the *Dunedin Double* with The Chills' side of the cover featuring a tiny hieroglyphic illustration of a joint was just everywhere!

The cops' and officials' excitement abated quickly. The dog was not at all interested, even in the multiple-copy Crystal Zoom overstocks on the top shelf where his handler lifted him for a sniff. Looking over The Chills cover, one of the visitors muttered, 'If there was anything here it would be like looking for a bloody needle in a haystack.'

Most of them left as quickly as they'd arrived, with a distinct air of disappointment. A couple stayed on to take names and addresses, including that of the work experience student. While the 'good' cop struggled with the spelling of our names, the 'bad' one showed me a photo of a postcard they had intercepted at the post office. 'To: GJ Productions, care of Flying Nun Records, Box 3000, Christchurch, New Zealand' was written in a crazed but slightly familiar handwriting — you got to know handwriting back then since everyone wrote rather than typed.

The card was from Melbourne. It had been split and a thin layer of hash had been inserted between the layers, which had then been reassembled. The cop said it was very neatly done, but the smell had made detection inevitable. I said I didn't know who — I mean what — GJ Productions was and of course I didn't know anyone in Melbourne. Suddenly feeling a bit of a smartarse, I asked, 'What is hash anyway, apart from being smelly?'

The tough cop suddenly got a bit tougher. 'Let's go to your house and see what we find there.' I immediately thought about the embarrassing number of empties by the back door and wondered if the dishes had been done. At this time my girlfriend and I were living in a rather nice flat in a small Art Deco block called West Avon. It's still there, opposite the Dux de Lux and the Arts Centre on the corner of Montreal and Hereford streets, just east of the Avon River.

I was kindly driven home in a police car and luckily my flat was looking reasonably clean and tidy. At least it was until they gave it the once over. Of course they found something and it probably did belong to me — a matchbox with a few marijuana seeds in it. Bugger, forgot about those. Now the cop formally arrested me and read my rights. But then he offered an option. I was in the music business and he knew I was well connected, not just in Christchurch but New Zealand–wide, so I clearly knew what was going on. He wanted to trade information. But I really couldn't help. I didn't know anything, even if I did have my suspicions about who GJ Productions might be.

Finally he left and didn't take me with him. He gave me his card and said I was to call with information if I heard or saw anything. I 'owed him big time' apparently. I felt extremely lucky not to have ended up in court with an inconvenient conviction. This was a time when the police still had moustaches and were unpredictable, not to mention downright hostile to bohemian lefties with an interest in music.

* * *

Ever since primary school I had enjoyed a bit of a daydream and I made sure my desk was next to a window. From the office my view was across to the front of the cathedral, where on most days a large group would gather in front of the steps to listen to the Christchurch Wizard pontificate. I never understood the appeal of listening to this middle-aged English bloke's daily, dull and meaningless rants. At least the Bible Lady had religious madness as an excuse.

Ray Comfort would sometimes speak. Ray was a Christian anti-drugs campaigner who had written the book *My Friends Are Dying*. The Square was a nutter magnet. If there were ley lines in New Zealand then a whole lot of them intersected in this very spot. As it is, word has it that the Square sits on top of an old Maori burial site, is tapu (sacred and off-limits) and has a whole lot of bad karma bubbling away under its surface. The bird man biked in daily to feed the seagulls and get shat on as thanks. I was rather fond of the older, kilt-wearing Chinese man who liked to flash his pink underwear at the schoolgirls. Less appealing was the middle-aged hunchback who would pursue young women across the Square on his adult-sized tricycle. Christchurch was strong on eccentricity, often with strong sexual overtones.

Outsiders often comment on the city's strange vibe: it's a city with a big sky above and a dark menace below. The rapes and murders always seem especially gruesome. Fascist, racist skinhead gangs are particularly visible. The wholesale nature of the sex industry staggers me. Maybe the Bible Lady was onto something after all. No doubt she would have seen the earthquakes that have hit the city since 2011 as some kind of divine retribution. But the earthquakes have just devastated the actual place rather than removed the weirdness that inhabited it.

Nearly all of the old Christchurch I grew up knowing and remembering was destroyed by the quakes. My mother's house in Aranui escaped serious damage but is surrounded by suburbs of wrecked homes, many empty, and the empty sections of demolished houses. The places I visited as a child, or worked in and saw bands play in as a young man, are all gone. The centre was destroyed, demolished and flattened. Thankfully, Christchurch Town Hall is going to be restored. It's an incredible building, despite its brutal concrete exterior. The interior makes me think of a kind of modern Renaissance palace. It has hosted some memorable shows over the years — the reformed Byrds, Devo, the Ramones, Motörhead, Talking Heads and The Fall among them.

Debate still swirls around what to do with ChristChurch Cathedral. I was often at the office on Sundays and I never really remember the cathedral having much in the way of a congregation. My recollections of the place are darker. There was a bit of a problem with 'jumpers' when I had the office in the Square. I would look out at the nor'wester blowing hot and dry across the open expanse, only to glance back moments later to see a circle of people formed around a familiar but distorted shape on the concrete below the cathedral spire.

As a kid, during the holidays I would climb the steps around the bells and up the spire to one of the lookouts. Once it would have been the best available view of Christchurch, when no other building would have been more than two or three storeys high.

Older people remember the spire being the only landmark on the horizon visible unobstructed from much of the city.

After iron bars failed to deter the jumpers, access to the spire was closed completely. That's when people started jumping off the Government Life Building next to us. There was an observation deck at the top, which was open for years before suddenly becoming supervised, then locked and finally closed. The landing was messier there, with an awning and parked cars below. The *whump* noise of the landing often suggested death may not have been instantaneous.

After that, the jumpers headed off to Whitewash Head, a huge sea cliff between Sumner and Taylors Mistake on Banks Peninsula, thirty minutes from the city centre. Sometimes a group of us would head up there in the summer, late after the pubs had closed, with some drink and cigarettes and sit talking in the long grass. The cliff was sheer and it was a wonder none of us ever accidentally toppled over. There were often people up there, alone, wandering about looking disorientated or agitated and obviously seriously considering jumping.

The cliff at Whitewash Head was a result of the erosion of the huge ancient volcanoes that made up the peninsula. These were originally 1500 metres high and have been scoured back and down to 900 metres or so over the last ten million years. I sometimes think that the part of those old volcanoes that has worn away exerts a negative influence on the city below.

* * *

While Christchurch seemed full of eccentricity and unease, Flying Nun was itself seen as a home for the musical outsider. Creative eccentrics flocked to be on the label, now perceived as a bridge that linked autonomous independent creativity with the real world of selling music around New Zealand and overseas. A massive international market for independently minded and made music had been opened up by punk, and the multi-genre explosion of post punk in its wake, and we were a part of that. Flying Nun was connected to that world, and the demand for new ideas and sounds drove a big increase in the number of bands we worked with, and the number of records we released.

The label had a strong backbone, with The Clean catalogue, Tall Dwarfs and the ongoing and ever-more ambitious recordings and careers of The Chills, The Verlaines and Sneaky Feelings. The Clean had spawned a couple of significant acts in The Great Unwashed and The Bats. These had been joined at the label by newer bands from Dunedin such as The Rip, The DoubleHappys, The Orange, Alpaca Brothers, The Puddle and Look Blue Go Purple. We also released records from Christchurch bands, such as Scorched Earth Policy and The Jean-Paul Sartre Experience. Significantly we started working with Auckland bands the Able Tasmans, Goblin Mix, the Bird Nest Roys and This Kind of Punishment.

And there were lots more. In fact, there was too much to do it all justice, though we did our best. There seemed to be so much good music being made and I felt we had to release it. The chances were that if we didn't, it wouldn't see the light of day. No other label had emerged to work the same or similar territory, and this was still well before the time when artists would consider taking on the complexities of releasing their own material.

For many of the bands, juggling ambitions and expectations was a tricky business. Often they weren't making music just for the sake of a career — they didn't want to be in covers bands playing the radio hits of the day or golden oldies. They were inspired by the punk revolution to make their own music and to see what they could do with it. Some backed themselves to have a crack and take it all the way, like Sneaky Feelings, The Chills and, later on, Straitjacket Fits and the Headless Chickens. Others thought about it, but kept their day jobs, finished their degrees and toured during the holidays.

Look Blue Go Purple were a case in point. Lesley Paris (who managed the George Street EMI shop and later played in Olla and ran Flying Nun Records when I left for the UK), Norma O'Malley (Chug), Denise Roughan (3Ds and Ghost Club), Kath Webster and Kathy Bull (Cyclops) were young women from the Dunedin scene who started playing together and writing rather nifty songs. Everyone loved them and they were a great counterpoint to the more macho guitar thing the guys did (not that you could accuse many of those guys of being genuinely macho).

In the accepting Dunedin scene, a group was allowed to grow up in public, playing gigs and getting better as they went. Look Blue Go Purple recorded three key EPs — 1985's ethereal *Bewitched*, 1986's more confident *LBGPEP2* (featuring 'Cactus Cat') and 1988's post-break-up *This is This*, and became very popular. They played a few tours with other bands, including one orientation tour, after which everyone agreed that playing the toga party at Lincoln College was a mistake.

Look Blue Go Purple well illustrated the depth and diversity of sounds on Flying Nun in the 1980s and their EPs remain an essential part of the catalogue. The members of the band always had proper job or study commitments, so they toured only during the holidays. Becoming a full-time band just seemed impossible.

We were so isolated from the major music markets that an overseas tour was an absolute commitment, an all-or-nothing call. A few bands had the opportunity and the means to go for it internationally, but most were happy to play when they could around New Zealand and release what they could, often on the EP format. They were all part of the rich Flying Nun–aligned scene that revolved around Dunedin but was intimately connected to bands and audiences in all of the main centres.

Flying Nun records straddled a huge range of material, from the pop-oriented Chills to the noise experimentalism of Wreck Small Speakers on Expensive Stereos. But it was all largely left field, with an emphasis on artist-controlled creativity rather than the professional career musician looking for a big budget to make material for radio and hit stardom.

It was an especially busy time for a group known as This Kind of Punishment. Essentially this was Graeme and Peter Jefferies from Nocturnal Projections, originally from New Plymouth. They had relocated to Auckland and initially got together with Chris Matthews and Johnny Pierce from Children's Hour. Musically talented and adventurous, open to collaboration and prolific, the group made a number of unique, offbeat recordings that we released between 1983 and 1987. Graeme Jefferies had since moved to Christchurch and set up a studio and home in some spare office space in the Dominion Building, on the other side from us.

Graeme didn't know many people in Christchurch. He was shy and reserved, but like most human beings remained a social creature. So he spent an awful lot of his time in our office, rolling cigarettes and humming tunes in his own very special low-voiced way. It eventually drove me nuts and I outrageously banned him from humming in the office. From then on he would sit just outside our front door and roll his cigarettes and hum away there, still perfectly audibly. And still he managed to get us to release his solo debut album, *Messages for the Cakekitchen*.

As well as recording in his rooms near ours, Graeme also got together with his brother Peter to make one last This Kind of Punishment record, *In the Same Room*. Both the band name and the title have sentimental resonance for me.

* * *

We were going to have to move as the Dominion Building's planned demise neared. It wasn't altogether unwelcome. The lack of sun made the space a bit gloomy and then there was the general nuttiness of the Square. So we found a new office around the corner on Gloucester Street, in the old *Lyttelton Times* building. Up a long flight of stairs was a whole floor of sunny office space. It had

With Gary Cope in the Gloucester Street office, from a November 1987 feature in *The Press*, 'Roller-coaster ride for Flying Nun Records' (courtesy of Fairfax Media NZ/*The Press*)

a partitioned section for stock and a giant walk-in safe for master tapes. Light, peaceful and perfect.

A number of musicians helped out in the office during this period. Shayne Carter was based in Christchurch for a while with his new band Straitjacket Fits and he was in great demand because he could type. This was a rare skill in our circle before the coming of the computer and its word-processing capabilities. Poor typing meant retyping things, or the extensive use of Twink.

Personally, I found handwriting much more efficient, although many had trouble reading my scrawl. Chris Knox complained that when I wrote 'Knox' it looked like 'Max', and perhaps named his long-running weekly comic strip *Max Media* accordingly. David Pine from Sneaky Feelings also came to Christchurch to help out and was a pleasure to have in the office, with his intelligence and sunny outlook, all the while unobtrusively making sure Sneaky Feelings remained a priority at Flying Nun. I remember David being particularly tenacious in pursuing a local Greek fish and chip shop proprietor in order to get a Greek Sneaky Feelings review translated. He didn't get a translation but we still have the review, now rather greasy, on file.

A young man named Bruce Russell also showed up. Bruce had just got back from some OE in London and was fully knowledgeable about what was worth knowing from there. He sported a Sandinista T-shirt and a Palestinian scarf, but his native intelligence undercut any suggestion of affectation. Bruce was smart, funny and blunt, and was a great help around the office. He was especially good at keeping things grounded and free of bullshit. He helped organise our foreign media relationships. For some time we had been inundated with correspondence, fan mail from fanzines and college radio. Everyone wanted to be on our mailing list and get free records. Bruce was furiously efficient about getting this updated and sorted.

He had a band called The Dead C, with Robbie Yeats (The Verlaines) drumming and Michael Morley (Wreck Small Speakers on Expensive Stereos) on guitar. It wasn't really music as many had previously known it, but I could see it was in the vanguard of something, and fitted with the general mood of change around the fringes of new musical thinking. It was sound art rather than the rock or song-based structures we were familiar with. We released the first couple of albums, we liked them, they were different to the other bands we worked with and we liked working with Bruce.

Christchurch seemed full of good people doing good things, but I had felt the urge to move for some time. An awful lot of my older friends and contemporaries had left town for overseas. Given the large number of bands we looked after in Dunedin, and the fun time I inevitably had when I visited, I briefly considered moving there. But it was small and even further away from the rest of the world than Christchurch. And the rest of the world was what we were increasingly trying to communicate with and where our sales and financial future lay.

Moving away wasn't an easy decision to make. It wasn't just about making the right move for the business, though it was certainly essential from that perspective. There were also personal matters to consider. Christchurch was my hometown. I had spent my whole life growing up here and virtually all of my immediate family still lived in the city.

CHAPTER 15

GOODBYE CHRISTCHURCH

In the end, the whirlpool pull of Auckland was irresistible. The PolyGram pressing plant in Wellington had closed down and we had moved our vinyl manufacturing to EMI in Lower Hutt. All the parts — parts being all the bits and bobs used to create stampers for making the records — had to be remade to be compatible with their gear. All the records that were current in the catalogue had to be re-cut and new stampers made when they were due for a repress. All this represented a considerable delay and outlay, far greater than the hit we had taken on the Fall album a few years earlier. Two years later, in 1988, EMI also closed.

By now, of course, compact discs had been slowly but surely becoming the dominant format. We had some titles available on CD that we had produced as a part of our overseas licensing deals, but generally our customers were still buying vinyl. With the EMI plant closing we would now have to manufacture our records in Australia. I knew that dealing directly with an overseas pressing plant wasn't going to work for us. We would be at the bottom of an even more pronounced pecking order, further out of sight and out of mind. We needed some help and somehow I got talking to one of the majors, WEA.

All the major record companies had quite distinct personalities. It stemmed from the type of artists they represented and who their most successful acts were at any given time, as well as their approach to sales and marketing. CBS had grown out of the old Columbia Records, home of Bob Dylan, Santana and Bruce Springsteen, with some megastar signings in more recent years such as Billy Joel, Meatloaf, Wham! and Michael Jackson. It was a relentlessly marketing- and promotions-driven company.

RCA was Elvis Presley's old record company and was strong on country music. It seemed a bit hokey and old fashioned, despite having been hugely successful with David Bowie and Lou Reed in the 1970s. EMI was a British corporation that had lucked in with The Beatles and then Pink Floyd's *Dark Side of the Moon* yet retained this Old World British Empire feel. PolyGram was Dutch (Philips) and German (Siemens) owned and, like the other majors, had grown out of its acquisition over time of a host of smaller record companies. PolyGram sub-labels included Mercury, Vertigo and Polydor, and big-name artists such as James Last, Genesis and Dire Straits.

Down this end of the world there was Festival Records, an Australian outfit co-owned by Rupert Murdoch's News Corporation and the Kerridge Odeon cinema group. They licensed independently produced international material for Australia and New Zealand and represented a real mixture of medium-sized labels from around the world, such as Island Records, Chrysalis, A&M, Arista and Australia's own Mushroom Records. Festival had an eclectic catalogue as a result.

And then there was Virgin, which was the smallest. It looked after Richard Branson's Virgin releases in New Zealand and licensed material from some smaller operations such as Cherry Red and Rough Trade, which is how the Fall albums found their way to the South Pacific.

WEA were very much a major and had a reputation for quality signings, with better taste than the others. The corporation was a collection of strong, formerly independently owned companies including Warner Bros., Elektra (the label of The Stooges, Love and The Doors, plus a whole lot of softer West Coast artists), and Atlantic Records (Ray Charles, Aretha Franklin, Led Zeppelin and Crosby, Stills, Nash and Young). WEA itself was the overarching promotional and distribution arm for these and a number of other strongly artist-oriented labels where the emphasis was on signing talent and releasing quality music, and not being too gauche in the marketing of it.

I liked the reputation of Tim Murdoch who ran WEA in New Zealand. All the local companies were run by larger-than-life characters in the early 1980s, largely because there was still plenty of money sloshing around the industry. As times got tougher, the big characters tended to fall away and the companies were increasingly run by accountants.

Tim was an old-style record company guy. He could be generous and ruthless in equal measure. Rumour had it he had made surfer movies when he was younger. At EMI he had been entrusted with going to the United States to negotiate a distribution deal with the recently conglomerated WEA. He came back to set up a new company, partially owned by himself, to distribute WEA's growing catalogue. Whatever else he was, he clearly loved music. He probably didn't love our music, but it mattered to me that he was a music man.

I wanted a manufacturing and distribution deal for New Zealand. The key was the manufacturing part. Stephanie Booth, who ran production at WEA, was the best and exactly who we needed to ensure we could get pressings out of Australia on time and at good prices. I wasn't ready to let the New Zealand distribution go, but I had to get the deal done. By this stage well over 50 per cent of our sales of finished product were exported and the overwhelming bulk of that was vinyl. I needed to ensure we could continue to manufacture that vinyl and this 50 per cent now took precedence over concerns regarding a distribution deal altering our relationship with local retailers. By now we were starting to import and distribute independent music from overseas. There just wasn't the margin to include this part of the company with our Flying Nun distribution deal, so we created a separate entity called Flying In.

At that time no one was importing finished independent records to on-sell to retailers. The majors shipped in bits and pieces but there was a huge amount of desirable independently produced music that wasn't turning up in New Zealand, apart from in the odd specialist store in Auckland. So I started buying finished product from the overseas companies we already sold to, including Rough Trade UK and US and Homestead Records, with the idea of tapping into what seemed like a big unfulfilled local market.

Flying In grew rapidly to become the local importer and distributor of everything that was good in the 1980s indie world. We were handling music from labels including 4AD, Creation, Sub Pop, Rough Trade, Blast First, Matador and virtually every other international independent that had any worthwhile acts. We ordered carefully but sometimes took punts on the bigger releases and managed to avoid getting stuck with unsold stock.

This wasn't fleetingly fashionable chart material that can burn brightly then fizzle out. This was music that would keep on selling through word of mouth and student radio play. Some of the titles we brought in were very big and successful releases by the likes of Sonic Youth, Dinosaur Jr, The Pixies, Big Black, Primal Scream, My Bloody Valentine and Nirvana. It turned the Flying In arm of the operation into a million-dollar business in its own right.

What we didn't know how to do was structure a manufacturing and distribution deal. Nor, it turned out, did WEA. They offered us an advance of $50,000, which we immediately accepted and spent on paying bills and due royalties. We paid it off over the coming months, but it certainly made the move to Auckland possible.

In fact, the WEA deal made the move to Auckland inevitable. We needed to be near their headquarters to make sure the production of our vinyl went smoothly. It wasn't so much about making sure Stephanie was doing a good job as Stephanie making sure we were giving her what she needed to do her job properly. I think we must have driven her nuts.

The Lesley MacLean–designed red-and-yellow generic labels were introduced at this time in an effort to limit confusion with labels, catalogue numbers and playing speeds. We produced the label copy with all the essential information and this was then overprinted onto the base labels. We were never completely happy with the design but we really needed to streamline as much as possible in the new production process.

Chris Knox also created a design. It was largely black and yellow and very much in his style, which I didn't think would suit all the artists on the label. Typically, I allowed him to use it on his solo *Seizure* release, which completely defeated the purpose of a generic label.

* * *

So in early January 1988 I moved to Auckland. I drove all my possessions north in a succession of Maui camper van trips. Maui needed vans in Auckland, where the incoming tourists tended to arrive, rather than Christchurch, from where they normally left. Maui paid for the petrol and the ferry crossing. I'm not sure Maui knows of its key role in the history of this New Zealand record company, but it was pivotal.

It took three book- and record-laden trips, incredibly heavy loads, to relocate my life and belongings. I found a dump of an office in an old building next to the Regent on Nelson Street and shipped everything up from the Christchurch office along with

Gary. Like the Dominion back in Christchurch, the building was waiting to be pulled down, so it was filled with young, marginal, arty businesses on month-by-month leases. It felt even less secure than that suggests. Day by day was closer to the general sense of impermanence. Eventually, a fire somewhere else in the building persuaded me we needed to move immediately.

This led us to a space on Queen Street, just up from Vulcan Lane, opposite Wyndham Street. The ASB Bank was on the ground floor and there was a modern lift. Some inner-city locals referred to the building as 'the nipple building', due to the double-dome effect on top. It was our best ever office, with a reception area, individual offices along the front wall with views of Queen Street and up Wyndham Street to the *New Zealand Herald* building,

Matt Campbell designed this logo for us in 1988, soon after we moved to Auckland

a kitchen, and plenty of space for the ever-expanding warehouse out the back. It felt a little bit grown up.

I liked the locale. Queen Street was busy enough to make you feel like you were in a major city. The bus stop to Ponsonby and Grey Lynn was right outside, next to a taxi rank. There were two pubs, the Occidental and the Queen's Ferry, just around the corner in Vulcan Lane, that were frequented by journalists from both the *Herald* and the *Auckland Star* (still going at that stage, and also based nearby). Behind us on High Street were Unity Books, De Bretts hotel for after-work cocktails, Rossini's for lunch, Le Brie for dinner and car parking buildings beyond. It was perfect for us.

The office would quickly grow. Gary and I were soon joined by Martin Phillipps's sister Rachel and then Lesley Paris, who had just moved up from Dunedin. Shayne Carter and Straitjacket Fits also made the move north, so he came in and typed — although we had by now acquired an underpowered computer. The Able Tasmans' Peter Keen came in to help pack orders rather than properly pursue his marine science studies.

Lesley's boyfriend, Paul McKessar, had also moved to Auckland and tried life in a suit at an advertising agency before joining us to look after publicity and promotion, in his jeans. Alan Holt took control of the warehouse and we soon had people dedicated to looking after the import side of things with Flying In. Richard Ram from Wreck Small Speakers on Expensive Stereos came in to work on the accounts and never really recovered. Royalty accounting was like that before computer software was invented to deal with it. We also had graphic designer John Pitcairn subletting a room. It was good to have someone close by doing the basic artwork and cover design, although the work was always queuing up.

Doug Hood and his Looney Tours had an office there as well. He was flat out touring overseas bands, including big names like Eric Clapton and MC Hammer, and organising the original Big

Day Out. Being connected to the business of live music like this was really useful. There were hook-ups with the overseas bands whose records we distributed in New Zealand, and our bands could get the support slots on the local legs of tours. Doug was still very much involved with The Chills, handling their affairs in New Zealand and providing a steadying voice of reason as their career heated up internationally.

The reality was that Auckland was just more connected with the rest of the world, and we were now largely reliant on international sales. As well as licensing our more established album artists such as The Verlaines, Tall Dwarfs, The Chills and Sneaky Feelings to overseas record companies, we had grown our export business steadily over the last five or so years. We were shipping quantities of finished product (made-up records in sleeves with royalties included in the sale price) to distributors in Europe, the UK and the US. Making sure this supply of vinyl was as uninterrupted as possible was a crucial aspect of the Auckland operation and one of the key reasons for the move north.

Being in Auckland allowed us to manage our arrangement with WEA more closely. Their distribution of our releases worked well enough for the higher-profile bands, but it was true the lower-profile releases suffered. I had feared this might be the case, but it was a cost we simply had to accept. It had become a strain looking after so many bands. Sheer necessity dictated that the focus shifted to our bigger artists to ensure we maximised sales of their significant releases. Those acts were busier and took up a lot more of our time. Consequently we had to sell more of their records to cover that investment of time. It is an undeniable law of economics that there is more profit to be generated from selling more of a few titles than selling fewer of many. Making a profit was an issue because there were always bills to be paid.

When we had been handling our own distribution we could generally break even on a minimum initial pressing of about 300 to 500 copies. This made most of the smaller or one-off projects possible. With WEA now looking after our local distribution, selling fewer copies of the smaller releases and also taking a percentage of the income as their distribution fee, many of those releases had gone from marginal to hopelessly unprofitable. One-off projects were now much harder to justify.

Some of the artists, especially now isolated in Christchurch and Dunedin, began to feel neglected and abandoned. When we had moved north, Bruce Russell had moved to Dunedin and started up Xpressway as an alternative outlet for the artists and music he enjoyed. As luck would have it, these tended to be the artists that were now feeling estranged from Flying Nun. Avoiding all the complex issues inherent in vinyl manufacture by being essentially a cassette-only label, Xpressway started picking up some of the bands we could now no longer realistically do justice to.

Bruce had learned a great deal during his time sorting through the media correspondence at Flying Nun. He would have come away with a thorough understanding of the power of word of mouth and networking, and a very good list of who was important and influential in music media around the world.

He cleverly emphasised Xpressway's difference from Flying Nun. The name itself indicated something fast and snappy, when Flying Nun vinyl releases had notoriously slow turnarounds. Bruce could run cassettes off in his workroom as he needed them. He also had a coherent aesthetic that he applied to both the selection of the music he released and the packaging he presented it in. In contrast to Flying Nun, where the different bands enjoyed using their own artwork without the confines of a house style, Xpressway releases all looked and sounded like a part of a whole. The covers featured a mix of typewritten lettering and old print imagery. Fixed costs were non-existent and manufacturing costs low. The material was generally simple live recordings, inexpensive to make and ideally suited to cassette release.

I found the Xpressway catalogue numbering particularly impressive. Flying Nun catalogue numbers had been all over the

David Mitchell provided the artwork for the 1990 Xpressway *Pile=Up* compilation
(courtesy of Bruce Russell).

place. Initially I didn't even want them on my releases at all, but the pressing plant demanded it so the records could be tracked as they went through the manufacturing process. I didn't take the system seriously for some time, allowing a profusion of vanity numbers to infest the catalogue: 'mee001', 'good001', 'cold001' and 'hideous001', for example. At the start it seemed funny. I was twenty-one, my sense of humour was that of an underdeveloped schoolboy, and I hadn't got into this to be a bureaucrat. When I finally saw the logic of a single sequence of catalogue numbers, it proved impossible to avoid missing out numbers as projects were delayed or abandoned. In contrast, Xpressway was a model of cottage-industry efficiency and ran straight from 'X/Way01' to an abrupt stop at 'X/Way23'.

Central to the Xpressway catalogue was Bruce's own band, The Dead C, whose discordant, rambling and loud art noise suited the label. When Bruce had come back from London he wasn't talking about the English bands he may have seen there, but the American band he had discovered called Sonic Youth. He was particularly proud of the double limited-edition (2000 copies) live album *Walls Have Ears* that arrived soon after his return via mail order. It came out between 1985's *Bad Moon Rising* and 1986's *Evol*.

Flying Nun released Sonic Youth's next one, *Sister*, in 1987, and looked after all of their early independently released catalogue up to *Daydream Nation* — before they 'sold out' to multinational evil in the form of David Geffen's DSG Records. I believe some money was involved, and everyone has a price. Sometimes that price is just enough to get by and live by playing and making music; sometimes it's the ticket to pop stardom and wealth.

But the *Walls Have Ears* album was from the time when Sonic Youth were still a guitar art-rock band, making a live album on the cheap to feed the hype that was building around them. The Dead C seemed born out of this phase of Sonic Youth's evolution, before they abandoned the guitar noise and became a rock band

and signed to a major record company. The key difference, I guess, was that Sonic Youth were a band of musicians looking for credibility by doing it awkward, whereas The Dead C were less accomplished, doing it awkward by necessity. Different approaches but equally valid in their own ways.

Flying Nun had released the first Dead C release, *DR503*, in 1988, followed by *Eusa Kills* the following year — around the same time Xpressway put out its first Dead C cassette, *The Live Dead See*. The early material is still largely song-based. Some of it, such as 'Scary Nest', feels connected to the more conventional Dunedin sounds from the early 1980s, but their sound moved towards experimental free rock over time, with loops, odd electronics and samples being added to the improvised guitar soundscapes.

Xpressway would later release a seven-inch EP, *The Sun Stabbed*, and the live *Perform DR503B* cassette. Most of The Dead C's music would come out on overseas labels such as Siltbreeze and Ba Da Bing, which extended and built on the networking web the band had created. The Dead C play infrequently but have made occasional overseas appearances, including at the All Tomorrow's Parties festival in the UK in 2006.

The Dead C are often cited as an international success story that has been little understood or supported at home. Being on the cover of a respected experimental music magazine like *Wire* is certainly an achievement, but the truth is that such a challenging form of music is of niche appeal wherever it is heard, internationally or in New Zealand. Obviously an overseas niche is always much bigger than a local niche, which is just a product of population and market size. Like most good New Zealand bands, The Dead C's success has been achieved on the backs of day jobs and obstinate longevity.

Other South Island artists previously associated with Flying Nun began releasing their music through Xpressway. Dunedin's Alastair Galbraith from The Rip made the jump, putting out some great cassettes. He was joined by some key former Flying

Nun disgruntleds in Christchurch, such as the Victor Dimisich Band, Scorched Earth Policy and The Terminals. All good and interesting. We supported the label by selling their catalogue via our own mail-order system and overseas distributors. I believe we were Xpressway's biggest customer.

Bruce was a forceful and confident character. The implicit message of the little guy doing good and acting as a 'lifeboat' for the Flying Nun 'rejects' seemed to resonate for many. The carping from the Xpressway camp about Flying Nun being a label of sold-out has-beens might have irked if I'd had the time to be bothered. We were busy enough working our own slightly bigger niche. As it was, by 1993 Bruce had had enough and wound the label up. My guess would be that dealing with the unrealistic expectations of musicians all became too much.

One of Xpressway's absolute triumphs to my mind was Peter Gutteridge's *Pure* cassette album, a solo showcase of his absolute talent. As well as being a founding member of The Clean, Peter had been an original member of The Chills and been in The Great Unwashed. With his own band, Snapper, he'd finally had success in 1988 with a self-titled EP. With Alan Haig (The Chills) on drums, Dominic Stones (Bird Nest Roys) on guitar and Christine Voice on keyboards, he established an impressive and influential sound — loud, dark, droning and menacing music that reflected a little of what was going on inside Peter's head. Stuart Page made an excellent video for 'Buddy' that depicted the band trying to look tough by riding pillion with bikers.

Peter was a happy, good-looking and smart boy who got stuck early in a cul-de-sac of drugs and addiction. Dunedin seemed to have its share of addicts and some were inevitably involved in the music scene. Chemist shops were routinely broken into and one character went to prison after being found hiding in a cupboard at the medical school. Addicts led broken-down, compromised lives every bit as bad as the local alcoholic derelicts.

Peter slowly deteriorated physically and mentally. The Snapper EP opened a lot of doors and generated expressions of interest from overseas, but his addled mind was unable to recapture the magic. Subsequent recordings dragged on and generally failed to live up to expectations. There were hard-to-understand obsessions, including one for guns. My fear was that any overseas travel would be dangerous. Dunedin was at the end of the supply chain. Peter was on methadone and anything else was hard to come by or of dubious quality. Exposure to the more readily available substances overseas seemed like a recipe for disaster. So while Flying Nun tried to encourage Peter to finish the various Snapper projects, we increasingly knew they were doomed to under-deliver on his potential. The dithering and indecision around the recording, and the chaos around his own affairs, were just too much.

At the same time, Bruce was in Dunedin and no doubt being supportive. There was none of the pressure to match the Snapper success, and Peter allowed Xpressway to release *Pure*. It's essentially a great collection of demos: quickly recorded, meditative, meandering, reflective and hopeful. I thought it was a way forward for Peter even on a practical level, leaving him free of the hassles of thinking about a band, complicated recording sessions or any of the logistics of playing a gig, touring or travelling in support of a release.

But Peter never really did get it together with Snapper again. There were some singles and two albums: *Shotgun Blossom* (1990) and *ADM* (1996). The former was financed by Scottish label Avalanche Records. This should have been an opportunity to build on the great reviews the Snapper EP had received in the UK music press. But Peter had had enough trouble getting the album together, let alone looking after the business side of things or getting overseas for a schedule of live dates. The record company can only do so much; ultimately the artist is responsible for putting together the music and making the plans that will dictate the course and velocity of his or her career. Interest waned and Peter never got to play abroad when he needed to.

I caught up with him in 2010 after I'd bought back Flying Nun and was keen to get the Snapper back catalogue sorted out. He was looking very haggard and needed a stick to walk. We convened the meeting outside in the Dunedin Gardens. I needed the fresh air, as he smelled decidedly off. It was good to talk but hard to stay focused on practicalities when Peter kept skipping ahead to make plans that were simply not feasible. 'What is the quality of grand pianos like in German venues?' he asked. I had never seen a grand piano in a German music venue and he never would.

I saw Peter play twice not long after. He appeared as part of The Chills' thirtieth anniversary gig at the Coronation Hall in Maori Hill. The latest Chills line-up cranked through a set and then the original line-up hit the stage: Martin Phillipps was joined by sister Rachel on keyboards, Alan Haig drumming, Jane Dodd on bass and Peter ... nowhere to be seen. I found him down the road having a smoke and encouraged him to get a move on. He made a grand entrance down the centre of the hall with his stick clattering and his mouth muttering. There was a bit of a stumble or two on the stairs up to the stage. It took him an interminable age to untangle his guitar lead, which was incredibly long and wound up in a shape like a giant bird's nest. The audience waited patiently as Peter wrestled it into submission. I found it incredibly sad and stressful and had nothing but admiration for Martin's patience and good humour, especially when the band finally started playing.

It was wonderful to hear this early Chills material played by these musicians. Jane Dodd's bass on these songs was a revelation, as she never recorded with the band. It was so poppy, innocent and delightful, and just about audible underneath Peter's fuzzed-to-the-max guitar noise. The original Chills played their historically faithful set, while Peter simultaneously played his interpretation after thirty years moving towards a black hole in a different universe. It was absolutely great and alarming and unsettling, all at the same time.

I next chanced upon Peter playing a Christchurch earthquake relief gig organised in Dunedin by Hamish Kilgour, who was visiting from New York. I missed the Buddhist monks' performance but there was a variety of music on offer and a small, friendly and receptive crowd. Hamish and Snapper drummer Mike Dooley (The Enemy and Toy Love) got together with Peter to play some songs. Everything was ready to go, except Peter wasn't. His equipment wouldn't work. Leads had to be found, unwound, plugged in and checked, switches switched, checked, rechecked and reconfigured. It really dragged on. The two other players waited patiently as Peter stumbled over and around his gear, trying to make it work. Finally after forty-five minutes came some noise, one song and then an announcement: 'Sorry, the guitar is out of tune.' It was all a bit too much and I ran away. That was the last time I saw Peter.

In 2014, he finally got to travel overseas. Using the royalties generated from licensing the rights of *Pure* to a US label, he went to New York to play a show, believing it would get his career rolling again. Peter was in a vulnerable state, though, having recently quit methadone cold turkey. There had been reports coming out of Dunedin of wild and erratic behaviour involving firearms, knives and naked yoga up the Leith River valley. He loved New York, but there were some awkward moments with him wanting to get on stage at a Clean performance, his behaviour was eccentric if not erratic, and he ran out of places to stay. On his way home he went missing in Los Angeles and failed to make his connecting flight. When he did make it back several days later, he was taken into custody at Auckland Airport and admitted to Middlemore Hospital, apparently for his own safety. He was upset and depressed, feeling that he had 'blown' his chance of achieving something on his first trip overseas. He committed suicide the next day while in the care of the hospital.

When I learned of Peter's death, I couldn't help think about the sad trajectory of his life. I played *Pure*, which on reflection seems to be the most open, optimistic and connected work he ever made — ideas recorded as simple starting points, initial sparks that he tried to translate into something denser and more technologically polished. It was a process Peter often seemed to find fraught and it often affected the quality of the finished recordings, but on *Pure* the beauty of bright new ideas prevails, rather than the crushing business of trying to turn them into something 'finished' and ready for a paying public to judge.

Pure was an ideal project for Xpressway, as was Peter Jefferies's solo project *The Last Great Challenge in a Dull World* (1990). It's post punk with a healthy dose of Brian Eno and nicely played piano. What I love about the album is its energy and momentum: it's going somewhere, and abounds with ideas and sounds. It even manages to transcend its main weakness, Peter's singing, which can be both mannered and monotonous. Here it is enclosed within such glorious soundscapes and set among simple but evocative piano that the whole is greater than the sum of its few parts.

That's the great thing about a release on an independent label. The ideas can be fragmented and strange, and the execution variable. But there is a tolerance and acceptance of what is being offered up creatively, something that is sorely missing in the commercial mainstream to which so many artists aspire.

CHAPTER 16

HELLO AUCKLAND

When I first moved to Auckland, I was sharing a flat with Pete Farnon (who managed the Sounds Unlimited record shop in Newmarket and later owned Beat Music on Victoria Street East) on Victoria Street West, right in the city. It was a small flat above a sex shop. The old building is still there opposite the casino, somehow missed by all of the redevelopment in the area. Central Auckland didn't have many residents in the late 1980s, so there wasn't anywhere nearby where you could buy food or everyday bits and pieces. It would have been intolerable if there hadn't been a Super Liquor Man just up the road, which sold good-quality imported Russian Vodka. Otherwise the lack of shops wasn't much of a problem for me, as I didn't really eat food. It was, however, a bit tricky slipping in and out of the flat via a doorway beside the sex shop entrance. People waiting at the bus stop directly outside would give me a knowing glance. Sometimes those people looked familiar and the glance was one of horror rather than disdain.

I found the Auckland summer heat unbearable. I could almost cope with the extreme dry heat of Christchurch, but the humidity factor in Auckland really threw me. I couldn't stop sweating and I

Relaxing with Paul McKessar in the office warehouse, Queen Street, Auckland

had to stop wearing my nice woollen knitted jumpers. Eventually the black jeans went as well and I resorted to T-shirts and shorts. I was an ugly sight, with my particularly white untannable southern skin pocked by festering mosquito bites and burnt red by the first direct sunlight it had seen for fifteen years. I suffered, and so did those who had to look at me.

I have the sweater's curse: extremely thick hair. Think hair that if I am not on top of things makes me look like I am some sort of Pre-Raphaelite fopster dandy, before it quickly grows into a wild escaped-prisoner style. It was Chris Knox who made the former comparison.

During my first summer in Auckland the heat eventually drove me to distraction and I decided I needed a haircut. I managed it myself in front of the mirror in the badly lit bathroom. If the razor wasn't blunt to start with, it was at the end.

I wasn't adjusting to Auckland well. I was overheated and dislocated and not really seeing many of my Auckland friends while flatting in town. The haircut gave me some relief though. The day after, I stumbled up to the Gluepot Tavern to see that night's live entertainment, I forget who. I grabbed a seat next to my recently made acquaintance, Colin Hogg from the *Auckland Star*, and started to yak away, before eventually realising that he clearly had little idea of who or what I was. Nothing is more startling than the look of shock, distress and concern that comes over the face of someone confronted by dangerous lunacy. I hit the toilets and had a good look at my hair in a proper mirror. It was a haphazard mow, tufts were left here and there, and in between were numerous cuts and scrapes. Travis Bickle in *Taxi Driver* had made a much better job of his haircut.

I never got used to the Auckland summer heat (or the constant Auckland winter wet, when I stop to think about it), but I gradually got better at presenting myself as a respectable, worthwhile human being. The hair growing out helped, as did my girlfriend eventually moving up from Christchurch to join me, as well as moving out to the more civilised suburb of West Lynn (on the Westmere end of Grey Lynn) to flat with Doug Hood and his partner, Victoria Oliver, on Francis Street, just around the corner from Chris Knox and Barbara Ward on Hakanoa Street. I wouldn't have admitted it, but I did need some routine and order if I was going to keep my life on the straight and narrow.

Soon my girlfriend and I got our own apartment at the top of College Hill in Ponsonby. It had just been vacated by Trevor Reekie and Sheryl Morris who ran Pagan Records from there, and Simon Grigg of Propeller Records had lived there previously. (Pagan was one of the few other New Zealand record labels around. It was a bit more mainstream than we were and had had considerable success through the 1980s with Shona Laing, the Warratahs, the Greg Johnson Set, Tex Pistol, and the Holidaymakers.) Murray

Cammick, the owner and editor of *Rip It Up*, lived in the flat next door. We were obviously meant to be there.

The building was directly opposite a local landmark, the Hydra Bacon Factory. While I wasn't sure about what went on inside, the huge 'HYDRA' neon sign gave the area a very interesting reddish-orange glow at night. We were also diagonally across from the Three Lamps corner, where Jervois and Ponsonby roads meet. The Gluepot Tavern was just across the intersection and I'd see a lot of bands play this famous old music venue — without ever really growing fond of the place.

Ponsonby was a good place to live at this time. It had been gentrified without yet becoming overdeveloped. It was still interesting, but not as intimidating as it had been on my earlier visits. You could eat cheaply and it was close to the city and the office on Queen Street.

We bought a car and got to know the city. More mobility and socialising helped normalise me for a while. I grew to love the geography of Auckland: the harbours, the volcanoes, the gulf and the islands. We looked at buying a house together on Hakanoa Street, a couple of doors down from Chris and Barbara, but my inability to pay myself much on any sort of regular basis meant we couldn't scratch together either a deposit or a loan for the $150,000 asking price.

I got on with work and Flying Nun got on with doing our best with the new WEA set up. All those vinyl records needed to be re-cut and replated for pressing in Australia. CD sales were finally increasing for us, but vinyl was still by far the biggest format for us. We needed to be making records to maintain our export business.

Flying Nun was still seen as a bit of a southern oddity in Auckland. We sold good quantities of music but were perceived as being out on the fringe — albeit a fringe that had steadily pulled the music-buying public towards it and away from the mainstream all through the 1980s. It was a process that would continue over the next few years, as we became more integrated into the

Auckland-based music industry and achieved more publicity and sales with the likes of The Chills, Straitjacket Fits and, crucially, the Headless Chickens.

The new offices in Queen Street were big enough to really spread out and get ourselves organised. There was room for everyone to have proper workspaces, if not offices, and a place for more filing cabinets to hold the increasing number of reviews from around the world. In the process of unpacking everything we found some artwork Paul Smith had drawn up in 1981. A black-and-white illustration of a person/thing with an exasperated pose floating freely in space with an 'f' in its 'flaming' hair and an 'n' on its jerkin. We liked it a lot. Paul had moved overseas years previously and was, I had heard, living in Australia, but we had lost contact. We liked this character, who seemed to suit the name 'Fuzzy', and he/she/it became our logo-cum-mascot. Fuzzy went on everything from the letterhead to the back of record and CD covers and labels, stickers and fridge magnets.

In times of stress, which was most of the time now, I would find myself thinking, 'What would Fuzzy do?' Leave the office immediately and go to a nearby bar and have a drink seemed to be the usual advice. I would go to the Occidental just around the corner in Vulcan Lane and often I would find some of the journalists from *The New Zealand Herald* or the *Auckland Star* already there before me. They kept odd hours and were also prone to the emotional frailties that required a drink or two mid-afternoon. It's funny how mid-afternoon can soon become mid-evening and then you don't have a care in the world.

Colin Hogg from the *Auckland Star* was sometimes there. He had eventually recovered from his encounter with the 'bald' me at the Gluepot on that hot summer evening and we had become quite good friends. Like most of Auckland, he was from somewhere else — in his case Invercargill, so we had lots to laugh about. And we had a bit more going on in our heads than a lot of the characters in the media or music worlds we inhabited. We were interested

Paul Smith designed Fuzzy's first appearance in the November 1992 Flying Nun newsletter

in and talked about things that weren't necessarily directly connected to ourselves. We weren't interested in discussing our cars (I think we both drove aged, rusted Holdens), or real estate or boats. The friends I was going to make in this town weren't going to be fishing or boating buddies. But nor were these friendships going to be based on music or the necessities of doing business. They would be about other, more abstract stuff: compatible ideas and attitudes, the kinds of things that shift and interact and make life complex. I got on very well with Colin and because we were both from the South Island we didn't always have to say much. Of course by mid-evening at the Occidental we often couldn't say much at all.

I wasn't totally neglectful of my Flying Nun responsibilities, however. I worked long hours, usually starting early at the office and coming in at the weekend as well. I felt I had to be there when no one else was so I could get stuff done. During office hours it was just meetings and a constant flow of the excellent people with whom I worked coming through my office door wanting a confirmation or a decision or a chat about something. On occasion I rose to the challenge with unbelievable energy and enthusiasm and would have been completely unbearable to be around. At other times I was the quiet retiring guy who really didn't see why he had to be consulted about much of anything. And if I was out of the office and Fuzzy didn't know the answer, they knew where to find me.

* * *

Gradually I grew to like Auckland and became part of the place. If I say I got to know it well, I mean I got to know the inner city well. I seldom needed to travel beyond the CBD and its surrounding suburbs of Parnell, Ponsonby, Herne Bay, Grey Lynn and Eden Terrace. The rest of this city of over a million people spewed out from the strangulated isthmus between the Waitemata and

Out on the town with Colin
Hogg, Auckland, early 1990s
(photo by Christine Webster)

Manukau harbours, but I never really needed to visit the huge tracts of homes and businesses that ran to the south, east, west and north of my little world in the centre.

Most of the musical life of the city was concentrated around the central city anyway. Bands tended to come in from the fringes to live and play. The Bird Nest Roys were one such group, and seemed exotic because they came from West Auckland. Even though they mostly lived in town, they had this aura of Westie strangeness. It took me a little while to realise that the private language they spoke might actually be unique to the imaginary world they'd created to insulate themselves from the banalities and brutalities of their place of origin.

Their confident attitude and collective sense of humour set them apart from other bands, and they were musically excellent, fantastic live, but just a little lacking when it came to recording. Some bands can never capture the magic of their live performances when they get into the studio. If the Bird Nest Roys had managed to translate their raw talent onto record better, it could have seen them cross over to mainstream success.

I'd started working with the Able Tasmans before my move to Auckland and we had released an EP, *The Tired Sun*, and an album, *A Cuppa Tea and a Lie Down*. With a settled line-up and a swirling keyboard dynamic to their sound, they quickly became a personal favourite. I always tried to make their live shows and now they'd started to make very good albums, too. I still play *Hey Spinner* (1990), *Somebody Ate My Planet* (1992), the *Shape of Dolls* EP (1993) and *Store in a Cool Place* (1995) all the time. The guitars and keyboards of Leslie Jonkers and Graeme Humphreys (aka Graeme Hill) played over the top of a solid rhythm section of Craig Mason (The Chills) on drums and Jane Dodd (The Chills, The Verlaines) on bass, while Peter Keen's majestic singing floated beautifully above it all. I liked them an awful lot, but they found it difficult to build a bigger audience in New Zealand. I think fans of the label overseas had trouble getting a handle on their keyboards-based sound. They were ever so slightly out of sync with musical fashion.

These bands had a lot of support from student radio around the country, but nowhere more so than in Auckland with bFM. They were always the biggest and best organised of the student stations. They had a large potential audience and could carve out a big enough share to generate decent advertising revenue. Marcus Lush, Mikey Havoc and Graeme Humphreys/Hill from the Able Tasmans were all breakfast DJs on bFM at different times and built their subsequent careers in radio on that experience.

We had always worked closely with the student stations. They were the only radio outlets for most of our releases and their listeners tended to be our bands' core audience. Being based in Auckland now we became even closer to bFM. We had distributed their *Outnumbered by Sheep* compilation in 1986, which mostly featured bands connected to the label. Debbi Gibbs was station manager and she was very motivated and highly competent — attributes she would bring to her next venture, managing Straitjacket Fits.

Straitjacket Fits' story starts back in Dunedin when Shayne Carter from Bored Games and Wayne Elsey from The Stones formed The DoubleHappys in 1983. They started out with a temperamental drum machine they named Herbie Fuckface before replacing him/it with a real person, Dunedin friend John Collie. The DoubleHappys ended with Wayne's tragic death in 1985. The band had been travelling back from Auckland by train when he climbed out of a window as a prank, and was struck and killed when the train entered a tunnel.

It took the band mates a while to recover. Shayne recorded the single 'Randolph's Going Home' (1986), with Peter Jefferies, about his friend's death. Shayne and John then formed Straitjacket Fits with David Woods (Working with Walt), later adding guitarist-vocalist Andrew Brough (The Orange). Andrew came with a mellower pop sensibility that counterbalanced Shayne's more aggressive indie rock guitar sound. It was a strategy designed with success in mind.

The band were good right from the start. They could all play, were stunning live and Shayne was intelligent, articulate and charismatic. The debut, *Life in One Chord*, was one of the best Flying Nun EP releases and sold very well. Straitjacket Fits were on their way, and linking up with Debbi Gibbs showed how serious they were about having a crack at the big time.

Only a few mainstream bands had real managers in those days. I can't think of any Flying Nun acts with management (who weren't family or friends) before Debbi came along. Essentially, the entrepreneurial types that might become managers were smart enough to see that the potential income was unlikely to make it worth their while. A very New Zealand paradox. While a good number of our bands enjoyed mainstream success, outsiders were also undoubtedly wary of approaching such obviously wayward and wilful characters. Doug Hood was involved with The Chills, but he would have seen himself as a friend helping out rather than a manager working to take a cut of their earnings. This lack of managers did make things tricky for the label, too, as we had to pick up many of those duties without any direct return for all the work. We helped out, but it took time and therefore cost money — just another example of having to do what it took if our bands were to keep moving, building their profiles and selling records. Like so many New Zealand businesses, we learned to multi-task.

At least our relationship with Straitjacket Fits was put on a professional footing by Debbi. We even had a contract. It was signed one evening in the old (now demolished) Aurora Hotel on Victoria Street. I probably needed a drink or two to calm myself down enough to sign my name on what was, in fact, the first such document we'd ever had drawn up. Debbi was helping to drag Flying Nun towards the business mainstream. In return there were benefits for the band being associated with Flying Nun. The label already had a name internationally and we could open doors beyond our own backyard.

The Straitjackets went back into the studio with Terry Moore to record their debut album, *Hail*. Terry was well on his way as a studio engineer and producer and knew Shayne from their days in Bored Games. He was seen as sympathetic to what the band were trying to achieve, and he had been a good choice as producer of the first EP. By the time of the album sessions, however, there were differences of opinion about how the recording should be approached. The process became a little tense.

Hail almost sees the band make the leap from making a brilliant EP to making a very good album. There's a great diversity of material between the differing styles of Shayne and Andrew: epic, noisy guitar songs juxtaposed with poppy, jangly numbers, with a cover of Leonard Cohen's 'So Long, Marianne' for good measure. It was a strong record.

Debbi had brokered a UK and European release with Rough Trade and the earlier EP tracks were added to bolster the album. We were all happy with the result and that the band had taken the important next step. It was deliberately not a blind leap into the unknown, but a measured undertaking designed to create positive press and start building a solid international audience, which in turn would make them attractive to a major record company.

The received wisdom of the time was that you jumped at the chance of being signed by a major. This was when the big companies had the money to spend. If you played it right, they would spend it on you and buy you the exposure that success demands. Even if it was a poor deal, you still signed it — if you did become successful you could always renegotiate afterwards with the success being a substantial bargaining tool. If the project failed, there would be a considerable unrecouped advance to the band and the percentages and detail of the contract would be largely irrelevant. Debbi used American lawyers to get the best possible deal with whichever company with the deepest pockets showed the most interest.

Arista was the record label set up in 1974 by Clive Davis after he was forced out of CBS. He was a lawyer who fancied himself a music man and who rose to the top of the industry at CBS, becoming as high profile as many of the artists he worked with. Check out his book *The Soundtrack of My Life* — he's portrayed as a Renaissance man on the cover of my old paperback and it's a fascinating read by one of the most unrepentant, rampaging egotists the music business has ever known. Arista had recently had huge success with Whitney Houston but retained some residual credibility from signing both Lou Reed and Patti Smith in its early days. Lou had given them some duds and Patti all of her best work.

I always felt the relationship between the Straitjackets and Arista was an awkward one. Clive was nowhere in sight. He would have been unbearable if he had been, but his personal interest would have guaranteed full company backing for the band.

The A&R man who signed them, I'm sure, totally believed the band were great and could be successful. The issue was, had he convinced the rest of the company? To me, the rest of the company looked very middle of the road and mainstream, and just a little thrown by this snotty band of awkward funny-talking foreigners.

The band and Debbi were totally professional and gave it their best shot. It is hard to convey the amount of sheer hard work a band undertakes when they sign a deal with a major US record corporation. The pressure to deliver something the company can sell is immense. While they will tolerate an evolution or development in sound, essentially they want songs that mainstream radio will play, and therefore have a chance of selling in the volume required to recoup their not inconsiderable financial outlay.

Touring is not just travel from gig to gig, city after city. The whole movement of personnel and gear from one stage setup, performance, load out and transport to the next is wearying, exhausting and boring enough. Then add the demands of constant promotion — meeting the local company reps, visiting the local college radio stations, fulfilling the local press obligations. Some of these people might be genuinely interested in an unknown band from nowhere, but most are probably not. It's a wearing, artificial kind of existence.

The deal was done and British producer Gavin MacKillop (Shriekback, PIL, Chills) was to produce the new album. They recorded *Melt* in nine weeks in an Auckland studio and the unadorned live sound was more to the band's liking. Shayne's songs were broken up with a couple of gentler pop offerings from Andrew, but the Straitjackets were by now seen by most fans as a highly distinctive guitar band led by an intense front man.

Flying Nun retained the rights to the album in New Zealand, where it was released in 1990 to very good reviews and sales. The band followed up their exploratory US visit of 1989 with a full-blown twenty-day tour to support the album. It was obvious that

Andrew was unhappy. Shayne would mock him musically and conversationally, and Andrew's only real response was to walk off stage or simply not turn up. He soon left to do his own thing with a band called Bike. Band friend Mark Petersen replaced him.

Mark brought more guitar to the band and you can hear it on the *Done* EP they recorded in 1992 with Mark Cohen in Melbourne. It's a raucous, noisy, weaving, guitar-driven statement of intent. They were reconciled to the idea that they didn't need a soft side to appeal; they just needed to be confidently true to themselves.

Paul Fox (Sugarcubes, 10,000 Maniacs) produced the new album, *Blow*, in early 1993 and encouraged the band to record as near to live as possible. The result is a natural progression from *Done* with the intense guitars now becoming rather extreme. I liked it a lot but wondered what Arista made of it all. The band bounded off to join the Noisyland package tour of the US and Europe — and that was it. They felt they had done all they could together and there was no point keeping on.

Shayne formed a new entity called Dimmer in 1994. Flying Nun and Sub Pop jointly released their fantastic debut single, 'Crystalator', before Shayne left to record a number of albums with various major record companies. Major changes had happened at Flying Nun and there was a dispute over his publishing contract. So things didn't end well, but I still think Shayne P Carter is one of the smartest and most talented people I've ever worked with.

He was at home in the company of the smart and creative personalities producing work through Flying Nun. If they shared one thing in common it was an unwillingness to compromise. Shayne, like the others, wanted as many people to like and buy his music as possible, and worked extremely hard to make that happen. But there comes a point when the audience has to move towards you, too. You can only remake your art so many times, twist it so many ways, before it's not what you created any more. There are limits to the compromises you can make, and that was the tension at the heart of so much of Flying Nun's work.

In 1989 it seemed like a good time for another compilation album. The feeling was that there was plenty of strong recent material that could be pulled together and showcased. We could market it in New Zealand and internationally. Importantly it would give us a high-volume-selling full-priced album that didn't require any expenditure for recording. And it would act as a sampler of recent band development, hopefully stimulating interest and sales in the bands featured. Just like *Tuatara* had done for us so effectively a few years earlier.

Deciding on a title was as tricky as ever, but The Clean came to the rescue with *In Love with These Times*. It's a slightly edited down version of the early Clean-written and Nelsh Bailter Space–performed song 'I'm in Love with These Times' — and of course it's the title of this book. Perhaps my use of the title was a little more naive the first time around, but the sentiments were unknowingly similar: a combination of the seemingly upbeat and genuine enjoyment of the time and the music set ironically against the by-now obvious financial struggles and a degree of personal malaise.

We hired Stuart Page (The Axemen) and Grant Fell (from the Headless Chickens) to put a cover together. Gary Cope was very keen on the video side of things, and there were some particularly strong ones around this time to match the songs on the album, such as Straitjacket Fits' 'She Speeds' video, Look Blue Go Purple's 'Cactus Cat', The Bats' 'North by North', The Chills' 'Rain', the Headless Chickens' 'Donca' and more. The idea was hatched to incorporate stills from the relevant music videos, generate some computer graphics for the individual band names and take a still photograph of the image on a television screen then assemble the images in a grid to make up the cover. I liked the approach a lot and it lent itself nicely to our one and only television commercial campaign. It seems a bit dated now, especially the voice-over, but we were well chuffed at the time and it might even have sold a few copies of the record as well, although I wonder if it was enough to recoup the cost of the campaign. Nevertheless, *In Love with These Times* showcased a strong line-up of artists and material and was a clear indication of the continued strength of the label's roster. And we shipped export copies around the world, where it effectively updated the old fans and helped attract some new ones with its view of what had been happening musically at Flying Nun since *Tuatara*. The *Melody Maker* review in May 1989 was highly complimentary, offering positive descriptions of many of the songs featured on the album, before concluding, 'None of this can properly prepare you for the full extent of the joy of *In Love with These Times*. Fall for it, rise with it. And kiss a cloud along the way.'

CHAPTER 17

MUSHRooM CLOUD OVER NUN

By late 1989 Flying Nun must have looked pretty good from the outside. I was working with some great bands that I loved dearly, had a rapidly growing business on the side importing and distributing music that matched my own and the label's outlook, and I was working out of a perfect office right in the heart of Auckland and employing people I had very high regard for. What could be better?

Actually, there was a problem — the general lack of money in the bank. It was starting to get dire. And as it got dire I found it difficult to cope.

It was clear that while the creative outlook was bright and always getting brighter, there were major financial problems. The business had remained hopelessly under-capitalised since the initial $300 investment I had made in 1981. Our funds were not sufficient to underpin the volume of business, which now exceeded one million dollars annually, and the outlay on recording projects we were now making.

Since I had begun working for Flying Nun full time my wage had always been basic. I had no property or assets or family money to fall back on. What I needed was investment money, preferably money that came with some added expertise. At this time a passive investor seemed an unlikely option, as few people really understood the music business (or could be made to understand it quickly enough to make a considered decision). If they did get it, it was immediately obvious that risk was a key feature of the industry. It was glamorous but hardly attractive.

In 1989 I met Simon Baeyertz through Doug Hood. Simon was a young head of promotions at Festival Records in Auckland. He was a self-styled Renaissance man who knew lots about music, art and cooking. But he didn't follow rugby, and he didn't know anything about The Velvet Underground, The Stooges or The 13th Floor Elevators, so he struggled with Flying Nun's mix of interests. Nevertheless, we got friendly because he was soon off to Melbourne to work for Australia's leading independent record label, Mushroom Records.

It was a good time for him to arrive at Mushroom. The company had just made a lot of money off the back of the huge international success of Kylie Minogue and Jason Donovan. Somehow, these young, rather dull-looking Australian TV stars had leveraged their soap success into becoming middle-of-the-road pop sensations (with the help of the Stock Aitken Waterman songwriting and production machine). This had allowed owners Michael Gudinski and Gary Ashley to sell half of Mushroom to Rupert Murdoch's News Corporation.

The income generated by Kylie and Jason, along with Rupert's investment, triggered a Mushroom expansion. The company began investing in new signings and label start-ups, and they expressed interest in working with us — the weird country cousins in New Zealand, with our strange electrified hillbilly music from way down south.

Simon must have made a bit of an impact when he got to Mushroom. I can see how his keen intelligence could have matched some of that Australian bluster. But he must have had a bit of steel in him, too, to cope with and conquer what is a pretty macho industry everywhere, and especially so in Australia.

I don't believe Simon had much idea of what our music was about or where it came from, though. Some of the older, more cynical Flying Nun characters perceived a shallow appreciation instantly. He was there to do business and saw the potential to sell some records, for which he could take some considerable credit if it all worked out.

This was particularly true of our international dimension. The Flying Nun bands had a credibility no Australian band could match, but they lacked the financial and industry know-how they needed to achieve overseas success. Simon could help make it happen.

I knew Mushroom had some money to spare, and that Simon was in there selling the idea that we could work together and that Flying Nun might be worth investing in, but I was also aware it wasn't going to be an ideal relationship. They were a successful mainstream record company, built on the back of bands who worked hard on the live circuit and got mainstream radio play in Australia, and I doubted many of our acts could fit into and flourish in that world. I was also sceptical about whether anyone there, including Simon, really knew how to tap into the serious international interest already created in the label and the bands it represented.

On the other hand, money was scarce and releases were being held up by a lack of funds to press them. I didn't have many options. I was extremely depressed, drinking far too much, far too often. I had to make a choice: I could wind the company back and let the bigger bands go off to sign deals with companies who could finance their development, or I could find a partner who would invest in the growth of the bands and the business.

Somewhat reluctantly I headed off to another New Music Seminar in New York in July 1989. It's a horrible time to be in New York, with its unpleasant humidity and heat. I stayed in a friend's non-air-conditioned Manhattan loft and found it very difficult to recover from the jet lag. I was at the end of my tether, dragging myself from one ice slushie seller to the next, desperately trying to reduce my core temperature — which was as much a symptom of anxiety as the East Coast summer heat.

I was isolated and somehow managed to avoid meeting up with old friends from the UK and Europe. The mobile phone was still pretty primitive then and I spent a lot of time pushing coins into pay phones on street corners, trying to arrange a key meeting or two. I did manage to get hold of a senior A&R manager at Warners. We had mutual acquaintances and she was very well informed about the label — enough to know there were some great bands making great music and that there was a buzz.

The buzz was the key bit. The world was full of great bands making great music but it was commercially meaningless unless they were creating a buzz. You could build the buzz and sell records. Nothing happened without the buzz. The buzz was about what was the coming thing. It was about fashion in music and the next big-selling bands.

We talked for a while. It really didn't seem to matter what was discussed because she simply wanted to say that my lawyers should talk to their lawyers so we could set something up. I was still jetlagged and perhaps she was as well, because the whole conversation seemed incredibly vague. I went away thinking, great, they are offering me a label deal, a lifeline with money upfront, and a direct route into the biggest market in the world.

The reality, of course, was that I didn't have any lawyers at all. Even if I found some they would be expensive and the process of doing a label deal would take at least a year. And if we did manage to make a formal arrangement, the Warners New York office was an awfully long way from New Zealand. It was great in theory, but any agreement was still a very long way from being clearly defined, let alone a done deal. And it was hard to assess just how it might work out in practice.

Later, when I mentioned the prospective deal to Simon Baeyertz, his response — or, more precisely, his complete inability to respond to what I had just told him — suggested he was deeply disappointed he hadn't been the one brokering it. It didn't matter though, as by now I knew the Mushroom deal would happen, even if it was a way from completion. I would be dealing with Simon, who I knew faults and all, and with a business based only three hours away by plane. The culture may have been different, but I knew the seemingly hip Warners would have been even more alien and ultimately more difficult to deal with.

At the end of 1989, Simon Young, Mushroom's head of business affairs, came over to talk the deal through and it was time to show them the accounts. I had put off finishing the current set because I knew they would be pretty dire. Flying Nun was technically insolvent. I had to move fast to close the deal and obtain an injection of cash, or I had to liquidate the company and most likely put it into receivership. It was make or break and rather stressful, and I was starting to fray a little, starting to come undone.

Being insolvent and with only one band contracted meant the company was essentially valueless. Mushroom wasn't going to pay me anything for a share, but would acquire 49 per cent of the existing company and inject $100,000 in working capital, thus making Flying Nun solvent again. Early in 1990 we established a new company, Flying Nun Australia, which would be 51 per cent owned — and therefore controlled — by Mushroom. We'd sign the bigger bands to this entity — bands like Straitjacket Fits, The Jean-Paul Sartre Experience and The Bats, all of whom were due to record new albums and had generated international interest. They would become Mushroom's playthings.

We also set up a joint venture publishing company. Mushroom Music was Australia's largest publishing independent, well run and successful. Music publishing is where the money has consistently been while the recording side of the industry has shrunk with the onslaught of music online, legal and otherwise. Publishing is less visible and less well understood, but it looks after songwriters' key interests. Artist royalties are generated by the writing and performance of music. In the old-school industry in which we were working in 1990, the royalties for the performance on recordings would often be advanced to a band so they could record or tour in support of a release. The publishing royalty would go to the songwriter and that is what he or she would live on. The non-songwriting members of the band would only see income from the performance royalties if the release went well and recouped all of the advances.

So publishing companies tended to have cash sloshing around if they were well run. To be well run they had to be administratively tight, methodically collecting all royalties due and reporting that income to the songwriters they represented. They also needed to actively promote the music, for instance by placing it in movies or advertisements for a fee. This part of publishing has become increasingly important over the last twenty-five years as the industry has come to appreciate the true worth of music to movie-makers and advertisers.

So off I went to Melbourne and Sydney to meet the folks at Mushroom. The company was at the height of its powers. The flash offices in Albert Park in Melbourne were full of employees with the usual music industry gender split — guys running things and women doing all of the work. But there were good people there. Head honcho Michael Gudinski was in his wild-eyed pomp. We really didn't have much in common but he loved music and the music business and had a finger in every pie — records, publishing, distribution, touring and merchandise.

It was pretty impressive and Gudinski ran and directed it all decisively, like a crazy old pirate captain. I liked that. We were very different: he was brash and unashamedly entrepreneurial, while I tended to sit back quietly and watch it all. For all that, Michael was possibly the only person who understood what I had been through, and said so — I had done well; he knew how tough it was to keep an independent record company going.

So the deal was signed and there had to be a few changes. Gary Cope left after years of extremely demanding work trying to make the financial side of the business work as well as looking after much of the day-to-day running of the company. It was probably a relief for him to finally get away from it all. Lesley Paris filled the gap and started to look after the day-to-day running of the company and Richard Ram became our in-house accountant. The investment money paid off the outstanding creditors, brought our artist royalties up to date and meant we could get on with our release schedule. Some key albums — The Bats' *The Law of Things*, The Jean-Paul Sartre Experience's *Size of Food* and The Verlaines' *Some Disenchanted Evening* — could finally be released.

A major change was in our New Zealand distribution. We moved to Mushroom's long-term distributor, Festival Records. Festival was run by industry character Jerry Wise. Jerry was a very big man who had come to New Zealand as the tour accountant for the Small Faces, who played some shows here in January 1968 as part of a package with The Who and John Paul Jones. This big gentle giant of a man, charged with looking after the money of a group of notoriously angry short men, had soon had enough, liked the look of New Zealand and decided to stay. He worked as Festival's accountant and ended up running the company. I believe the key role of a tour accountant was to make sure the band was paid what it was due in full on the night of the performance and before they left town. If they weren't, they would almost never get their hands on the cash. Few would have argued with Jerry.

I liked him a lot. He was an accountant but loved the music and understood the music business. He had a tough exterior and was physically very imposing, but he would do anything to help and came to our rescue a couple of times. And Jerry had some very nice and hard-working people with him at Festival. It was a good business and helped make some of our key releases very successful over the next few years.

* * *

Things were looking up. There was a burst of new bands and renewed recording activity in 1990. Our finances had been shored up (not that the stress of managing the books ever went away), the ship had been steadied and we were under way again. Some of the older bands were getting a second wind, too, or just kicking on with their careers, making good records.

The Bats had visited the UK on a three-month working holiday in 1986. During the trip they had recorded the 'Made Up in Blue' single, which became an *NME* single of the week, and made a start on the *Daddy's Highway* album. By this stage they had established themselves as a formidable live band, playing melodic pop songs, propelled by a driving rhythm section, that you could dance to. The standout song on the album was live favourite 'North by North', for which Alister Parker (the Gordons and Bailter Space) and film-maker John Crisstoffels (The Terminals) made a very good video.

Video was now having a major impact as a music marketing tool, and it worked well for some of our acts too. The right band with the right song making the right video could garner repeated plays on *Radio with Pictures* late on Sunday nights, which in turn might help grow the fan base. There weren't all that many videos that really did the trick but — as with The Verlaines' 'Death and the Maiden', The Chills' 'Pink Frost', The Jean-Paul Sartre Experience's 'Flex' and Straitjacket Fits' 'She Speeds' — the 'North by North' video sold the record and helped establish the band.

The Bats were now one of Flying Nun's major signings, and were highly motivated and organised. They toured, saved their money and got overseas to promote themselves and to have a bit of a sightseeing holiday as well. They liked to maintain the kind of work–life balance that wasn't always possible in the rock music world.

The *Law of Things* album was released in 1990 and built further on their established sound, with 'Mastery' and 'Smoking Her Wings' the highlights. The release had been delayed while Flying Nun was finalising the deal with Mushroom Records, and when it came to recording their next album, *Fear of God*, the band came up against the harsh realities of the music industry proper.

Mushroom was by then a full Flying Nun partner and willing to finance some of the bigger and more internationally connected artists. The Bats had been overseas, their records were licensed to overseas labels and they'd been released on Flying Nun UK and Europe, so they had some profile and following. The Mushroom-led plan was to 'improve' their sound, and thus broaden their appeal, by bringing in a name producer.

Nick Sansano might not have been A-list but he had strong credentials, having worked across genres as an engineer and producer with Public Enemy, Ice Cube, Run DMC, Sonic Youth and the Jon Spencer Blues Explosion. Most importantly he was willing to travel to New Zealand to record the album. Unfortunately, it wasn't a match made in heaven. The band were used to a relaxed approach to recording and they found him obsessive in the studio — obsessed with getting everything 'right', in the way traditional studio folk can be.

It seems obvious that you would only blow large amounts of money in the studio, chalked up as an advance against an act's future earnings, if there was a decent chance of a potential commercial hit record at the other end. But The Bats' Robert Scott was never going to be Michael Stipe, and The Bats weren't R.E.M. heading for mainstream crossover via some commercial radio play.

If anything, the trend was moving in the opposite direction. There was a gradual shift within the 'alternative' music world towards what the Flying Nun bands, such as The Bats, had been doing all along — being themselves, doing their own thing, cutting back on excessive recording budgets and other big music business trappings. People were beginning to see that a band from left field didn't have to aim for a deal with a major record company and chase radio play and chart positions. You could stay true to your music and how you wanted to approach it, and build a successful career with an independent music business outside of the majors and their suffocating budgets.

Fear of God was mixed in New York by Nick Sansano, without the band's involvement. Despite the folky nature of the album, the tighter playing and general precision, it all feels a bit bland. If I had thought the band's *By Night* recording had been underdone, then this effort was most certainly overcooked. It is still a good album, with 'Boogey Man' and 'The Black and the Blue' being highlights, but the whole project left the band a little disappointed.

It did help confirm the growing awareness that bigger budgets were not necessarily the way to go for all of the more ambitious bands. The differences in approach, not just to the music itself but to the way the bands wanted to pursue their careers, were more complex and varied than anyone originally appreciated. *Fear of God* was to prove to be one of many expensive learning experiences for Flying Nun and its artists during this period.

The Bats became part of the 1993 Noisyland Tour of the US and Europe, along with fellow hopefuls Straitjacket Fits and The Jean-Paul Sartre Experience. This ambitious tour was financed by Mushroom, Straitjacket Fits' international record company Arista, and Music New Zealand (a short-lived industry- and government-financed export initiative). When the decision was made to wind up Music New Zealand as a going concern there was an unspent lump sum sitting in its bank account. Flying Nun put forward a proposal to spend it on the Noisyland Tour and was successful. Generating some activity in overseas territories would theoretically help some or all of the bands take the next steps towards international success.

Instead, the gruelling nature of the tour (which was by no means unusual for international acts) almost killed off the bands involved. Instead of one band going it alone, we had three bands of friends in an uncertain hierachy. There was a little ego and insecurity involved and this was amplified by the boring and exhausting nature of the touring. Who was the audience there to see on this particular night, and who should headline? It was never resolved — perhaps it could not be resolved — and so tension built as the tour proceeded.

The Bats' *Couchmaster*, released in 1995, was the eventual laid-back, climb-back-on-the-horse album, since which they have persisted in making music when and how it suits them, all the while getting better and better. The 2011 *Free All the Monsters* album (released on a by then resurrected Flying Nun) saw them continue to grow. It was a fine, self-assured album of glittering, understated guitar intricacy. Robert's singing was quieter and softer, giving him more control and tunefulness, and he had never sounded better. Kaye Woodward's delicate guitar playing and vocals added depth, and it was all built on an immaculate rhythm section.

It says a lot about The Bats' strength as a band that they survived it all and continue to play and record, on their own terms, when it suits them and fits in with the rest of their lives, jobs and families.

CHAPTER 18

HEAVENLY POP HIT

The Clean got back together in 1989 to do some shows in London, and decided to record an album while they were at it. *Vehicle* was a pretty good effort, but what was most heartening was their new way of working. Though the international touring for the release of the album was hard work, the band then found a balance. They realised they could get together, play some shows and record new material whenever they felt like it. From here on this would work well for them, especially now that the rest of the world had caught up with the band's early '80s output that we had continued to actively promote, export and license internationally, and they were held in deservedly high regard. The casual approach suited them: there was no pressure, other than a finite number of shows and the occasional one-off recording, and they were never together long enough to get on each other's nerves. The shows were usually pretty magical and some great records were made. I particularly loved 2009's *Mr Pop*.

David Kilgour was also making solo albums from 1991, or recording with his band the Heavy Eights — ten albums in total and all worth hearing. He has successfully worked with poet Sam

Hunt in recent years and I go to see him play whenever he is in town. Aside from anything else, he's a fantastic guitarist, and it always takes me back to those earliest days, when Chris Knox and I got so excited about making Flying Nun something more than its rather humble origins. We had been so inspired by what David was achieving with The Clean that it became more than just a case of documenting what was happening in Christchurch and Dunedin at that time, and turned into a belief that people elsewhere really needed to hear this music, that we could sell more than minimum runs, that there was a greater demand, and we could keep on growing because we knew the music was so good.

Other bands were really starting to come through in 1989. The Jean-Paul Sartre Experience had relocated to Auckland and we finally got to release their excellent *Size of Food* album that year. They had simplified their name to JPS Experience by this stage from the mouth-filling orginal, supposedly following legal threats from the estate of the late Jean-Paul Sartre. We had already released their self-titled EP and then the *Love Songs* album a few years earlier, but now they'd really started to build an audience and were looking to try and do something overseas. There was strength in the fact that there were three songwriters and they were such good players. They'd really created their own sound, which was just right for the times. And then they changed everything around and in 1993 made *Bleeding Star*, which was noisier and more guitar heavy. Now they were a psychedelic band and the mood had changed.

Suddenly JPS Experience looked like contenders. Like a lot of Flying Nun bands they'd found a unique sound, one that was all their own yet still broadly appealing. The cool New York label Matador licensed *Bleeding Star* for North America. Everything looked very bright until the hard lessons of international touring life were learned during the career-crushing Noisyland Tour.

Bailter Space were another band beginning to get more serious. After kicking off as Nelsh Bailter Space, and then shedding the

'Nelsh' and various members, they were essentially the Gordons revisited, revised and reborn with the same guys back together. But while the Gordons had been John Halvorsen's band, Bailter Space were very much Alister Parker's. They were also hugely loud, but the sound had evolved to become less angular and more spacey. Again, it was perfectly in sync with what was happening around the world in music, while remaining totally their own thing. They weren't picking up ideas or riffs from other bands; this stuff was coming straight out of their own heads. It was rather awe-inspiring — a large atonal mess of a sound that was still somehow highly melodic.

Bailter Space released a great sequence of albums, starting with *Tanker* in 1988, followed by *Thermos* in 1990, *Robot World* in 1993 and *Vortura* in 1994, before the quality began to slip. They also left Flying Nun and signed to Matador Records, though they were later dropped by the label. Alister can be intense and I could imagine he drove others around the bend the same way he'd done to me when still based in New Zealand. He was very creatively talented, be it playing the guitar or taking photos. He would throw himself into projects, encourage others to join in and help, produce amazing results — and then blow the whole thing up. It made for great music, but didn't do wonders for his ongoing relationships with those around him, or the band's career.

The stresses of running a record company weren't all about money, then. Difficult and demanding creative personalities also took their toll — although it has to be said the point of friction was almost always money. The artists needed more of it and I wanted to spend less of it. I assumed that such stresses were the cause of my terrible bouts of depression — my moods and my ability to work swung alarmingly and I would attempt to self-medicate by drinking copious amounts of imported Russian vodka. But to be fair, the majority of artists I worked with were fine and intelligent people with whom I remain friends to this day, and who have been nothing but positive influences on my life.

Martin Phillipps had got The Chills back on track, too. The 1987 *Brave Words* album had done its work and attracted interest from a bigger record company with a fatter wallet. He had signed a deal with Slash in the US and London Records for Europe, and kindly allowed us to remain his record company in New Zealand. Slash was a larger US independent label that had been set up by Bob Biggs but by this time was funded by one of the majors, Warners, and owned by Roger Ames's London Records. The upshot was that we could potentially have a hit record for absolutely no financial outlay, and the band would generate royalty income for itself from the first sale in New Zealand because no recoupable advance was made towards the recording. All of those costs were covered by Slash, Warners and London.

The latest Chills line-up of Justin Harwood on bass (Big Sideways and, later, Luna), keyboardist Andrew Todd and new drummer Jimmy Stephenson (replacing the tinnitus-stricken Caroline Easther) looked very solid. They were well rehearsed and ready to record the masterpiece that had been swirling around inside Martin's head for some years now.

Released in 1990, *Submarine Bells* is a very fine record. It's everything Martin wanted to achieve in the making of an album. It was recorded at Jacobs Studios and produced by Gary Smith (Pixies, Throwing Muses, 10,000 Maniacs, Billy Bragg), with enough funding to do it all properly, to be able to capture all the sounds and textures in Martin's imagination, with elaborate arrangements, and it spans a real diversity of material, shot through with different moods and tempos. Some of it was a little baroque, and some of the lyrical sentiments were a bit mawkish for my tastes. Generally speaking, I feel lyric sheets are unnecessary because I prefer my lyrics to remain a little obscure, vague or misheard. Sometimes printed lyrics simply highlight the shortcomings and oddness in the writing. Mystery can be a powerful and useful tool in the development of an artist's career.

But these are minor, subjective quibbles. The album is an artistic success and as the record company guy I loved the fact there was an undeniable hit single on it. Bigger record companies are smart like that: they simply won't release an album without a song that has a good chance of generating radio play, as it's what will sell the record. In this case we had 'Heavenly Pop Hit', and it seemed perfectly made to order. As soon as I heard it, I knew we had a winner that would expand the band's audience into the mainstream.

With Festival Records' help we put a plan together and budgeted the promotional activities around the release and national tour the band would undertake to promote the album. It was very successful and a welcome money-spinner, culminating in a triumphant return to Dunedin in July 1990 with a show at the Town Hall. The single went to number two and the album to number one in the same week. I think we sold around 20,000 copies all up in New Zealand, which was very respectable, not to mention good for the band's bank balance, and ours.

The Chills also toured extensively in the US and Europe. The single climbed to number seventeen on the main Billboard rock chart and came within a whisker of generating the radio play in London that would have kicked the band on to the next level. Everything was going in the right direction, but they weren't there yet.

Then things started to unravel quickly. Due to exhaustion, the band cancelled a tour of the USA to support the second single release off the album, 'Oncoming Day'. Justin Harwood and Andrew Todd left the band.

Slash obviously had concerns, but I was surprised to learn they had forced Martin to drop the band's manager, Craig Taylor, and replace him with someone they had chosen. This was unheard-of interference in a band's affairs. Martin obviously felt he had no choice, but at this level no good ever comes of appointing a manager at the behest of the record company. There's the obvious conflict of interest, but one has to question the effectiveness of any manager who is there simply to look after a band's affairs after all the major deals have been signed. This all happened at a time when the prime motivation for a good manager was to obtain a recording and publishing deal with a major record and/or publishing company as well as the biggest possible expression of faith in a band — a large cash advance. The 20 per cent or so a manager took was his reward. Coming in to work with a band after these deals were done became a day-to-day job, not the passionate relationship it needed to be if the band were to succeed.

The Chills' follow-up album in 1992, *Soft Bomb*, was a darker, more sombre affair. There was more highly arranged material and a contribution from one of Martin's idols, the singer-songwriter and Beach Boys collaborator Van Dyke Parks. It's a good album but a bit narrower in appeal compared to *Submarine Bells*, and it lacks variety. The cover seemed to reinforce the overall mood, and the single, 'Male Monster from the Id', definitely wasn't 'Heavenly Pop Hit'.

It felt to me that Martin hadn't been quite ready to record. He was still trying to replace Justin Harwood and Andrew Todd. It can be hard enough to find the time to write songs when you are busy with a working band, but it's even harder when you are trying to completely rebuild one. This time Martin felt he had to look beyond New Zealand for players, and the international nature of the subsequent line-up must have added logistical complexities. It became obvious that *Soft Bomb* wasn't going to match the sales of *Submarine Bells*, either, and I worried about the implications for Martin and his recording contract. Sure enough, Slash pulled the plug halfway through the American tour supporting the album release. The Chills had been dropped.

Martin was devastated, and it left him in the lurch financially. It was unusual for an artist to be left with debts. Unrecouped advances were one thing — you never had to pay them back, they simply recouped themselves from ongoing sales. But these were actual debts that needed to be repaid, so this was a blow. I know Doug Hood helped as much as he could, but he had his own business to worry about and very little leverage as only Martin's de facto New Zealand manager.

The fall was spectacular. Back in Dunedin, with no international deal, no band and no money, Martin hit rock bottom. He developed a nasty homebake heroin addiction and contracted hepatitis C. He has been bravely candid about these problems and has taken years to recover and get his life back into some kind of functioning order.

* * *

The Chills' experience with Slash would not be the only time Flying Nun crossed paths with that US label. When The Verlaines outgrew our ability to support their international activity, they too signed to the LA-based company.

Graeme Downes had followed an interesting path, even by Flying Nun standards. From the original, critically lauded side of the *Dunedin Double*, through the iconic seven-inch single 'Death and the Maiden' and the perfect twelve-inch EP *10 O'clock in the Afternoon* in 1983, it was an amazing trajectory. Graeme had studied music at Otago University. He was a bit of a star student, eventually becoming a senior lecturer. He could and would write and 'orchestrate' highly elaborate albums, beginning with *Hallelujah All the Way Home* in 1985.

When he formed The Verlaines, Graeme was also a gifted cricketer. Roy Colbert, who was then a cricket reporter for the now defunct Dunedin *Star*, described him as having provincial representative level potential, if not more. I always wondered about Roy's cricket reporting, because he was as blind as a bat. But his evaluation gained more credibility when Graeme played

The 'Looney Nuns' cricket team, including Australian ring-ins The Go-Betweens

in a friendly match between a Looney Tours/Flying Nun team and a New Music Management team later in the 1980s.

I had never been so close to someone able to bowl a ball so quickly or whack a ball so damn hard. Our team, led by Doug Hood, was a bit loose, but we had co-opted Grant McLennan and Robert Forster from The Go-Betweens, who happened to be in town on tour. We figured they'd be naturally gifted at the game, being Australians.

Grant was obviously worried about my supposed role in the team when he instructed me with some dismay to 'get off the grass'. It was actually a pre-game drink that was causing the problem with my warm-up, but it was the ball he was talking about. I had lazily let it roll across the grass, which apparently would affect its shine. Who would have thought?

Shine or no shine, I couldn't see it much altering the velocity of any ball bowled by Graeme as it hurtled towards the head of some poor unfortunate from Hello Sailor. New Music Management was owned by old-style promoter Mike Corliss, who managed

Hello Sailor. They were all there late on this Sunday morning and well into the spirit of the event. I even held a catch — an insanely difficult one, given the number of beers I'd consumed — to dismiss Hello Sailor front man Graham Brazier. Graham and I probably had more in common than we realised, being roughly on a par in terms of both cricket talent and drinking ability.

Anyway, as The Verlaines became more of a priority, Graeme rapidly descended the Otago cricket grades before finally giving it all away. The Verlaines' music is hard to describe. It was post punk in the sense that Graeme had been inspired to form a band after being directly inspired by The Clean, and the playing of David Kilgour in particular. And, like many of his Dunedin contemporaries, Graeme brought some 1960s influences — Bob Dylan and Van Morrison especially. But unusually, his music was also informed by his classical training. It influenced the song structures and the way the songs related to each other on albums.

I became quite close to Graeme. I enjoyed his intelligence and intensity. He was serious about his music but was and remains unpretentious. He also had a bit of a rugged southern man aspect

The Verlaines on stage at the Gluepot, Auckland, 1985

to his personality. When I see those ads for undrinkable Dunedin beer featuring faux southern hard nuts, I think of Graeme out-shooting or out-fishing, and out-drinking, the lot of them ... while simultaneously finishing his doctorate on Mahler. We both enjoyed a drink or two while we watched the rugby. It was always whisky.

We drifted apart as his studies and academic career became more serious. I'd moved the office to Auckland, was getting to Dunedin less often and had started drinking vodka instead of whisky. I was stressed and feeling isolated by the growing pressure of trying to keep the many artists we represented happy, building sales and all the while trying to keep costs down. Nothing unusual with any of that, except I was doing it from tiny little New Zealand, miles and miles from anywhere that mattered in the music world or where the record-buying masses lived. I was beginning to understand the paradox of the Flying Nun phenomenon. The very isolation that had created the conditions for the music to develop the way it did — exactly what made it special and unique — was also the main barrier to communicating and selling that music internationally.

Graeme and The Verlaines would record some excellent albums for Flying Nun: *Hallelujah* in 1985, *Bird Dog* and a compilation of the early material, *Juvenilia*, in 1987, and *Some Disenchanted Evening* in 1989. They were touring internationally and needed more support than we could give them. And perhaps they were mistrustful of the new setup with Mushroom. I loved the band, but it had become increasingly difficult to sell their albums of complex song structures and monumental arrangements. They didn't appeal to a mainstream audience, and the music could be obtuse and hard to fathom. I wasn't hearing those standout, stand-alone songs that so defined their early career the way 'Death and the Maiden' had. So off they went and signed to Slash.

The Chills had signed to Slash for the US and London Records for Europe and they seemed to know what they were doing. Slash's original founder Bob Biggs had always struck me as one of those mini-major record company types. Major record companies were often run by larger-than-life characters — I'm thinking of Ahmet Ertegun at Atlantic, Clive Davis at Sony and Chris Blackwell at Island. These were very talented music people with charisma, drive and crazily outsized egos. The smaller, more successful independent label guys often shared those attributes, but in differing ratios. While they would be successful, they wouldn't reach the heights and they often wouldn't last. They eventually got worn down by trying to survive rather than succeed.

Of course, my own complete lack of nous precluded me from such company. I wasn't the usual record label owner, manipulating artists and their recordings to maximise profit and achieve world domination. My perceived role was more modest. I saw myself as a facilitator, someone who was there to help the artist get something together and help sell it. I wasn't going to interfere with the recording, and the band could work out the covers themselves — although I did intervene in the case of the original cover for The Verlaines' *10 O'clock in the Afternoon* by Jane Dodd, which I thought looked too much like our earlier *The Last Rumba* live compilation album cover. I don't know what I was thinking. Which was exactly the problem. This was *all* new. There was no way of knowing how things should be done. If I had known how it was meant to be, it might never have happened. I sometimes feel the lack of drive for personal success on my part had the knock-on effect of selling the artists short. Perhaps if I'd been more driven, it would have helped them achieve more, make better deals, sell more records and make a better living from their music. Then again, if that had been the real me perhaps I would have given up on this music business lark quite quickly and sold houses or used cars instead.

My relationship with Graeme Downes and his wife, Jo, who managed the band, became fraught after Mushroom bought into Flying Nun. There was a bit of a conflict with Simon Baeyertz, and they were offended by the money on offer for the proposed next album. I think they were willing to put up with the previous Flying Nun chaos because of the strength of our personal relationship and they knew I was doing my best. But with Mushroom on the scene there was a correct expectation for more professionalism and this inevitably manifested itself around the money that was on offer; plus, they did not feel confident that Simon Baeyertz was going to looking after their best interests.

Slash had deeper pockets than ours and signed The Verlaines directly. The band had a following and college-radio support, and Slash believed they could grow that by funding new recordings and touring. The idea of touring the US is pretty frightening — it's a huge country, there are enormous distances to travel, and it's a real test of any band to undertake it again and again. The first Slash album, 1991's *Ready to Fly*, was to a degree about the wrench of Graeme leaving Flying Nun. The Verlaines had a good crack at making it in the US, working hard at touring, but in the end good reviews and decent but unspectacular sales for *Ready to Fly* and 1993's *Way Out Where* album weren't enough. No matter what a band does, or how it does it, eventually all is measured against sales. It might be the fortunes of an individual album or the trend over a number of albums over time, but in the end the numbers talk.

Radio play was still the key, whether the band filled clubs or stadiums. At an indie level that meant student radio in New Zealand and college radio in the US. As time went by it became harder and harder for radio to pick up on individual tracks from Verlaines albums. Fashions change even on the fringes of the indie world, maybe more so. If there is a new thing, then there is also a new old thing. 'Hot' new bands appear and new styles and genres develop and dominate. It's a treacherous river of eddies, whirlpools and fast-moving currents. The sales trend for a band that has made a few records becomes important. Are they building or has interest peaked? It has absolutely nothing to do with the quality of the music.

I always found dropping bands very hard, but proper record companies seem to find it pretty easy to do. It costs money to keep them on. Any doubt and an act will be dropped to stem the flow of money that is now no longer perceived as an investment, but as throwing good after bad. One has to be tough and resilient. Unlike Martin Phillipps, however, Graeme had his career in academia and eventually The Verlaines became an adjunct to that. It proved to be a great way of keeping it going, making the records and satisfying that core of faithful fans around the world.

CHAPTER 19

UP AND DOWN IN LONDON

Everyone seemed to get it together in 1990. Maybe Mushroom's involvement in Flying Nun was seen as a stabilising influence, opening up solid opportunities to get an actual contract and get ahead. Whatever it was, it translated into a tangible creative upsurge. There was some great music being made and it couldn't all be classified as being part of the so-called Dunedin Sound. Bands from all over the place were doing it, though to be fair some of them were transplanted southerners. Straitjacket Fits and JPS Experience had moved north from Dunedin and Christchurch to Auckland. But the great Dunedin band the 3Ds were actually mostly from Auckland in the first place.

I loved the 3Ds. The 'D' came from the first initials of the original three members — David Mitchell (Exploding Budgies, Goblin Mix), David Saunders (Battling Strings) and Dominic Stones (Bird Nest Roys, Snapper). They were all displaced Aucklanders but they sounded like a Dunedin band. That might have been due to the fourth D, Denise Roughan (Look Blue Go

David Mitchell's Goblin Mix poster design featuring 'Leper Lager' was a pun on the early New Zealand beer brand 'Leopard Lager'.

Purple). The male trio first visited Dunedin while touring with their previous bands, fell in love with the place and the people who made music there, and stayed.

They were a great band. Everyone could play well, and the twin guitar attack and dual songwriting of Mitchell and Saunders was a real strength. David Mitchell was also an astonishing guitarist — one of the best I have seen. Watching him play live is an immersive experience. His influences were not the usual American blues players, but seemed to derive from Celtic roots via traditional and 1960s folk music. It was wild, intense stuff. He never seemed to notice that his fingers were bleeding.

I had first met David when he was recording the Goblin Mix album in 1986. We had agreed to give them $5000 to record it, which in hindsight was a considerable amount of money. I guess we must have had it at the time and we saw a band with potential that had no other means of financing a record. I was in Auckland visiting The Chills, some of whom were living in Pompallier Terrace in Ponsonby. It was a sunny day and we were sitting on the front porch drinking beer and chatting. David appeared, pushing an empty shopping trolley up the street towards the shops, and stopped to talk; the recording was going well and they were going back into the studio that evening, he said, and off he headed. Twenty minutes later he came back with his trolley now absolutely full of alcohol — beer, wine and spirits. I have no doubt whatsoever that helped partly explain the alarmingly high recording budget.

Money well spent probably. The 3Ds were to become an important band for us. Goblin Mix might not have recouped the money we gave them, but we had at least established a relationship with the band members, one that would carry over to their later bands. By this time a lot of Dunedin musicians had aligned themselves with Bruce Russell's Xpressway label. The 3Ds were a bit more ambitious, though, and I think they understood that what the band wanted to achieve would not be possible by that route. They wanted to make records and tour and have a decent budget to do both, not to scrimp and save and try to pay for it all by themselves. They knew what they did was special and that there was potentially an international market for their music.

The band embraced the now traditional Flying Nun model of first recording and releasing two EPs, *Fish Tales* in 1990 and *Swarthy Songs for Swabs* in 1991. They went on to record three albums and undertake some tentative overseas tours. The LP *Hellzapoppin'* came out in 1992, followed by *The Venus Trail* in 1993, and then there was a gap before they made *Strange News from the Angels*, a break-up album, in 1997. While David Saunders was motivated and wanted a crack at indie-rock success, other members of the band either had pre-existing job commitments or temperaments that just weren't suited to spending huge amounts of time abroad doing the hard touring that successful rock-music careers are built on. They had made some of the best music released by the label in the 1990s but were never in agreement about what they wanted to achieve or how.

Following the demise of the band, I became firm friends with David and Denise after they moved to London and formed The Ghost Club with Jim Abbott. They confessed they had always thought of me as a businessman but had come to see that I was actually an alright person. I was slightly taken aback by the businessman bit.

The truth was, my connection to the 3Ds had always been a bit personal. The whirling guitar attack seemed to match certain things that were going on in my head back then. The stress of running the label had been unrelenting. The money worries had been temporarily eased by the Mushroom deal, but we were incredibly busy with recording projects, there was more happening overseas than ever, people at Mushroom to deal with daily, and our Flying In subsidiary was still growing rapidly.

Fortunately, Lesley and Paul were very capable — not that delegation was one of my strong points. In all honesty I was not particularly well suited to running a business of the size Flying

Nun had become. I had no gift for organisation or efficiency. I was a fan who had let his enthusiasms get the better of him. The label was built on a wild love of the music rather than a business model with turnover and profit as its prime objectives. Decisions were often made for aesthetic reasons, or in the best long-term interests of a band, not always with an eye on the bottom line. I was a dreamer who had somehow got to live the dream. I managed to keep the whole show going, but there was a cost. I was increasingly hit by bouts of depression. Madness seemed frighteningly possible.

By now I had learned marijuana wasn't for me. The paranoia it induced was terrible. But there was a bit of cocaine scattered around Auckland at that time. Friends would offer it to me and I began to spend more and more time in the bathrooms of inner-city restaurants and bars. I enjoyed the stuff: it made me feel invincible, which was a nice change from my normal default setting of self-doubt and anxiety. I could certainly see how people became addicted — and I observed a few friends doing just that. So I made a point of never buying any myself, and somehow I didn't have to. Friends and even strangers were very generous. Sometimes you would find a line just waiting and ready to go when you innocently went to the toilet. People were so off their trolleys they were inadvertently leaving free samples on cistern tops all over town.

But my interest in cocaine didn't develop much further than that of a social dabbler, mainly because my primary preoccupation was drinking. I was a drinker because it most effectively blotted out the stress of work. Booze turned my normal shyness into something more social. It lubricated and loosened my awkward inhibitions; it turned me into someone acceptably functional and it made me forget. It was very effective, but the short-term euphoria, the feeling of being warmed up to the point of being tipsy but still coherent, came with longer-term consequences. It amplified my depression and made other problems worse. I was pouring petrol onto a fire.

* * *

The music kept on coming, though. By the late 1980s the band to watch around Auckland was the Headless Chickens. I was aware of Chris Matthews, who had been in Children's Hour and released some records with us in the early 1980s. This ferocious and fine band had come to an end in 1984. Chris then recorded with the Jefferies brothers in This Kind of Punishment, before he and Children's Hour bass player Johnny Pierce got together with Michael Lawry in 1986 to form the Headless Chickens, making a strange and dark self-titled mini album which I liked a great deal. Sadly Johnny committed suicide in August 1986. After recovering from the shock, Chris and Michael added old friends Grant Fell and Bevan Sweeney from Children's Hour and Rupert E Taylor from the Bird Nest Roys and continued as the Headless Chickens. They were making a name for themselves, and in 1987 put themselves forward for the Rheineck Rock Award.

The award was sponsored by Lion Breweries and carried a $60,000 prize to be spent on recording an album. The judges were Colin Hogg, Doug Hood and bFM station manager Jude Anaru. The previous year's prize had gone to South Auckland soul-dance band Ardijah — deserving winners who made excellent funky pop music. When the next year's award went to the Headless Chickens, there was instant uproar. Mainstream media considered it an outrageous left-field decision, but anyone who bothered to listen to the music could see the Chickens deserved the prize. They were special. It was mainly the name of the band that antagonised people.

The award was announced at a big event held in a nightclub on Nelson Street. Everyone who was anyone came, the band played, and everyone was happy on the free beer. There was a giant fridge along the back of the bar. On the right-hand side there were bottles of Rheineck, and on the left-hand side its more sophisticated cousin Steinlager. At the end of the night all of the Steinlager was gone and not a single bottle of Rheineck had been touched.

The only known photo of the original Headless Chickens line-up of the late Johnny Pierce, Michael Lawry and Chris Matthews, 1985

The Headless Chickens recorded *Stunt Clown* with their prize money. It went way over budget and we had to find the extra money at a time when cash flow was very poor. But it seemed clear the band was a good risk and would do well commercially. Their use of technology was a little at odds with the tastes of the traditional Dunedin Sound fans, who liked electric guitars but not sampling. But making music has always been about using technology to make new and interesting sounds, so this was all just part of that progression. Soon enough, it would be accepted as the norm, but at the time some southern eyebrows were definitely raised.

Released in 1988, *Stunt Clown* sold well enough and charted at number eighteen. It wasn't the breakthrough album we'd hoped it would be, but it did raise the band's profile, to the point where they were on the way to becoming New Zealand's biggest. It took a while and the addition of vocalist Fiona McDonald, and a lot of live and studio work, before it all came together.

The stunning 'Gaskrankinstation' single in 1990 was the statement of intent, followed by the *Body Blow* album the next year. Three singles from the album — 'Cruise Control', 'Donde Esta la Pollo' and 'Juice'/'Choppers' went top ten. The album itself failed to chart until an expanded version was released in 1993 that went to number seventeen. The Chickens continued to pioneer the use of samples in New Zealand rock music, and made a point of using recognisable splices of our musical history, such as Shona Laing's '1905' and The Crocodiles' 'Tears'. They were ahead of their time and breaking new ground, and before such techniques became accepted and routine they attracted a fair amount of criticism.

The commercial high-water mark came with the release of the 'George' single in 1994. We had been close before, but finally Flying Nun achieved a number-one single, our one and only. Unfortunately, it didn't feature on an album until *Greedy* was released in 1997, so no one got to capitalise properly on that success. By the time of *Greedy*'s release Fiona had left and the band had lost its momentum. What I'll remember most, though, is an

Admiring the Headless Chickens' gold disc for *Body Blow*, 1994

unforgivingly ferocious live band, an amalgam of guitars, sampled sound, human and electronic rhythms and patterns, and a lot of great songs.

* * *

While things were going well with bigger bands, we also had the confidence to continue to do things around the fringe, working with bands like Solid Gold Hell, Fatal Jelly Space and Skeptics. Skeptics were an early post-punk band out of Palmerston North. Like many alternative bands from smaller, more isolated places, these guys were highly motivated. They had collectively found a way to cope with and react against the stifling nature of their hometown. Palmerston North is a 'scientific centre of agriculture', an international hub of grass science, a big farming service town and not an obvious or easy place to be making strange modern music. But it's often off-the-beaten-track towns like Palmerston North that throw up the most interesting examples of outsider music. Skeptics' early material was highly original, idiosyncratic and not always easy to listen to, but over time they developed into something truly formidable. They became one of my favourite bands.

They had a couple of tracks included on the 1982 Furtive Records *Three Piece Pack* compilation and then released the *Chowder over Wisconsin* EP through Flying Nun in 1983 and we distributed the *Ponds* LP in 1985. The band had their own club, Snailclamps, for a while before David D'ath, Don White and Nick Roughan departed for Wellington.

Many best know the band for Stuart Page's 1988 video for 'AFFCO', off the *Skeptics 111* album released in 1987. The video has a few 'shocking' freezing works scenes, as well as David D'ath splattered with fake blood and wrapped in gigantic quantities of clingfilm. Apparently it's not really an anti-meat song advocating vegetarianism but instead just a song about meatpackers. There was mild controversy around TVNZ's reluctance to show it at the time, and I thought that the controversy overshadowed the music itself, which was starting to get very interesting by this stage.

Skeptics 111 was recorded in the band's own Wellington studio setup, Writhe. Nick Roughan became the key technical guy, along with Brent McLachlan from Bailter Space, and between them they recorded some very good music. They built Writhe from scratch in the old SIS building on the corner of Taranaki Street and Martin Square. I remember the place as a bit of a rabbit warren, but it became a key New Zealand studio, recording important material by the likes of JPS Experience, Snapper, Head Like a Hole, Shihad and many more, and established itself as the musical creative hub in Wellington. 'Ownership' of this studio facility gave both Skeptics and Bailter Space the time and space to fully develop their own sounds and recordings. The bands became close: Bailter Space's John Halvorsen joined Skeptics on guitar around the time of their move to Wellington (replacing Robin Gauld) and Brent McLachlan played with them at later gigs as part of a formidable twin-drum setup.

While recording *Amalgam* in 1989 singer David D'ath discovered that he had leukaemia. Perhaps this provided an impetus that saw the band flourish in the studio and live over its last year or so. The farewell shows, including those that I saw in Auckland's Gluepot, were remarkable events and some material from the shows surfaces in Simon Ogston's excellent 2013 documentary about the band, *Sheen of Gold*.

For me, the most important legacy is the *Amalgam* album itself. Released in 1990, soon after David's death, it is one of my favourite Flying Nun records. It's a brilliant album, with strong-muscled songs stretched to their limits and walls of guitars and synthetic keyboards crashing together to create rich layers of musical texture. With David D'ath's commanding, impressionistic singing swooping around and through it, it made for powerful, unforgettable listening. The late-period material that appears here is set apart from their earlier material by a very real sense of urgency and momentum. I would play it loud when I was working in the Flying Nun office alone at weekends. It seemed to help me get the royalty accounting done.

To honour David's unreasonably early death, in 1992 we released a four-disc Skeptics box set, comprising a remastered *Skeptics 111* and *Amalgam,* along with a collection of earlier material called *Sensible* and some live material collected under the *If I Will I Can* title, along with a booklet of David's line drawings. We pressed up 300 copies and watched them slowly sell. Perhaps we were asking a lot of the record-buying public to all rush out and splash out on a box set of uncommercial musical strangeness, but it seemed important to me to make the statement that this stuff was good enough to collect and present in this way. It is music that has proven to be timeless and quite apart from anything else ever made.

* * *

We all liked to celebrate at Flying Nun and for anniversaries we would pull out all the stops and try to do something really special. For our tenth anniversary, Paul McKessar and Ian Dalziel worked on a special set of trading cards. Each card had a theme, with an illustration on one side and the story on the other. They were mainly about the bands, but there were also some cards on topics such as 'Departed Friends', 'Student Radio and Orientation', 'Garage Magazine' and 'Xpressway'. The pack fitted neatly into a cassette-tape case. For the lead card, Ian designed the now-famous 'Flying Eyeball', and we used the central feature of that image — a cherubic flying baby with an eyeball for a head cradling a record — as our logo for the next few years.

We also put out two compilations: one highlighting our current stable of artists, called *Pink Flying Saucers over the Southern Alps,* and another that was a double retrospective, *Getting Older 1981–1991.* Andrew Mueller at *Melody Maker* went a bit over the top when they eventually reviewed the latter collection in August the next year:

ABOVE: The Flying Eyeball's first outing as the cover card for the 1991 tenth-anniversary trading-card set, designed by Ian Dalziel. RIGHT: The 1991 tenth-anniversary laminate. I only read it properly and got the joke days after the event.

'Motown? Amateurs. Sun Studios? Chancers. 4AD? Creation? Not in the same league. Factory? Sub Pop? Part-timers, each. Sarah? Blast First? Gimme a break. Ladies and things, may I present for your edification and enjoyment, 20 unfailingly sublime moments in the wonderful 10–year life of the greatest record label of any status, anywhere in the world, of all time ever. A rousing ovation and a volley of roses, if you would, for Flying Nun.' At the time I thought what he was saying about those other labels was especially true of Flying Nun. But the rest of the article correctly and gushingly reviewed the actual music, and what it said was true: it really did stand up, it was special and it held its own against anything from anywhere.

Unfortunately I got into a bit of trouble with this compilation. I managed to forget to include a Sneaky Feelings track and the band were correctly offended. It was entirely unintentional: I was starting to get tired and emotional on a daily basis and just beginning to unravel. Indeed, by about 1992 I was worn out and up and down and not much fun to be with. My lifestyle was a bit wonky: bursts of activity followed by periods of feeling down and being unproductive, with other times of agitation and anxiety. I thought it was all due to the stress of the job, and that certainly didn't help. I was so wonky I broke up with my long-standing girlfriend and went to live alone in the converted dog pound at the top of Queen Street. I had a huge space there in which I rattled around all alone. Colin Hogg was also in the process of splitting up with his long-term partner. I think he thought we would be safer flatting together rather than on our own, so we got a place on Wellpark Avenue back in West Lynn. Apparently, it had previously been a brothel, which would explain the strange men constantly knocking on the door at all hours.

With Mushroom being a major shareholder in Flying Nun, I now had an employment contract and a modest but regular salary. So I was a stressed mess, but slightly more presentable and sociable, and the label was suddenly fashionable in the eyes of the Auckland trendy set. I was also single, so I was seen as eligible and available. Yet I was essentially a shy young man and the attention rattled me. Indeed I wasn't at all equipped to cope. Despite appearances, I was really just a husk of a man.

* * *

Mushroom now had new money to spend following the investment from News International, which enabled it to establish an office in London and release its own records across Europe. This in turn eliminated the need for third-party licensing, which was always problematic. I had long experience of the problems myself when dealing with overseas territories. If you license to an overseas company, the income has to be split between yourself and the artist, meaning you are attempting to balance the income needs of both parties from a single royalty payment. The difficulties are all the more pronounced when your home territory is a tiny, distant market like New Zealand, where both label and band always struggle to sell enough music to achieve any critical mass.

Quite early on, the idea was floated that I could shift to London to oversee a Flying Nun presence within the Mushroom empire. We knew we had to keep developing our overseas business, that selling records in New Zealand would never be enough in itself, so it was a huge opportunity.

It also appealed personally. I had set up Flying Nun when I was just twenty-one years old and had been working hard at home while most of my friends had made it overseas for extended stays or relocated to other parts of the world. I had had the opportunity to travel to the US, the UK and Europe on business, but this was a different prospect. Business trips were sheer hard work — never more than a few days in any given place, lots of meetings and obligations, then home again to resume contact via fax and phone. I thought a change of scene might be good for me.

So I set off late in 1993 for a look around and I decided it could work. I was home for Christmas then back permanently living in London early in 1994.

Gary Ashley, Michael Gudinski's co-director and partner in Mushroom Records, was charged with setting up the London office at 555 Kings Road — down near the Fulham end of the famous street, close to the Fulham Broadway tube station and Chelsea Football Club's Stamford Bridge ground. Gary was quite a brash chap and I worried about working with him so closely. The music they were pushing was very mainstream and they would be working in quite a different way from the Flying Nun operation I envisaged.

Gary hired a range of people for the new operation. There were music-mad kids as well as some more experienced types from the big UK indie distribution world, so there was enthusiasm and know-how. There was also the presence of a team working for another Mushroom affiliate company, Korda Marshall's Infectious Records. Crucially I warmed to Gary as I got to know him. He was Australian, brash and blustery, but admirably human underneath it all. He had huge energy and quickly built a record company from hits for the likes of Peter Andre and Garbage. Garbage was an interesting phenomenon — Nirvana producer Butch Vig's band fronted by Scottish singer Shirley Manson — and they broke big in the UK.

I managed to kick things off by getting very sick with a particularly nasty flu. I became delirious with a very high temperature. As it turned out, it was the perfect time to get sick. I hadn't long settled into my new flat on Southgate Road on the Islington–Hackney border and I'd fallen for my flatmate Catherine Marks. Despite Catherine being a lawyer from Hamilton, I was smitten. She seemed to quite like me, too.

Once I'd recovered, we went on a romantic holiday to the Loire Valley in France. Then on my return to London I was struck down again by post-viral fatigue. I simply couldn't get out of bed. Using the bathroom was a nightmare, as I had trouble getting back up the stairs afterwards. The doctor said it would take me a year to start feeling better and he was spot on. I had to take three months off work and then slowly ease back into it. I think thirteen years of overwork, stress and an associated poor lifestyle had finally all caught up with me. My weakened system was flattened by the flu and it wiped me out for a long time.

Once I was back at the office, we started to work on our New Zealand releases in a more coordinated way across Europe. Artists and bands such as David Kilgour, the Headless Chickens and the 3Ds came over to support their records, but it quickly became clear that sporadic touring in itself was not enough to build a profile and sales in this extremely competitive market. To succeed, artists would have to relocate to the other side of the world — which is exactly what Love's Ugly Children and Garageland did.

Former *Radio with Pictures* host Karyn Hay had introduced me to Garageland and I was instantly wowed by the material that would eventually appear on their *Come Back Special* CD EP debut. Vinyl had gone completely by this stage, but the EP format still had some life in it on CD. I loved the band. They were doing well in New Zealand and made the bold move to London. We set them up in a house in Tooting, and Mushroom's in-house publicist, Rob Jefferson, who was behind much of Garbage's success in the UK, took them under his wing and worked very hard with them. There were little victories, but the bigger fairy-tale success proved elusive.

I also hired a publicist, as I needed someone on a similar wavelength in the office who could work on Flying Nun projects exclusively. There were all kinds of other interests and priorities within the office, so getting someone to support me would help ensure we were focused on the crucial UK publicity. It was essential for a simple reason — increased profile equalled increased sales. The new guy had been at another indie label and worked freelance, so he was well connected with the music press and knew how it all worked.

In hindsight, this probably meant he knew where everyone drank. Relationships with the music press were usually maintained over a pint, so on certain afternoons he would head off to the West End with a bag of samples; other afternoons he would go to meet with one of John Peel's producers. The job was to pass on the new releases, talk about them, talk them up and generate reviews, features and airplay. He also provided another point of contact with the wider music scene and industry and could report back on who was playing where, who was on the way up and who was looking for a record company.

I liked the guy. For starters, he wasn't too hyped up. In fact he was quite relaxed, introverted even, especially for a publicist. It wouldn't have suited the label and the music we represented to have someone too over the top, after all. But I soon began to realise that he was perhaps a tad too retiring and that he might have a drinking problem.

I wasn't shy of a drink myself, but with my new life in London, the stresses of running Flying Nun in Auckland behind me, and my new relationship with Catherine flourishing, I was a happier person. My recent illness had slowed me down, too; not only was there less need to drink, I couldn't drink as much anyway.

It was, however, relatively normal practice for record companies to have lunch at the pub — something to eat, a couple of pints and a bit of a natter. My new publicist liked at least a couple of pints of Guinness, whereas I found a smaller bottle of lager set me up for an afternoon doze. I remember him changing his drink when the summer heat arrived — lager and cider mixed together. Very refreshing, he said. For some reason it was called a snakebite and it had a reputation for making people crazy.

So at first I was only moderately intrigued when I was told one morning that he was drinking beer in the office. Nothing unusual in that, I thought — except it was only nine o'clock. Then he was spotted drinking pre-mixed vodka and tonics on his way to the office from the tube station. Another time I was driving back through Camberwell from a day trip to Kent, when I pointed out a sad sight on the side of the road — a tramp dragging his bad leg along the footpath. It took me a few seconds to realise it was our publicist, dragging his gout-prone foot home from the pub.

The drinking during work was one thing, but my main concern was the lack of press we were generating. John Peel hadn't played anything of ours for an age. Before we had set up in London we'd had successive singles and albums of the week in the UK weekly press. The *NME*, *Melody Maker* and *Sounds* had given good space to releases by The Clean, The Chills, Snapper, The Verlaines, Sneaky Feelings, Tall Dwarfs and The Bats and more — glowing reviews that were in part responsible for our international reputation. But they had dried up completely and I couldn't understand why.

I finally get to meet John Peel (along with Judith Tizard, then Associate Minister for Arts, Culture and Heritage) at Flying Nun's twenty-first-anniversary bash (photo by Gemma Gracewood).

Publicity is a hard business. You're always getting knocked back, and having to pick yourself up and knock on the door again. Perhaps the new guy's personality wasn't quite right for the job, perhaps he didn't connect with the music well enough, or perhaps his heart just wasn't in it.

I was at a gig when the general manager of a very successful and highly respected label stopped for a chat. Our publicity guy's name came up early in the conversation. The manager was fishing. I confirmed that, yes, indeed, our guy was absolutely brilliant at his job. I gave him a glowing testimonial without seeming too eager, and sure enough a couple of weeks later he sadly announced he would be leaving to join the other label as head of publicity. Apparently the job came with a mobile phone.

The penny didn't fully drop for another five years. John Peel was visiting Auckland at the same time I was back for Flying Nun's twenty-first anniversary celebrations in 2002. I had first spoken to John in the early 1980s on my first trip to London. He had returned a call very late the night before I was flying home and said some very nice things about our music. He had been quoted as saying Flying Nun was the best label in the world, so he was an obvious fan.

I attended a talk he gave and in response to a question from the audience he said that, for some reason, he hadn't received any of our releases since the early 1990s. So our publicist hadn't been off visiting the BBC every Tuesday afternoon after all, he had been going to the pub. That also explained why some of our pre-release samples had been turning up in the local record shop.

* * *

As mentioned earlier, we at Flying Nun liked to party. So when 1996 and our fifteenth anniversary rolled around Lesley Paris and Paul McKessar came up with 'Nunfest'. It would be a New Zealand–wide celebration of the label, focused on a string of live shows, starting in Dunedin and moving north to finish in Auckland — 28 bands playing 10 shows, two record fairs and a golf tournament.

I figured it would be a good idea to take some overseas journalists with me from Europe to New Zealand for the shows. Sharon O'Connell and a photographer came out from *Melody Maker*; Laurent Didailler from our French distributor PIAS and JD Beauvallet from French music magazine *Les Inrockuptibles* also made the trip. It was a chance to see some of the by then legendary bands from the 1980s plus some of the more recent signings.

I got back to discover a special batch of beer called Roger's Ruin had been ordered from Macs Brewery. It was a hard slog for the Flying Nun staffers and our overseas guests as we travelled north following the shows, staying up late for parties afterwards and drinking far too much Roger's Ruin. But it was also great fun (despite the terrible hangovers) and yielded extensive press coverage in *Melody Maker* and *Les Inrockuptibles*.

The special Nunfest 1996 beer label designed by David Mitchell

All of this was in turn beneficial for the label profile, but what we really needed in London was something close to hand to actively sell. Gary suggested I do some A&R and perhaps sign some UK bands — not a bad idea on the face of it, but the scene was completely different from New Zealand, where groups had largely begun as hobbies rather than career ambitions. A few got lucky and made a living from music, but most had low expectations and just wanted to be creative and make some worthwhile music. The whole scene in Dunedin was laid-back and cooperative because the very idea of turning it into a job or having any financial success seemed so remote.

By contrast, London was one of two or three international capitals of the music business. The place was full of bands and their managers fighting each other for attention. It was a twenty-four-hour, seven-days-a-week bun fight. Bands would burn brightly just long enough to fuel a bidding war between companies and generate the all-important big advance. I went to a lot of gigs around this time and some of the audiences were completely made up of industry insiders trying to make eyes with whatever buzz band was buzzing that week. A real audience of punters and fans was often conspicuous only by its absence.

I got friendly with some other like-minded characters, including Laurence Bell of Domino Records. I mentioned to him my reservations about competing with rival companies and their big chequebooks, and that maybe I would have to get out into some of the remoter parts of the UK and find bands there. Maybe the music would be more interesting there, before the London industry bent and twisted it out of shape. I guess that is what Laurence went on to do when he signed bands like Franz Ferdinand from Glasgow and the Arctic Monkeys from Sheffield.

My publicist was still with me at this stage. He had connections in Londonderry, Northern Ireland, and we'd heard there was a band there that might be just the ticket. We flew into Belfast a couple of weeks after the IRA ceasefire. The checkpoints were abandoned but the architecture of occupation was still there and startling: roadblock infrastructure, military and police buildings behind wire cages, empty watchtowers. It must have been hell living there during the Troubles. We drove across the country to Londonderry. 'What do you think of the Irish mountains?' asked my publicist. They were bleak and moorish and about the size of the sand hills at New Brighton Beach.

I soon caught on that the people I was mixing with did not live in 'Londonderry'. Only the colonial English Protestant imperialists called it that. We were in Derry. We met the band's managers, nice chaps. 'I'm not politically minded but …', one said at the beginning of a two-hour tour of the city: Bogside, Bloody Sunday, the giant political murals and the deserted military and police checkpoints. You knew where you were by the types of flags flying, Union Jack or Irish, and the alternating colours of the kerbstones: blue, white and red, or green, white and orange. Everything here was religious, historical, social and absolutely political.

Dinner was at a local Chinese restaurant. The band members were nice young people, big music fans who wanted to find a way ahead and out of Derry. I enjoyed our meal. It was a family-owned restaurant, with a pragmatic approach to the tastes of its customers — you could have rice or chips with your meal, or both if you wished to explore fusion food at its most basic.

Somehow I managed to spend the evening in a pub. There was, of course, live Irish music. The people absolutely loved it, but it was very much a live thing. They played it live and people listened to it live. In Ireland music buying in the form of records or CDs was far below the quantities elsewhere in Europe. It just wasn't how they wanted to hear their music. I think connecting with the emotion of the music and the moment was paramount. A bland studio-recorded version didn't cut it.

Anyway, we were all having a jolly good time and then the raffle came around. Everyone was keen to buy a ticket. I innocently asked what the prize was, in case it was a tray of meat I would have to drag back to London with me. There was a sudden and total silence. I was given no answer and the ticket sellers simply moved on. It turned out there was no prize; they were just systematically collecting money for the IRA.

At the end of the evening we all stumbled out onto the cobbled streets, feeling very jolly. Then a large military armoured car pulled up. It had strips of iron hanging along its sides to stop bombs from being rolled underneath it, and phone numbers stencilled along the body in case you wanted to dob somebody in anonymously. Out stepped these incredibly tall Royal Ulster Constabulary officers, and it was all on. Things became very verbal and the cops dragged a couple of pub patrons off somewhere. It was pretty obvious they were going to be beaten senseless.

I wasn't sure how to get back to the hotel, so I thought I would grab a taxi. There was a queue of old and tired-looking London-style black cabs and I jumped in the one at the front. It already had people in it. They were waiting for it to be full before they set off, dropping the customers off one by one to save money. When I told the driver the name of my hotel he gave me a startled look and there was muted but audible panic among the other passengers. After a long moment considering his response, the driver suggested in a measured, deliberate tone that I was in the wrong cab at the wrong rank. I should head around the corner and try my luck there.

Sure enough there was another taxi rank, this time with nice-looking, late-model cars. I was the only customer and the driver was happy to take me home to my hotel. I discovered the next day that the first cab rank was for Catholics, who shared their rides to save money, and that no driver would dare cross the river to take me to my hotel on the Protestant side of town, for fear of being shot. I was lucky my accent was strong enough to distinguish me as a naive Antipodean rather than English. A confused Englishman might not have made it back to his hotel.

We didn't get to work with the band. They wanted a large advance to record and live on, and to set them up for the next step of their career. It seemed like too much of a punt and would have been a huge investment for us. Anyway, I really didn't see it as a priority. I wanted us to spend money on getting our own bands from New Zealand to the UK and trying to make a success of them. After we'd turned the Derry band down, their management ditched them and there was a minor personnel reshuffle before they surprised everyone and signed to the huge multinational Geffen. So they got their big advance but I'm not sure they ever got to release a record. I suspect it didn't work out, but I hope they had some fun before it turned sour.

I did sign a few American bands for European distribution, mostly instrumental post-rock acts (not that we knew to call it that back then). Dynamic and bouncy San Francisco band Pell Mell were one I loved and still play. Labradford were a bit more austere and intellectual, and Cul de Sac were truly crazed and wonderful. The money was more realistic, the sales were modest but satisfying, and the music was really good. I also did a bit of work distributing London band Stereolab in Europe, and got to like them a great deal as a band and as people.

Pragmatism won over when we released Ween's 1994 *Chocolate and Cheese* album. They weren't a band at all to my taste. They were overly clever types whose vaunted sense of humour I thought appealed mainly to boys. But sometimes a sale is a sale and we needed some. *Chocolate and Cheese* sold very well for us. The only problem was that a few of us from the office had to accompany the band on their European tour. We got a little tired of the prima donna Dean and Gene double act and spent our nights partying without them.

The Ween album sales pumped some proper money into our account, but I could sense there was a general drain on cash in the Mushroom UK operation. There had been big successes, but these had cost considerable amounts of money to make happen. Peter Andre had had an enormous-selling debut album, but how did you approach a follow-up? When expectations and promo budgets are set high, it can be a financial horror story if something fails to fly. Garbage were also a big success, but I imagine the cost of launching them was immense. You could spend too much money figuring out how everything worked, before suddenly having to trim your costs and trying to make the business run smoothly. And, as I would soon discover, things rarely run smoothly for long.

CHAPTER 20

ALL OR NOTHING

The Tall Dwarfs travelled overseas only a couple of times, notably to Nijmegen in the Netherlands for the Fast Forward Home Tapers Festival in February 1994. They still weren't sure of the terminology at this stage and perhaps the translation did not help, but it was about artists who tended towards DIY recordings that may have been recorded at home or in a small studio and may or may not have been lo-fi. The Tall Dwarfs were trailblazers in this world. I went along for the ride, as did Alastair Galbraith, Peter Jefferies, Smog, Sebadoh and Canada's Mecca Normal, and a surprisingly good grouping of other international acts were also at the small, relaxed event, which was no doubt subsidised to the hilt by the European Union.

Nijmegen was a bit out of the way, inland on a big bend in the Waal River (the Dutch part of the Rhine), close to the German border. It must have been eighty kilometres from Amsterdam and at least twenty minutes by train, so by Dutch standards it was quite remote. The venue was like a local youth club with a café attached. This being the Netherlands, the café sold pot.

It turned out the venue was one of the Netherlands' oldest and most famous. It was called Doornroosje, or Sleeping Beauty

— an apt name given my experiences there. Lots of bands had played the place, including Pink Floyd, Joy Division, Sonic Youth and now Tall Dwarfs. Originally it had been a meeting place for hippies, and it was housed in an old school on the outskirts of town. It had also been one of the first venues to make hash and marijuana openly available.

There were lots of Germans there, for the pot as much as the music. Well, when in Rome (or Holland), I thought … and I needed something to go with the beer and vodka I had been consuming throughout the afternoon. The nice man behind the counter was describing his wares to some of the other customers. This kind didn't just get you stoned, it 'came on strong and then plateaued for a good time before tapering off gently'; another one, perhaps called 'Moroccan Madness', 'crept up on you slowly and peaked violently a number of times before falling off, but you will never be the same again'. Being a New Zealand pro, I bought some of the stronger stuff and chatted with the café owner over another couple of beers on what was a rather pleasant late summer's evening.

The sun was going down and so was I. The conversation and the owner both drifted off and I entered something like a catatonic state. Pot paranoia never seemed far away in those days and suddenly it was upon me. There I was, sat on a stool, way out in the middle of nowhere, alone except for the two other people I knew — one of whom would undoubtedly take cruel advantage of my fragile state if he found me like this. I slipped off the stool and slithered across the floor, out the door and across a lawn to lie under a tree and gaze at the stars.

It was reassuringly peaceful and I dozed off for a couple of hours, while healthy and sober young Dutch couples frolicked in the shrubbery around me. I was eventually able to find my feet and head back inside to catch up with the music. Chris hadn't missed me at all, having been busy tormenting Peter Jefferies, who seemed to be flirting outrageously with Jean Smith from Mecca

Chris Knox designed this ad for US music magazine *Forced Exposure* in 1987.

Normal. I could almost talk by the time Tall Dwarfs came on stage.

Alec had consumed hash cake for the first time and had made the novice's mistake of thinking the first lot wasn't working, gobbled even more, then had the whole lot kick in. To his credit he played a splendid set while horribly high in front of a crowd of strangers.

Chris was forty by now, Alec and I were in our mid-thirties, and we couldn't seem to avoid behaving badly. On the greater spectrum of rock and roll behaviour it was pretty tame stuff, but the trouble with getting out of it with Chris was that it always seemed to magnify the maliciously mischievous side of his personality. If you were in a psychically or emotionally weakened state he would invariably exploit the situation and torment you into an even worse place. Despite my twenty-four-hour party tendencies I became very careful about the state I let myself get into around Chris.

* * *

Listening to the later Tall Dwarfs albums now, they still seem remarkable — the amount of material, the sheer diversity of styles and songs; there is so much going on with the songwriting, arranging, instrumentation and playing. At times it all seems like too much. And I wonder if this might have been the problem as Tall Dwarfs' audience slowly shrank over time— just too much music. But that music is still fabulous, still there to explore, and it's a stunning collection of work.

I think Chris sensed the gradual decline in Tall Dwarfs' stock. Making records with Alec was an on–off affair anyway. Alec was a family man and had always worked proper jobs, as a graphic artist when he could. He had to fit Tall Dwarfs activity in and around his domestic and professional life. Chris felt he could play solo and began writing material with that in mind. Before long he was planning to record solo, too.

Working both at home and in some smaller studios, he produced the *Seizure* album in 1989. It was his first solo effort since those earliest four-track experimentations on *Guppies* in 1982 — he was essentially collaborative by instinct. The Enemy's and Toy Love's songs were all seen as group efforts, and Alec was integral to Tall Dwarfs. Despite all his apparent confidence, Chris remained unsure of his talent and abilities. The bravado was partly a façade that disguised the uncertainties and insecurities. So the transition to performing and recording solo was also a sign that he was becoming more comfortable in his own skin.

Seizure is a surprisingly pared-down, song-based album. Gone is much of the experimentation that distinguished his collaborative work, in favour of unadorned expressions of the personal and intimate. The album title references the epilepsy he had endured much of his life, and it contains his greatest ever non-hit, 'Not Given Lightly', a love song to Barbara, the mother of his two children, Leisha and John. It was never a conventional chart topper, but over time it struck a chord with people. It even became a bit of a money-spinner as the soundtrack to a TV advertisement for Vogel's bread that ran for nearly ten years. I believe people play it at their weddings — although it must seem a bit odd when the names of Barbara, Liesha and John pop up as the adulated ones.

Croaker followed in 1990. Like *Seizure*, its cover features Chris's favourite colour combination of black and yellow. In fact, it's the same cover, with a papier-mâché model of Chris's grinning head smashing through its centre. Like *Seizure*, the new album showcased Chris's lyrics and vocals, backed with his frantic, insistent guitar or a bit of Casiotone and some primitive, looped percussion. It was as idiosyncratic as ever, in an age of new corporate conformity.

Chris went on to record another four solo albums. *Polyfoto, Duck Shaped Pain & Gum* (1993) was another awkward package consisting of a full album and an EP (*Gum*) — except it was all on a CD. *Songs of You and Me* (1995) was a return to a more straightforward approach, followed a couple of years later by *Yes!!*

The title of 2000's *Beat* alluded to the beat of music and of the heart, and featured a stylised heart on the cover. But I couldn't help feeling it referenced a different kind of beat. Plain beat. Worn out, and a bit over it all.

Chris's output over twenty years was extraordinary, with bands and as a solo artist, covering an enormous range of styles. But he hadn't stopped moving and growing. Tired of making records by himself for a dwindling audience, he went back to collaborating. This time it was another full band — The Nothing. It was a word with history: The Enemy's van had been christened 'Nothing' and one of their songs was called 'N.O.T.H.I.N.G.'; The Tall Dwarfs had kicked off with 'Nothing's Going to Happen'.

The Nothing made a couple of very good albums, a self-titled effort in 2005 and *A Warm Gun* in 2008. The latter is a funny record, with some surprisingly conventional sounds made by musicians playing conventional instruments. *A Warm Gun* is also notable for containing some of the most heartfelt material Chris ever recorded. I saw them play underneath a Grey Lynn villa that year. It was a great show for family and friends, capped off with a stunning version of The Beatles' landmark song from *Sgt. Pepper*, 'A Day in the Life'. The song builds and builds to a looming wall of noise that ends with the famously extended chord that fades out into an unintelligible, barely audible vocal coda.

It's hard not to see it as an omen in hindsight. In June 2009 I received a call saying Chris had just had a stroke. Barbara had found him immobile on the bathroom floor. Initially she thought he had suffered yet another epileptic fit, but she quickly realised this was different and much more dangerous, and that he'd been on the floor for a while. It turned out to be a bad stroke, meaning there was significant brain damage. Vital bits of his bright, sparky brain had been killed off.

It was such a shame. Chris had been in the middle of presenting a television series about New Zealand artists. He was rather good at it — engaged, interested and enthusiastic. He was older, the kids were older, he was calmer and much more mellow. He was still drawing *Max Media*, a weekly cartoon strip for the *Herald*, as well as reviewing music and film for various publications. He was knowledgeable, analytical, opinionated and respected for his views.

After years of relative hardship, life was a bit easier. There was some money to spend on music and DVDs of the unpretentious, non-mainstream movies he loved. The home movie theatre was finally set up. He drank a few quality beers before it became fashionable, but avoided excessive consumption. He ate vegetarian, could make cheese, and he exercised fanatically to keep the weight at bay.

I travelled up to Auckland to see him the following week. He was in rehab, monotonously exercising to try to regain some use and strength along the right side of his body. Lots of visitors were strumming Beatles tunes for group sing-alongs, and playing endless rounds of cards in an effort to get his brain reconnected and working again. The visitors kept coming to help reignite the old Chris they all so clearly loved.

There was the same trouble-making glint in his eye, but he looked tired, dishevelled, much older and unusually vulnerable. There were words, but they came as separate, isolated exclamations, and he couldn't string them together into sentences. There was improvement, but not enough. He seemed to be in there trying to get out, trying to express and connect, but he couldn't manage it. Chris was now quite clearly a different person.

When the news of his stroke broke, there was a great deal of shock among the Flying Nun community, which quickly rippled out through the international independent music world. Many artists wanted to assist or help, and it was decided that the best way to channel this concern was to record a tribute CD and stage a couple of benefit concerts.

The double tribute CD, *Stroke: Songs for Chris Knox*, involved artists from around the world: The Clean, The Mountain Goats,

Jay Reatard, Shayne Carter, David Kilgour, Bonnie 'Prince' Billy, The Bats, Jeff Mangum, Will Oldham, Don McGlashan, Yo La Tengo, Peter Gutteridge of Snapper, The Mint Chicks, Lou Barlow, The Verlaines, and Tall Dwarfs as well as The Nothing all feature. Each artist covered a Chris-related composition (which could be from The Enemy, Toy Love, Tall Dwarfs, The Nothing or his solo catalogue) and donated their share of any income to Chris's rehabilitation fund. Like many tribute compilations, the material varies in style and quality, but the level of sympathy and respect that these many busy artists from around New Zealand and beyond convey is palpable. It's a fantastic collection of Chris's songs interpreted by many of the artists he himself admired and befriended. Fittingly, his oldest musical buddy, Alec Bathgate, designed the stunning yellow-and-black packaging.

The first benefit concert was held at the Kings Arms in Auckland, in November 2009, to mark the launch of the *Stroke* tribute album. The second took place at the Le Poisson Rouge arts venue in Greenwich Village, in New York, the following May. Both allowed Chris's fellow musicians to express their support and raise money for his rehabilitation.

I thoroughly enjoyed the Auckland show. David Kilgour, Alec Bathgate, Dimmer, Neil and Sharon Finn's Pajama Club, Don McGlashan and the Bellbirds all played to a packed house of old friends and fans, including family, Members of Parliament, famous actors and previous collaborators. Chris spent most of the show seated at the back of the room but with a good view of the stage, and acquaintances and strangers alike spent a little time each seated next to him. It was genuinely quietly heartfelt and touching. And, to the surprise of everyone, Chris was on stage at the end, performing with limited vocabulary, but performing and loving it, and the ecstatic crowd loved him back.

The New York show was organised by Ba Da Bing label owner Ben Goldberg and was invariably more international: Yo La Tengo, The Clean, Portastatic, Shayne Carter's Dimmer,

Claudia Gonson and Sharon von Etten all played and, to everyone's amazement, Jeff Mangum made an appearance after years of hermit-like silence, prompting many to later note that this performance was pivotal in the subsequent reunion of his legendary band, Neutral Milk Hotel (Chris and Barbara were big fans).

And that wasn't the end of it. In July 2010, just over a year after Chris's stroke, MGMT came to Auckland to play three sold-out shows at the Powerstation, at which the Tall Dwarfs had originally been invited to perform as the support act. While in town for those shows, MGMT found the time in their busy schedule, at the height of their success, to spend a night performing a DJ set to a packed audience, with all proceeds going to Chris's fund.

Since then, Chris has learned to paint again, using his non-dominant left hand, and does so rather well. The work is still recognisably his, including portraits of friends and family. Whether the portraits are insightful or intuitive, it's sadly hard to tell. Chris can be very alert and attentive but struggles to communicate. He still only manages single words, and some of them are rather rude. Sometimes he forgets things that have just happened; at other times he seems completely aware of the here and now and then. There is clarity and there is confusion. It's such a cruel fate for someone whose life has been dedicated to expressing thoughts and feelings. Routine is important now, with a daily walk for fitness. And occasionally he plays a live show with a backing band. Single words and noises. He still pulls the poses of a front man, but for me it feels like a gesture. A gesture he finds exhausting but necessary to make.

CHAPTER 21

THE END, AND NEW BEGINNINGS

I loved being in London. Catherine and I shared lots of interests beyond music: books, film, theatre. Whatever you happened to be interested in culturally, you could be sure the best on offer would swing through London sometime soon. The bookshops were fantastic, the food was great, the city had some of the best galleries in the world and it was cosmopolitan, and I think I finally found myself there. I'd fallen in love, matured and become a better person. In the process, a bit of the allure of the music business faded. It was a heartless, ruthless scene in London. Everyone was on the make and it felt cut-throat at best, borderline unethical at worst, in a way I'd never experienced in New Zealand.

There were the obvious stresses and tensions at work. Money was short in Mushroom's London office and while I could see they had achieved a lot, it had come at a price. The cost of starting up in a big, competitive market and wanting to compete from day one sucks up the cash. I felt quite close to Gary by this stage. He'd got me over to the UK because he believed I could do good things and sell some music. I never imagined he knew what I really liked about music or how I would have approached its promotion. But I felt we were on our way to establishing something credible, with good international releases on top of our core New Zealand acts. I was confident we could make these records work without spending stupid major-record-company amounts of money.

The reality was that Michael Gudinski, back in Australia, was worried about the cash his London operation was eating up, and about where the music business in general was headed. Both he and Gary had been courting a Japanese company as another prospective partner. I seem to remember sitting in a corporate box at a massive but mostly empty suburban Aussie Rules stadium in Melbourne, talking to three Japanese executives. The most interesting of them was the long-haired-professor type responsible for long-term technological planning. He wasn't interested in anything that might happen within ten years, but in the potential value of the catalogue when the online and digital tidal wave arrived. I should have been taking more notice of this guy.

That all fell through. News Corporation, part owners of Mushroom's Australasian distributors, Festival, got wind of the negotiations and expressed an interest and ended up buying Mushroom entirely. Gary was pushed out, as was the head of business affairs, Simon Young. Both had been running the company with Michael for years and were shareholders.

I could see the writing was on the wall. I respected Michael's ability and reputation, but I was never one for corporate hierarchies and, being based in London, I hadn't really got to know him at all. I was out on a limb and I knew it.

Sure enough, the day came and I was out. In March 1997 I composed an email to my colleagues announcing that I had been accepted for astronaut training at Cape Canaveral, which half of them apparently believed. No one seemed to realise that I had an employment contract, and it took an age to reach a settlement. Michael demanded that I surrender my remaining shares in all of the Flying Nun companies. That sort of thing wears you down; you are thinking about it every day and it's hard to get on with anything new. And in this case it dragged on for well over a year.

It was a stressful time, and then we learned that Catherine was pregnant. I felt I needed to settle the whole thing so we could get on with our new life. The final settlement certainly wasn't for a whole lot of money, and was simply based on what I was due under my employment contract, as it was hard to argue my Flying Nun shares were worth anything. And, to be fair, Mushroom had pumped a good deal of cash into Flying Nun projects in New Zealand and the UK over the years they were involved. It was July 1998 and I was out.

Convinced that our lives were about to change forever, we went on holiday to the Grand Canyon and wandered around Arizona and Utah for three weeks. It was great to get away from all the stress that had been swirling around me for the last few years. The Grand Canyon and the surrounding desert were perfect places to get a perspective on things: big skies and vast open spaces.

Then it was back to London in my new capacity as a father and house dad in Shepherd's Bush. We were in a flat off Askew Road. It was fun hanging out with this new person in our lives, called Missy. I had got into the habit of calling Catherine Missy Teka, after the wife of Maori singer Prince Tui Teka, and the name seemed just right for our tiny little redhead. Our mothers didn't approve at all.

With Catherine back at work, I started getting quite accomplished in the kitchen. London is great for food, the restaurants are unbelievably good, but for me the fun was in being able to buy any ingredient you wanted. Everything was available and the quality absolutely top notch. I became an avid cookbook collector. I also turned out to be a pretty good dad. I fussed and fretted and was overwhelmed by the love I felt for this small quirky character. Being in London, I was surrounded by other house dads and things to do that keep suburban neurosis at bay.

Despite this, I became increasingly aware that something was not really right. My behaviour could be erratic and occasionally just a little bit crazy. I shuffled around or flew off the handle. I had no insight when I was in this place and it was increasingly hard for Catherine. We sought help but I didn't seem to tick any of the usual boxes.

We bought our own terrace house in Homerton in Hackney in 2004. Britain's worst street for gun crime was five minutes to the west and one of the country's most notorious estates was just over the back fence. The old Matchbox toy car factory was just around the corner on the banks of the River Lea. I liked it there. Then our second daughter, Lulu, came along, and we were a proper family living in an amazing city.

I was still going to see live music, and reading about music, and I discovered the kind of strange passions for it that middle-aged men do. I liked it loud, with guitars and other sounds, and wasn't too hung up on hearing the human voice and meaningful lyrics. Songs were good but so were grooves, though not necessarily dance ones. I've never been able to dance. I'm a white guy from Christchurch.

But my episodes were getting worse and more frequent. Catherine somehow managed to stick with me and was tenacious in her determination to find a way through. Our friends in London also provided invaluable support. A breakthrough came when I was eventually diagnosed at the handy nearby Homerton Hospital as being a manic depressive. And a rapid-cycling one at that — the ups and downs could come and go very quickly.

My condition had probably always been there; in fact it had probably contributed to the development of the label. The symptoms — extreme focus, increased energy, increased productivity and creativity, grandiose ideas, reckless behaviour and poor judgment — summed things up pretty well. A normally functioning person would have thrown the whole Flying Nun exercise away very early on. My slightly altered perspective had helped start the thing up and, crucially, ensured the thing kept going. There was judgment and good sense involved a great deal of the time, but I think when the chips were down the madness got me through.

The old, little-understood drug of choice for the condition, lithium, flattens everything out and allows me to live a life those around me can cope with.

I still get the occasional twinge of manic uplift but nothing too extreme, although the depressive troughs can be harder to manage. Overall I am in a better place, a place with lots to think about and do, with people I love who now seem to quite like having me around too.

* * *

Flying Nun in New Zealand was left relatively unscathed by the changes at Mushroom in Australia and London, but over time there were changes and rationalisations. Lesley got ground down by the stress of trying to balance creative integrity with good business and left. Paul did his best to integrate Flying Nun into the new Festival Mushroom Records (FMR) entity run by my old acquaintance Roger Grierson. Unfortunately, the Flying In part of it wasn't properly understood or its potential appreciated, and it was badly managed, run down and eventually closed. It wasn't the best time to be owning a record company, with the shift to digital downloads starting to have a big impact on sales. Eventually, News Corporation was able to sell FMR, including Flying Nun, to Warner Music.

The Warner Music New Zealand office did its best to look after the catalogue but it wasn't a priority and the profile of the label began to fade. In 2006 Charlotte Ryan approached me to put together a four-disc box set to commemorate twenty-five years of the Flying Nun label. I had just returned to New Zealand with my family. Catherine had applied for a job in public law in Wellington. Initially I'd announced that a return would only

Catherine, Missy and Lulu,
Moeraki, 2014

happen over my dead body; three weeks later we were all on the plane on our way home.

With our two girls — Missy was now six and Lulu was one — we set up house in Wellington. It was a bit of a shock after London but on reflection it seemed like a good time to return. Missy had been at school in the East End and was starting to sound like a little Cockney. I was braced for the day she would come home and utter her first 'innit'.

We struggled with the weather but gradually got into the things that were good about Wellington: the coffee, Unity Books, the second-hand bookshops, Slow Boat Records, Cuba Street and the bucket fountain, the regular film and arts festivals, and the sheer child-friendliness of the place after London. Over time I have become rather fond of Wellington.

I enjoyed putting together the box set track listing. It was designed to be comprehensive: four discs and eighty-odd songs running in a rough chronological sequence, accompanied by a detailed booklet, represented a huge amount of listening and compiling work. I had always played some of the old Flying Nun releases at home for my own pleasure, even after I left the company. But a lot of it had slipped to the back of my stacks or was packed up and in storage. That's often the case with a record collection: you make space for the new as your tastes and interests evolve. So the experience of being back in New Zealand and trawling through the Flying Nun back catalogue was a true reconnection. The music did stand up; it was still relevant, and there was an audience keen to hear that music and learn about the bands who had made it.

I could see that the Flying Nun catalogue had been fully absorbed into Warner Music. Without the care and attention it once received as a separate entity, the titles were slowly, one by one, becoming unavailable. The overall idea of the label was slowly fading, along with the sales and profiles of most of the bands.

So I began the protracted process of trying to buy Flying Nun back from Warner Music. Major record companies get bigger by buying up smaller labels and rarely sell off those parts once they're acquired. It's tricky to shave off a bit that has been completely integrated into the parent company. In the end, I think Warner Music in New Zealand was persuaded that Flying Nun represented something significant that was best preserved as an independent business entity. I also think they found it tricky dealing with the long-signed artists, so called 'heritage acts', with whom they had no real historical relationship. Practically, a lot of relevant documentation had been lost in the various changes of ownership, just as the vast store of institutional knowledge had evaporated as the dedicated staff had dwindled and disappeared. For this to work I had to be involved. I wasn't at all concerned about going back and revisiting my past; it seemed like the right thing to do.

It took a while to get everything arranged. Warner Music Australia had to be persuaded, followed by the regional headquarters in Hong Kong, before it went to the business affairs committee in New York. I still had a few connections in the music business in the States and a couple of them sat on that committee, but the powers that be must have thought it was the right thing to do, to sell me my label back.

Having talked Warner Music around, I then had to finance the purchase. The price we were looking at was not based solely on the perceived value of the rights to the catalogue: it also represented the work required to disentangle something from an integrated whole. There was a bottom line to how much all that grief and effort was worth, so we were going to have to pay a bit more than we wanted, and I would have to find a way to fund it.

Neil Finn's involvement was crucial in making things happen. His profile and stature in New Zealand music and society generally signalled that the buyback was serious. Crucially, Neil understood the importance of the label, the music it represented and the need to preserve it. The best way to achieve that was by making it active again, re-releasing the catalogue and working on new releases with new bands. With Neil involved, two others — my old friend Graham Cockroft from the Netherworld Dancing Toys and businessman and acquaintance Peter Rishworth — came in as partners. A new Flying Nun Records company was set up and the deal was done just in time for Christmas 2009.

Of course that wasn't the end of the story. There was a huge amount of work to be done. I hired a young man named Matthew Davis I'd met running the Victoria University on-campus radio station, who had impressed me with his intelligence and organisational abilities. We set up office at my home in windy Wadestown. The first major task was to re-sign all of the existing artists to new contracts. These were contracts that reflected the new realities of the music business world and made it worthwhile for the artists to stay involved in the ongoing process of repackaging, digitising and re-releasing their music.

It was a very different landscape from the one I had left ten or so years earlier. Where had all the record shops gone? Of course I knew the answer. Everything had changed with digital, and the CD sales base was eroding as steadily as the West Antarctic ice sheet. The problem was that increased digital sales weren't rising as fast as predicted — or was it as hoped?

Yet there were signs that vinyl was making a comeback. Indeed, the increased sales of that format has certainly been a key industry development over the last five or so years. The resurgence of vinyl has been a real boon to the genuinely music-loving section of the industry (as opposed to the mass-marketing commercial end), but it does present problems. Records have always been hard to manufacture. It's a dirty, physical process and things go wrong. Our problem now was that they went wrong in a factory on the other side of the Pacific Ocean, on the outskirts of Los Angeles rather than on the other side of Wellington in Miramar. That factory was also very busy trying to meet the steadily growing demand. Turnaround times were becoming longer, around 180 days, which made planning difficult, particularly in the context of the near-instantaneous distribution of digital music.

Price is also an issue. It's way too low. The high cost of making and distributing vinyl (which includes covering exchange rates, customs clearance charges and significant shipping prices for such a heavy product), leaves little margin left to be shared between the label and the artist. In the early days of the vinyl revival, record releases were seen as a loss-leading promotional device and were costed and priced accordingly, and that low price remains the expectation among customers. Yep, they seem expensive already, but to be really worthwhile for the artists and label investing in producing them, they should sell for a whole lot more.

We got a lot done in the initial two or three years, but sales could have been better. Costs came in as expected but generating sales was much harder work — a war of attrition, fighting for small volumes here and there. There was more detail to administer due to the smaller, fragmented markets we were dealing with. I am good with bigger ideas and not so attentive to detail; my concentration really isn't steady enough for that sort of work. I felt I had done my bit. We moved Matthew and the office north to Auckland, where it really needed to be once again, and made some economies by putting it together with Ben Howe's Arch Hill label. He would do a better job with the administration.

Making this thing called Flying Nun work has been a long-term project — thirty-five years now, and I'm sure we're nearer to getting it right all the time. I'm a Flying Nun Records company director and obviously have a responsibility to take an active interest in what's going on. We're keen to work with more new artists and I plan to involve myself in that. It could be fun.

EPILOGUE

While I was finishing the writing of this book I had to make an unplanned visit to Christchurch. My mother had been taken to hospital on Christmas Eve, 2015. She had left her home of fifty-five years for the last time in the back of an ambulance. From hospital she would move into a rest home on the eastern side of Christchurch, to be nearer the remaining family members living in the city. Her home would be cleared and sold in the New Year.

The finality of it all hit me hard. My mother had vowed never to leave the home that she and my father had built and moved into just months before my birth. Now the frailty of age had forced her out. In the process, my own conflicted connection to the home in which I had spent my first seventeen years was being severed.

My father had died in this house in 1998. It was only when Catherine and I had visited from London that we had realised how ill with cancer he actually was. He was to meet Catherine for the first and last time on that visit. 'When I heard you were a lawyer I thought you'd be a snotty bitch, but you're okay,' he told her. He was never one to beat about the bush when direct offence could be given.

Yet his once-sharp mind was ever so slightly blunted; the cancer was at his brain. He declined rapidly and died suddenly three weeks later. Thankfully it was a heart attack, we think, in the dead of a Christchurch night, while we, having returned to the UK, munched crab sandwiches for lunch in that primal old place, Zennor in Cornwall.

Back in the family home collecting a few things for my mother, I realised how little she would need to take with her to her new life in the rest home. My younger and closest brother, Frank, announced he was moving away from Christchurch, too. He had had enough of the devastation wrought by the earthquakes, and the ever-so-slow rebuild.

Driving around on that visit I could see his point. The city centre was more of a flattened catastrophe than ever, the eastern suburbs still torn to bits. The sound of hoons blatting about in souped-up cars (as you might experience in The Hutt or Hamilton) had been replaced by the sound of ordinary motorists bouncing and banging their way down still potholed and broken roads. It was a mess. Most of what I remembered was gone, and the family home would shortly also become just a memory.

Good people remain in Christchurch, of course. I ran into Roy Montgomery at the hospital and we skirted around the reasons we were both there by talking about the relative merits of various rest homes. Bruce Russell has consciously committed to staying and helping the city rebuild. Other old friends such as Alec Bathgate, Ian Dalziel and Jason Grieg have also chosen not to leave.

But what is happening to the city is not really a 'rebuild'. Whatever replaces the old Christchurch will be a new and different place. It will naturally evolve over generations due to real economic and demographic forces that no amount of planning can account for. The stark personal reality is that there are now fewer than ever real connections to my life there. While some hang on, I feel I've finally left.

Yet, if I've disconnected from Christchurch, I do still feel very connected to the central focus of my entire adult life, my work. I've learned that people and places are left or forgotten, but the ideas — the good ones that is — tend to linger longer.

* * *

Early on in the Flying Nun story, the premature and unfair deaths of Wayne Elsey, Johnny Pierce and David D'ath shook everyone in the label's wide and extended community of musicians and audience. More recently, Chris Knox's stroke has focused minds on the passing of time and the inevitability of one's mortal end. At least, my mind focused on those things, and in a rather alarming way. It made me wonder whether I might be experiencing some sort of delayed mid-life crisis.

Don't get me wrong, I was happy with my family life and felt no overpowering need to buy a red convertible. But there was a new urge to review what I had done, to remember things, events and people that I had known in my 'other', younger existence — the life that had swirled around Flying Nun Records in the 1980s in particular.

Memories are always unreliable and selective, and I was under no illusions about the state of mine when it came to the writing of this book. It's not a detailed history but a highly personal memoir, an interpretation of my past and what I've spent a great deal of my past doing — running a funny little record company called Flying Nun Records on the edge of the world.

It became a book about how the hothouse of punk and post punk affected me in Christchurch and like-minded characters in Dunedin — Chris and Doug, The Clean, Martin Phillipps, Graeme Downes, Shayne Carter and many, many others — a book about setting up the label and how it evolved, in fits and starts and largely through the collective spirit of a larger scene, into a proper kind of business. I remain grateful that it retained its quirky character while growing thanks to the involvement of a great number of talented artists, and that an impressive run of records found support with a small but important network of helpers, friends and fans worldwide.

I've written more about the business than the music. I hope readers will be encouraged to explore or rediscover the music themselves, including material that space limitations forced me to leave out. There are many people and events I haven't included here, which is inevitable but still unfortunate.

I have always known that I've had a lucky life. A largely unplanned and unexpected one, but a lucky one all the same. It's been a privilege, right from the start, to be involved with the music I love through Flying Nun. The success I have always measured wholly in terms of the artistic achievements of the artists I worked with. Writing this book has given me a new, redefined admiration for the people who made the music and for their reasons for doing so.

The music industry is a fraught business. We aren't making widgets. Talented people are ingeniously creating original and usually highly personal music. The ability to collaborate is often key to their success. So a record company needs to balance the creative and the commercial, with all the skills that demands. I can't say I really had any of those skills in abundance, but I was lucky enough to be surrounded by many who did. And somehow Flying Nun managed to harness just enough of those skills, in some sort of balance and for long enough, to make the whole thing just about work. We learned and developed quickly enough to cope with the growth in the number of bands we were working with, the number of releases, and the sales around New Zealand and overseas. And, as the bands developed and the sales grew, so we grew up.

Even in the nooks and niches of independent music, fashion reigns supreme. So whatever music you are making is measured against the broader shifts in musical fashion, and there is a tension and excitement that comes from working in that environment. If we were ever cool at Flying Nun it was because we really didn't care. We knew what we were doing was right, and thankfully enough people seemed to agree.

The label was notoriously disorganised and chaotic. It was part of the package. If the business had been slick and streamlined, we'd have appealed to a different kind of artist and it would have been a different thing musically. I'd rather have it chaotic and crazy any day. Nothing ever became standardised or worked to a formula. Economy of scale isn't greatly rewarded in New Zealand due to the country's size. We tended to approach each artist, each recording project, as the unique experience it was. That lack of a template suited the creative and the original.

Relationships with artists are key and by their very nature unstable. There are contrasting if not conflicting expectations. Often everything boils down to money or the lack of it. Strong friendships can falter. At best there are ups and downs. But I've come through writing this book on a bit of an up. The original causes of many disputes have been forgotten (did the fact that the record cover was upside down really affect sales in the long term?) and the triumphs — the music and the personalities that made that music — are remembered and celebrated for their true, fine, real worth.

I was the guy who happened to be there at the right place and time with the idea of starting a record label. It was born out of a positive combination of enthusiasm and naivety. The bands and all of those involved at Flying Nun collectively battled our own ignorance and made the thing work. Good people came full of optimism and some left burnt-out wrecks. I left for London and our fates became embroiled in bigger shit-fights and larger incompetencies.

Yet throughout it all, good music was made, as it still is today by many of the talented musicians we first worked with all those years ago. Shayne Carter has just finished recording an album of new material. Main Verlaine and international Mahler expert Graeme Downes continues to produce astonishing Verlaines recordings and performances. In 2015 The Chills, still led by Martin Phillipps, released their first album in nineteen years; *Silver Bullets* is a fine return to form after years battling adversity, addiction and illness.

We savour the highlights and do not lament the inevitable missteps and creative lulls that define most lives. Original Clean member Peter Gutteridge, co-writer of 'Point That Thing Somewhere Else' and 'I'm in Love with These Times', always struggled, but managed to pull it together a few times in The Great Unwashed and Snapper and in his solo demo recordings to show off his extra-special talents. That was enough for us as an audience. But as an artist he wanted more, and the disappointment killed him.

The Clean continue to mesmerise. Playing occasionally and recording now and again on a whim, they really are the ultimate cool, independently minded band. Internationally recognised, they do what they want, never constricted by industry or career concerns. It works for them, where it would spell doom for many. Talented, individualistic and wayward, they showed us the way.

There were countless others — writing songs, playing in bands, designing covers, organising gigs, typing letters and answering phones. It all coalesced into a dynamic whole that helped produce some timeless music.

In time I came to understand my own erratic productive energy. It was an illness that helped propel the risky venture early on, and then kept it going against all the odds and common sense. I was fortunate to be able to rein in what is a serious illness and control it when it threatened to become too much of a liability in my newly domesticated life. But once I had a young family, the drinking that I used to self-medicate had to be dealt with. I don't touch a drop these days. Things can still be a little up and down, but it's a much smoother ride than in the past.

I'm lucky that I met someone special and could have a family. I had been in serious relationships before, but things with Catherine were different from the start. We really clicked, fell hopelessly in love, and Missy and Lulu are the best things that could have happened to me. I have been fulfilled and happy in a way I never imagined possible.

But the record business is always there, nagging away. It's impossible to escape it for long. Flying Nun has stuttered at times, but it keeps on going. Its most recent reincarnation has seen the re-release of much of the best material from the 1980s, made available both digitally and on vinyl yet again. But Flying Nun cannot just be a reissue label. New things need to happen to keep it vital and alive, to propel things forward and help make sense of the immense history it is built on.

So I'm still listening to new music and thinking about audiences and working out how to bring the two together, as well as reconnecting with music from the past and finding ways to draw it to the attention of new generations of listeners. It's a collaborative, sharing business, but it's also a selfish one — wanting to hear what's new, what's next, listening for the possibilities and looking for the potential. Music is a shifting, dynamic and transformative necessity. A bit like fresh air: essential to life.

ACKNOWLEDGMENTS

I owe a great deal of thanks to all the bands and artists that I have been touched by during the course of my life, especially those I had the great privilege of working with during what became my career at Flying Nun. Because of the lack of space, and the nature of the book itself, many are not mentioned by name, but they are still the core of the story.

A special thanks to The Clean, who changed my life and the course of music in New Zealand forever, and to Chris Knox and Doug Hood, who came on board at Flying Nun because of their shared appreciation and enthusiasm for particular bands. Without these guys' participation, Flying Nun would never have become the vibrant and wonderful thing that it did.

At the start I had a number of 'helpers' who took the records around the shops: Roy Colbert in Dunedin; a team in Wellington, led initially by Ian Dalziel then Chris Lipscombe, followed by Kevin Jenkins; and Chris Knox in Auckland. I was also lucky to have a number of smart and empathetic co-workers, starting with Hamish Kilgour and then Gary Cope and Bruce Russell. Lesley Paris, Paul McKessar, Alan Holt, Rachel Phillipps, Natasha Griffiths, Sandra Hopping and Richard Ram all came to work with me at the Auckland Queen Street office. I was lucky to work with some excellent people in the London office who really cared about the music, the bands and the label. Back in New Zealand,

Andrew 'Hat' Meier, Dylan Pellett, Emily Crowther, Jonathan Hughes, Simon Woods and Charlotte Ryan all made a difference after I left Flying Nun, and more recently Matthew Davis and Ben Howe have been doing the hard work. These are people who can do things I never could. A special thank you to Matthew Davis for helping source images, his general encouragement and his injections of common sense, usually when sorely needed.

I would like to thank the photographers and artists who have made their work available for inclusion in this book: Carol Tippet, Barbara Ward, Stuart Page, Alec Bathgate, Robin Neate, Ronnie van Hout, Jeff Batts, Christine Webster, Alister Guthrie, Jonathan Ganley, Jane Walker and Gemma Gracewood for photos; Ronnie van Hout, Chris Knox, Robert Scott, Paul Smith, Alec Bathgate, Stuart Page, Matt Campbell, Lesley MacLean, Ian Dalziel and David Mitchell for artwork. Despite best efforts, a few photos remain uncredited.

Thank you to Bruce Russell for permission to use David Mitchell's *Pile=Up* illustration. Thanks to Bill Direen and Allen Meck for allowing the reproduction of The Bilders' *Soloman's Ball* cover and to Simon Grigg and John Collie for locating scans for inclusion in this book. Thanks to Robbie Burton at Potton Burton for locating The Verlaines photo. And thanks to Ian Jorgenson for the use of his scanner.

There are a few books that provided me with invaluable background information: Wade Ronald Churton's *Have You Checked the Children: Punk and postpunk music in new Zealand 1977–1981* (Put Your foot Down Publishing, 1999); *Kiwi Rock: A reference book* by Tim Davey and Horst Puschman (Kiwi Rock Publications, 1996); and *Positively George Street* by Matthew Bannister (Reed, 1999).

Writing this book has been an incredible education about the nature of writing and I have learnt a great deal about myself as a result. I am extremely grateful to publisher Finlay Macdonald and project editor Scott Forbes for their encouragement, sheer hard work and guidance; thanks also to copy editor Eva Chan, and to Alan Deare for his excellent cover design. All worked well beyond the call of duty to add shape and polish to my sometimes sprawling story.

I also need to thank my friend Colin Hogg, who seemed to move to Wellington especially to cajole the natural procrastinator and prevaricator in me to achieve the impossible and finish writing this book.

To my family, Catherine, Missy and Lulu, thanks for being unbelievably supportive and allowing me not just the time to write but to also sit absently, distractedly, contemplating.

I'd also like to pay tribute to my father, who died in 1998 and would probably have hated this book as much as Hunter S. Thompson's *Fear and Loathing in Las Vegas,* which I once foolishly recommended he read, and my mother, who was astonished that her somewhat lazy son could complete the writing of a book and is only spared the shame and shock of actually having to read it by poor health.

INDEX

Page numbers in *italic type* refer to illustrations.